SKYPE
HACKS ™

Other resources from O'Reilly

SKYPE HACKS™

Andrew Sheppard

O'REILLY®

Beijing · Cambridge · Farnham · Köln · Paris · Sebastopol · Taipei · Tokyo

Skype Hacks™

by Andrew Sheppard

Published by O'Reilly Media, Inc., 1005 Gravenstein Highway North,
Sebastopol, CA 95472.

O'Reilly books may be purchased for educational, business, or sales promotional use. Online editions are also available for most titles (*safari.oreilly.com*). For more information, contact our corporate/institutional sales department: (800) 998-9938 or *corporate@oreilly.com*.

Editor:	Mike Loukides	**Production Editor:**	Colleen Gorman
Series Editor:	Rael Dornfest	**Cover Designer:**	Marcia Friedman
Executive Editor:	Dale Dougherty	**Interior Designer:**	David Futato

Printing History:

December 2005:   First Edition.

 This book uses RepKover™, a durable and flexible lay-flat binding.

ISBN: 0-596-10189-9
[M]

Contents

Credits

About the Author

Andrew Sheppard has been fascinated by technology and science since childhood, and it's an indulgence that has continued to this day.

Since discovering Skype in 2004, Andrew has been using and hacking Skype in all sorts of weird and wonderful ways—if Skype came with any sort of warranty, he voided it long ago! Although his initial foray into using Skype was to find ways to save money on his phone bill, the true potential of Skype's ability to do things that no regular phone system can do soon overtook that initial interest and replaced it with a fascination and desire to see "how deep the rabbit hole goes" (to borrow some words from the movie *The Matrix*). He's still burrowing!

Andrew is the publisher of a couple of online electronic magazines about Skype: *Elpis's Skype Power User Magazine* (ISSN 1747-8421) and *Elpis's Skype API Developer Magazine* (ISSN 1747-843X). The concept behind Elpis (*http://www.elpispublishing.com/*) is that knowledge, without the tools to take advantage of that knowledge, is rather powerless, while the converse is a path to empowerment. Elpis Publishing's aim is to provide its readers with both the knowledge and the software needed to best use that knowledge: Knowledge + Tools = Empowerment.

After earning a first-class honor's degree in astrophysics, Andrew made the mistake of going on to earn higher degrees: a master's in astronomical technology at Edinburgh University (UK) and a master's in business administration at the London Business School (UK). This period of time and that which followed was punctuated with work as a scientific researcher at Oxford University, as a software developer, and later, as a "Rocket Scientist" at Bankers Trust Company in the financial square mile of the city of London, as well as in New York and Tokyo. A lot of heartache and financial anguish could have been avoided throughout had he become what is clearly the optimal career choice for anyone anywhere: a master plumber. Nowhere on the planet is there a poor or unemployed master plumber! Too late to correct past follies, Andrew now makes his living writing software, and writing books and magazine articles.

Contributors and Reviewers

The following individuals contributed hacks, helped with hacks, or reviewed material for this book:

- Adam Harris (contributor and reviewer) is the number-one poster—by a wide margin—on the Skype forums. His knowledge and depth of expertise on Skype are second to none. Adam brought a rigor and passion for accuracy that raised the bar for the author and other contributors.

- Lawrence Hudson (reviewer) has been a pioneering user of various technologies for more years than he cares to remember. This has worked to his advantage, and to his disadvantage, throughout his career as a businessperson and entrepreneur. Nonetheless, his fascination and enthusiasm for all things technological remain. Nowhere was this more apparent than in his enthusiastic support for, and thorough review of, this book.

- Jason Terando (contributor) is the author of the ever-useful ActiveS component that you can use to interface applications with Skype on Windows. Many of the automation scripts in this book use ActiveS, so a great debt of thanks goes to Jason for making ActiveS so liberally available through a BSD-style license. You can download ActiveS from the KhaosLabs web site, *http://www.khaoslabs.com/*. Chapter 12 would not have been possible—or, at least, would be only a mere shadow of what it is—were it not for Jason.

- Theodore Wallingford (reviewer) is the author of the book *VoIP Hacks* (O'Reilly). Ted provided valuable feedback on early chapters of the book, and a whole lot of encouragement to do more! Not only is Ted an expert in VoIP technologies (*http://www.macvoip.com/*), but he's also an enthusiastic and accomplished writer, having published an earlier work on VoIP, *Switching to VoIP* (O'Reilly).

- Kevin Delaney (contributor) is a cofounder of KhaosLabs and is an active member of the Skype forums.

Acknowledgments

Writing this book was a rather nightmarish experience. Not only is Skype moving faster than a speeding bullet, but it is also clearly a technology that needed to be written about, and written about in a timely fashion. This put quite a lot of pressure on me to write the book, but rather more on my family. To my son Nathaniel, who lost a whole summer with his dad because of the book, and to my wife Susan, who put up with being growled at from my computer keyboard in a hotel room in Hawaii while on vacation, all I can say is thanks, and that I hope to make it up to both of you.

Mike Loukides, my editor, was the inspiration for this book. When Mike suggested I write a book on Skype hacks, I didn't know what a great undertaking the book would be, or how much I would learn from the experience. Nor, frankly, how much fun Skype as a technology would be. Mike was also (together with Lawrence Hudson, mentioned earlier) a constant pillar of support and encouragement, and was someone to bounce ideas off of during my early days before sitting down to write the book, when I was completely replacing my home phone system and otherwise hacking around with Skype.

Kelly Larabee at Skype was a joy to work with. She was very professional, and she cut through a lot of red tape to get the book reviewed by the Skype development team. Many thanks go to her, to Kat James, and to the team at Skype.

The Skype community who are active on the Skype user forums are a wonderful resource for anyone using Skype—and for authors of books on Skype, they are doubly so! Too numerous to mention by name, my thanks go out to all the regular, and irregular, posters to the Skype forums. Special mention goes to Bill Campbell and the *Skype Journal* (*http://www.skypejournal.com/*), for his encouragement during the writing of this book and for his insights into the world of Skype.

I've been enamored with O'Reilly as a publisher since the days of its X-Windows book series, and I've been a constant reader of all things O'Reilly since then. So, when the opportunity to actually write for O'Reilly came about, I felt both flattered and privileged by the opportunity. The crew at O'Reilly didn't disappoint. In terms of both the caliber of the staff and their professionalism, O'Reilly made *Skype Hacks* a reality in record time.

Lastly, in the final analysis, all authors must shoulder the responsibility for their work. So, any errors or omissions that remain in this book are not from want of effort to remove them, but are the result of the fallibility of the author. However, I do make the commitment that I will share any such errors or omissions that are brought to my attention with all readers of this book, through its web site, *http://www.oreilly.com/catalog/SkypeHacks/index.html*. This is also the place to check for errata and updates to code listings.

Preface

My involvement with Skype began in 2004 when, after getting tired of seeing the outrageously high proportion of fixed charges and taxes on my phone bill each and every month, I decided to do something about it. Over the space of a few months, I gradually replaced my old phone system with Skype. In the process, I shaved 82% off my phone bill!

But after a short while, Skype's potential to save lots of money was slowly eclipsed by the realization that Skype could also do far, far more than any existing phone technology, whether making free calls over the Internet to someone on the other side of the planet, having your phone number and calls follow you wherever you go, or being able to send text messages, for free, from a web browser—even with just a formatted URL—on a machine without Skype installed and have it delivered to any Skype user, wherever he might be. This is a technology that is limited only by your imagination. As you will discover, you can do things with Skype that you simply cannot do with your existing telephone system or by using other VoIP offerings.

As you get to know Skype, you will become aware that Skype is unlike any telephone system you have known before. And after a short while, like Dorothy in *The Wizard of Oz*, you might find yourself mouthing the words: "Toto, I have a feeling we're not in Kansas anymore."

Skype Hacks is a book that shows you how to save money by using Skype, and how to remove the boundaries imposed by having lived within the confines of your regular phone system for so long, a system that has been in stasis for decades—dumb, lifeless, and unmoving. It is a book that hopes to liberate your imagination and show, in a practical hands-on way, how Skype can do amazing new things—sometimes things that even its creators never envisioned. If after reading this book, you find yourself with the urge to hack around with Skype, the people at O'Reilly and I will have succeeded in our jobs—and in the process, hopefully, we will have helped you to save a bundle of money.

Are you ready to journey onward to the "land over the rainbow"? Let's go!

Why Skype Hacks?

The term *hacking* has a bad reputation in the press. They use it to refer to someone who breaks into systems or wreaks havoc with computers as their weapon. Among people who write code, though, the term *hack* refers to a "quick-and-dirty" solution to a problem, or a clever way to get something done. And the term *hacker* is taken very much as a compliment, referring to someone as being *creative*, having the technical chops to get things done. The Hacks series is an attempt to reclaim the word, document the good ways people are hacking, and pass the hacker ethic of creative participation on to the uninitiated. Seeing how others approach systems and problems is often the quickest way to learn about a new technology.

Skype has very little in the way of documentation, particularly for the Skype user taking any steps beyond the basics. So in one sense, *Skype Hacks* is a how-to guide for getting things done with Skype—like a road map to Skype's basic features and beyond.

On the other hand, it is also a book that shows you how, with a little imagination, you can make Skype do interesting and new things—filling in the details on the map where before, there was only "here be dragons." Hacking around with Skype is easy, fun, and rewarding. Skype is a technology that encourages experimentation, so the book helps to equip you—the reader—with the mindset and toolset for you to hack around with Skype on your own.

Skype is a new technology, moving very fast and definitely worthy of being written about. Moreover, it is a technology that needs to be written about *now*, given the dearth of available independent sources of information. By being published now, *Skype Hacks* aims to be one of the first sources for useful and timely information on Skype. And, by being constantly updated in print and through the book's web site (*http://www.oreilly.com/catalog/ SkypeHacks/index.html*), it is hoped that it will remain a useful resource for all Skype users for a long time to come.

How This Book Is Organized

You can read this book from cover to cover if you like, but each hack stands on its own, so feel free to browse and jump to the different sections that interest you most. If there's a prerequisite you need to know about, a cross-reference will guide you to the right hack.

The book is divided into several chapters, organized by subject:

Chapter 1, *Start Using Skype*

This chapter is for readers who are new to Skype. It explains what Skype is and how it works, and introduces Skype's main features. It also builds a "Skype vocabulary" of concepts and terminology that will help when more advanced hacks are encountered; and, in this respect, it helps the reader to grasp some of the links among hacks in the book that would otherwise remain hidden.

Chapter 2, *Save Money with Skype*

Skype has the potential to save a lot of money for most current users of landline phone services. This chapter focuses on the economics of Skype and the ways of figuring potential savings. It suggests ways of maximizing your savings by mixing Skype services with your existing phone service, or other alternative Internet phone services. This chapter suggests ways to avoid potentially costly traps and pitfalls that may trip up the unwary.

Chapter 3, *Configure Skype*

Skype configuration really falls into two distinct categories. The first is configuration to get Skype to simply work, and this chapter helps a little in that respect. The second is configuration to get Skype to work the way you want—that is, improving performance, and customizing Skype to meet your individual needs. The focus of this chapter is most distinctly on the second category.

Chapter 4, *Tweak and Tune Skype*

In many ways, this chapter expands on the theme begun in the previous chapter—that is, configuring, tweaking, and tuning Skype to work the way you want it to work.

Chapter 5, *Skype at Work*

Skype in its current form is not targeted at business users. But more and more business-ready features are making their way into Skype with each new release. Even now, as this chapter shows, Skype has a lot to offer the workplace for those willing to give it a try.

Chapter 6, *Mobile Skype*

Skype is only now beginning to show its potential impact on mobile telephony. But that impact will no doubt be as ground shaking as it has been on fixed landline telephony. This chapter shows how, by hacking around with Skype, you can improve and enhance your communication while on the move.

Chapter 7, *Skype Fun and Play*

From having fun with creating your own ringtones, to practicing a foreign language with native speakers, this chapter shows the fun and playful side of Skype.

Chapter 8, *Skype Chat and Voicemail*

Sometimes it's easy to forget that there's more to Skype than just voice calls. This chapter redresses that balance by showing you how to hack around with Skype's other major features; namely, instant messaging or "chat," and voicemail.

Chapter 9, *Security and Privacy*

Security and privacy should be a concern for anyone who is part of the Skype online community. Some hacks in this chapter will help you to have only the visibility you desire within the Skype community, and other hacks will help secure you against some of the more common risks encountered by Skype users.

Chapter 10, *Quirks, Gotchas, and Workarounds*

Skype has its limitations, and you'll learn how to deal with them in this chapter. Moreover, where possible, you also will receive suggestions for workarounds for the most obvious quirks and gotchas.

Chapter 11, *Skype Add-Ons and Tools*

Skype has a burgeoning market for add-on products and tools that use the Skype API to extend Skype's functionality or that use Skype's services. This chapter gives a glimpse of what's currently available, and a sense of what is yet to come.

Chapter 12, *Automate Skype*

In this chapter, you receive an introduction to the Skype API and you learn how to extend Skype's functionality and automate repetitive tasks using scripting methods: VBScript on Windows, Python on Linux, and AppleScript on Mac OS X. In addition, these API scripts are mixed with shell scripts and scripts that drive Skype's GUI directly to achieve what no one method alone can achieve. This mixing and matching of complementary scripting methods provides greater flexibility in terms of automating Skype. Throughout the chapter, the emphasis is not only to provide you with a collection of useful scripts that you can use as is, but also to equip you with the necessary knowledge and tools to start writing your own scripts and, in that way, to automate Skype for yourself.

Financial Exchange (FX) Rate

Skype prices most of its services in euros, which is the common currency of the majority of the member countries of the European Union. The symbol for euros is €. To make the book more palatable to American readers, prices in the book are often given first in euros and then again in U.S. dollars. The conversion factor between any two currencies (not just euros and dollars) commonly is referred to as the financial exchange (FX) rate, or simply FX rate.

Moreover, sometimes it is also common practice to refer to a currency not by name, but rather, by a standardized and unique three-letter code. Every national currency in the world has such a three-letter code. For the euro, the code is EUR, and for the U.S. dollar, it is USD. Sometimes currencies are referred to in the book by their three-letter codes.

FX rates are not constant. In fact, they can and do move around a lot. But because a book is not a "live" document, it must use a fixed exchange rate. Therefore, unless stated otherwise, euro-to-dollar conversions were carried out at this FX rate: 1 EUR = 1.25 USD.

Skype Software Versions

Skype is advancing very quickly and new releases are frequent for all of Skype's supported platforms: Windows, Linux, Mac OS X, and Pocket PC, at the time of this writing. Without a doubt, this is good news for you, the Skype user. But, from an author's point of view, it makes the job of keeping the book up-to-date very difficult. Even during the writing of this book, on several occasions, I had to retest hacks already written for compatibility with new releases of Skype. Table P-1 outlines the versions of Skype I was using as the book went to press, together with the minimum system requirements for each platform.

In terms of testing Skype on its respective platforms, I used these operating systems and applications:

Windows
    Microsoft Windows XP SP2

    Microsoft Internet Explorer 6.0.2900.2180

    Microsoft Office 2002 Professional SP3

    Skype Toolbar 0.9 (beta) for Microsoft Internet Explorer

    Skype Toolbar 0.9.107 (beta) for Microsoft Outlook

Linux
    SuSE 9.3 Pro with the KDE desktop

Mac OS X
    Apple OS X 10.4 (Tiger)

    Skype Widget 1.0.2

Pocket PC
    Microsoft Windows Mobile 2003 Second Edition

Table P-1. Skype's minimum hardware requirements

Windows	Linux	Mac OS X	Pocket PC
Skype 1.4.0.56 (beta)	Skype 1.2.0.11_API	Skype 1.3.0.8	Skype 1.2.0.4 (beta)
2000 or XP	SuSE 9, Fedora Core 3, Mandriva 10.1, Debian 3, or newer	10.3 (Panther) or newer	Windows Mobile 2003 for Pocket PC or newer
400MHz processor	400MHz processor	G3, G4, or G5 processor	400MHz processor
128MB of RAM	128MB of RAM	128MB of RAM	WiFi enabled
15MB of disk space	10MB of disk space	20MB of disk space	
Sound-in device	Sound-in device	Sound-in device	
Sound-out device	Sound-out device	Sound-out device	
Broadband Internet connection, or minimum 33.6 Kbps dial-up	Broadband Internet connection, or minimum 33.6 Kbps dial-up	Broadband Internet connection, or minimum 33.6 Kbps dial-up	

I also feel obliged to explain the rationale behind using Skype "betas" on some platforms. Writing a book is a process that necessarily spans several months, and even once the book is written, preparation for production, and production itself, add many more months before the book hits the shelves at bookstores. For many subjects, this is of little consequence. However, when you're writing about something as fast moving as Skype, there is a distinct danger that much of what's written will be out of date by the time it gets into readers' hands. To mitigate this problem I have used beta versions of Skype wherever possible on the assumption that the functionality in those will more closely match the functionality available to this book's readers. This combined with frequent revisions between print runs and timely updates posted to the book's web site should make the book both useful and relevant for a long time to come.

 One reason to consider the hardware requirements of Table P-1 as being the absolute bare minimum requirements is that Skype is advancing at a phenomenal rate, with each new release bringing you new features and improvements to existing features. All of this new functionality must surely come at the cost of increased hardware resources.

Conventions Used in This Book

The following is a list of the typographical conventions used in this book:

Italics

Used to indicate URLs, filenames, filename extensions, and directory/ folder names. For example, a path in the filesystem appears as */Developer/ Applications*.

Constant width

Used to show code examples, the contents of files, console output, as well as the names of variables, commands, and other code excerpts.

Constant width bold

Used to highlight portions of code, typically new additions to old code.

Constant width italic

Used in code examples and tables to show sample text to be replaced with your own values.

Color

The second color is used to indicate a cross-reference within the text.

You should pay special attention to notes set apart from the text with the following icons:

This is a tip, suggestion, or general note. It contains useful supplementary information about the topic at hand.

This is a warning or note of caution, often indicating that your money or your privacy might be at risk.

The thermometer icons, found next to each hack, indicate the relative complexity of the hack:

 beginner   moderate   expert

Using Code Examples

This book is here to help you get your job done. In general, you may use the code in this book in your programs and documentation. You do not need to contact us for permission unless you're reproducing a significant portion of the code. For example, writing a program that uses several chunks of code from this book does not require permission. Selling or distributing a CD-ROM of examples from O'Reilly books *does* require permission. Answering a question by citing this book and quoting example code does not require permission. Incorporating a significant amount of example code from this book into your product's documentation *does* require permission.

We appreciate, but do not require, attribution. An attribution usually includes the title, author, publisher, and ISBN. For example: "*Skype Hacks* by Andrew Sheppard. Copyright 2006 O'Reilly Media, Inc., ISBN 0-596-10189-9."

If you feel your use of code examples falls outside fair use or the permission given here, feel free to contact us at *permissions@oreilly.com*.

How to Contact Us

We have tested and verified the information in this book to the best of our ability, but you may find that features have changed (or even that we have made mistakes!). As a reader of this book, you can help us to improve future editions by sending us your feedback. Please let us know about any errors, inaccuracies, bugs, misleading or confusing statements, and typos that you find anywhere in this book.

Please also let us know what we can do to make this book more useful to you. We take your comments seriously and will try to incorporate reasonable suggestions into future editions. You can write to us at:

O'Reilly Media, Inc.
1005 Gravenstein Hwy N.
Sebastopol, CA 95472
(800) 998-9938 (in the U.S. or Canada)
(707) 829-0515 (international/local)
(707) 829-0104 (fax)

To ask technical questions or to comment on the book, send email to:

bookquestions@oreilly.com

The web site for *Skype Hacks* lists examples, errata, downloads, and plans for future editions. You can find this page at:

http://www.oreilly.com/catalog/skypehks/

For more information about this book and others, see the O'Reilly web site:

http://www.oreilly.com

Got a Hack?

To explore Hacks books online or to contribute a hack for future titles, visit:

http://hacks.oreilly.com

Safari® Enabled

 When you see a Safari® Enabled icon on the cover of your favorite technology book, that means the book is available online through the O'Reilly Network Safari Bookshelf.

Safari offers a solution that's better than e-books. It's a virtual library that lets you easily search thousands of top tech books, cut and paste code samples, download chapters, and find quick answers when you need the most accurate, current information. Try it for free at *http://safari.oreilly.com*.

## CHAPTER ONE

Start Using Skype
Hacks 1–12

This chapter is targeted at readers who are new to Skype, or who have only heard about Skype and would like to try it. Experienced Skype users might want to skip this chapter and move on to more advanced stuff in Chapter 2 and beyond.

By reading this chapter, you will achieve three important goals: you will know what Skype is and what it can do; you will acquire a "Skype vocabulary" that will help you make better use of the hacks that follow in subsequent chapters; and you will be able to make a smooth transition to becoming a dyed-in-the-wool "Skyper." Moreover, you will achieve these goals in an action-oriented way—by doing hacks!

Additionally, by reading this chapter—an alternative title for which could be "A Whirlwind Tour of Skype's Features"—you will also see links among later hacks that would otherwise remain hidden. In short, if you are new to Skype, this chapter is for you.

What Is Skype?

Skype is both software and a bundle of services. It is an implementation of *Voice over IP* (VoIP) that enables people to have two-way telephone conversations over the Internet using a *softphone* (a piece of software that emulates the functions of regular phone hardware to make and receive calls). Many VoIP offerings are available. What makes Skype so different, and revolutionary, is that it is based on *Peer-to-Peer* (P2P) technology similar to Kazaa (this is not surprising, really, given that Skype was developed by the same people who brought us Kazaa). Using P2P technology means that Skype runs on a mesh of interconnected PCs spread across the global Internet (see Figure 1-1). This provides two important benefits to Skype users. First, Skype scales very well and there is little risk that it will run out of resources.

Second, because the Skype user community provides the resources to run Skype, it requires very little of its own infrastructure, so its services can be offered at little or no cost.

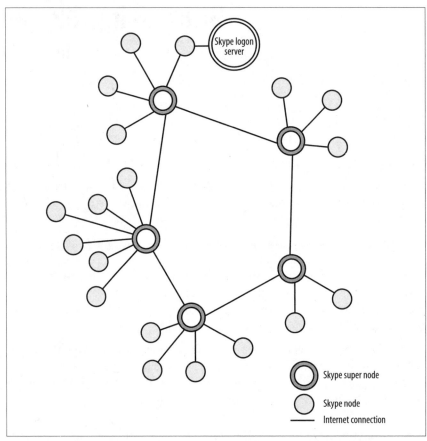

Figure 1-1. Skype runs on a mesh of computers that span the global Internet

In Figure 1-1, a *Skype node* is simply a computer running the Skype application (also sometimes called a Skype client). Likewise, a *super node* is also simply a computer running the Skype application, but Skype has nominated it to take on some of the administrative and coordinating activities of its P2P network. As Skype has not made public the rules under which a node can become a super node, becoming a super node is not something over which you have any real control; though, clearly, your chances of becoming a super node are greater the more P2P friendly your Internet connection is. Of course, in reality, there are millions of nodes and thousands, or perhaps tens or hundreds of thousands, of super nodes.

A node must register and authenticate itself with a Skype server during login. Once a call is established between two nodes, where possible, a direct Internet link between the two is used. By directly connecting two nodes for calls, Skype minimizes network routing overhead and therefore can deliver better voice quality.

Skype-to-Skype calls are free. Similarly, Skype users can conference call, chat, and transfer files with each other at no cost. A *conference call* enables several people to participate in the same call, just as though they were sitting around the same conference table. *Chat* is a generic term for what people generally refer to as *instant messaging* services, which allow instant text communication between two or more people over the Internet.

All Skype traffic is *encrypted* end to end (which makes your communication more secure by obscuring information from eavesdroppers along the communication path), so it's somewhat more secure than most alternatives, including regular phone lines. End-to-end encryption means that you and the recipient of your communication have free and open access to the exchanged information, but at any point along the communication path in between, that same information is unintelligible. Skype-to-Skype calls are encrypted end to end. Incoming calls for SkypeIn and outgoing calls for SkypeOut are only encrypted while on the Skype network and are *not* encrypted for the part of their transmission that goes over the public telephone network.

If this were all that Skype offers, Skype would be an island unto itself and of rather limited interest. However, Skype also offers six prepaid add-on services—all at extremely low cost—that allow Skype users to make and receive calls to regular phones (as well as make free calls to other Skype users), and much more. In brief, here are the six services:

SkypeOut
> Allows you to call regular telephones, anywhere in the world, at very low rates—as low as €0.017 (about $0.021) per minute. However, rates do vary, and calls to mobile phones and some destinations can cost substantially more than €0.017 per minute.

SkypeIn
> Gives you a dial-in telephone number that regular phones can call. The number will be routed automatically to wherever you happen to be logged onto Skype. Phone numbers are available for several countries and their regions. Currently, a SkypeIn number costs €30 (about $37) per year. As an added bonus, SkypeIn comes bundled with voicemail.

Voicemail
> Allows you to receive voicemail messages from anyone and listen to them at any time and from anywhere you are logged onto Skype. Using

this service, you can also send voicemail to other Skype users, even if they are not subscribers to Skype voicemail.

Skype Zones

This software add-on for Skype gives mobile Skype users access to thousands (more than 18,000 at the time of this writing) of wireless hotspots dotted around the globe from which to use Skype and its services. It is important to note that this is a Skype-only service and it does not support other Internet activities—for example, web browsing.

Personalise Skype

Allows you to buy custom ringtones and pictures for your profile from Skype's online store to give a personal sound and look to your Skype experience.

Skype Groups

This Skype service simplifies the management of, and payment for, other Skype services for groups of people. Using Skype Groups, an administrator for a group can allocate SkypeOut credits, SkypeIn numbers, and voicemail to all members of a group. And all this can be done without the need for multiple credit cards and separate payments! Plus, reports can be generated to keep the managers and accountants happy.

You should also be aware that Skype is unlike any telephone system you have known before. It is based on technologies totally unlike your existing *Plain Old Telephone System* (POTS) that uses the *Public Switched Telephone Network* (PSTN), which is run by large telephone companies that we've all come to know, and in many cases hate! Nor does it use industry-standard protocols, such as the *Session Initiation Protocol* (SIP), which means that it does not interoperate with other VoIP services. Also, Skype has only rudimentary *Private Branch Exchange* (PBX) features (which allow phones within an organization to connect to each other as well as to the outside world), though this may well change as Skype matures.

Skype delivers surprisingly good voice quality calls over the Internet using surprisingly low data-rate requirements. The data rate that an Internet connection can support usually is referred to as its *bandwidth*. Dial-up modems have typical connection bandwidths in the range of 28.8 to 56 *kilobits per second* (Kbps), or 3.6 to 7.0 *kilobytes (KB) per second*, where 1 byte equals 8 bits. Broadband connection speed is typically measured in hundreds of kilobits per second, and possibly in *megabits per second* (Mbps) for fast connections, where 1 Mbps equals 1,000 Kpbs. Skype typically consumes between 3 and 16 kilobytes per second (24 Kbps to 128 Kbps). However, obviously your Skype experience will improve with higher available bandwidths. This is especially true if you are doing other things—such as browsing the Web or downloading files—while making a Skype call.

Skype works with almost any type of Internet connection: *dial-up* (where you connect with a modem over a regular telephone line); broadband *Digital Subscriber Line* (DSL, or its cousin, *Asymmetric DSL* or ADSL); *cable broadband*; *local area network* (LAN); *Personal Area Network* (PAN, usually using Bluetooth, which is a short-range wireless technology); *Wireless Fidelity* (WiFi) or *hotspot* (a public wireless connection); and even *satellite* Internet services (which usually connect through a radio dish pointing skyward at a geosynchronous satellite in space). Given any one of these types of Internet connections with enough bandwidth, and chances are you'll be Skyping in no time! However, you should understand that good call quality depends a great deal on having sufficient bandwidth and low latency, which is a challenge if your connection is through dial-up (poor bandwidth) or satellite (poor latency).

As you will no doubt discover, you can do things with Skype that you simply cannot do using your existing telephone system or other VoIP offerings. These "things" are not just technological, either, as many of them represent ways to save money that were just impossible before. Skype is revolutionary because of the technology it uses. For that reason, you are limited only by your imagination. Happy hacking!

> Mac OS X and the Pocket PC platforms don't support the mouse right-click action. In the hacks that follow, for those cases where an item of functionality is supported by Mac OS X or Pocket PC but is not available through right-clicking, the equivalent actions to access such functionality are stated explicitly.

HACK
#1

Make Your First Skype Call

If you're new to Skype, this hack will have you talking online quickly and with a minimum of fuss.

Works with: all versions of Skype.

Not surprisingly, Skype has gone to great lengths to make it easy to install and use Skype. Instead of duplicating what Skype has put in place for new Skype users, here I simply intend to act as your friendly guide.

Just like when you test-drive a car, the goal is to get you on the road as quickly as possible and put Skype through its paces, all the while avoiding the potholes and other obstacles that might get in the way.

Follow these steps and make your first Skype call with a minimum of aggravation and fuss:

Check minimum system requirements

Table P-1 in the Preface gives a quick overview of system requirements for each platform Skype supports. At the time of this writing, Skype supported Windows (2000 and XP), Linux (SuSE, Fedora Core, Debian, and Madriva, formerly Mandrake), Mac OS X (10.3 Panther or later), and Pocket PC (Mobile 2003). For the latest requirements for each Skype platform, check the download page for the version you are interested in, at *http://www.skype.com/download/*. Remember, these are *minimum* system requirements, so you may want to build in a little margin of error when deciding whether your machine is up to the job. This is especially true if you intend to use your machine for other tasks while you talk.

Check out Skype's look-and-feel online

Before installing Skype, it's well worth it to first familiarize yourself with the look-and-feel of Skype on your preferred platform (see Figure 1-2). That way, when you first run Skype, you'll be looking at something familiar. You can familiarize yourself with Skype by visiting Skype's web site, at *http://www.skype.com/products/screenshots.html*.

Figure 1-2. Familiarize yourself with Skype's look-and-feel by flicking through screenshots online (in this case, for Windows)

Download and install Skype

Go to the download page of Skype's web site, *http://www.skype.com/ download/*, pick the install package for the platform of your choice, download it, and follow Skype's installation instructions. Skype has made a good effort to make these steps easy and trouble free.

Start Skype and configure options

After starting Skype, either as the last step of the installation procedure, by double-clicking its icon, or by directly running the Skype executable, select Skype → Tools → Options... (Skype → Preferences... on Mac OS X) to open the Configuration Options window. The two areas where a new Skype user is most likely to have problems are with sound devices and network settings, which you can find under the option categories listed in Table 1-1. Click on each configuration category in turn and review its settings. For each setting, ask yourself whether its value is compatible with what you know about your machine and network configuration; if it isn't, make any necessary changes before saving your Skype configuration options.

Table 1-1. Skype's audio and network settings

Platform	Options category	What to look at...
Windows	Sound Devices	Check that the audio-in and audio-out devices are the ones you want to use to make calls.
	Connection	Check that the port number for incoming connections is compatible with your network setup; if it isn't, change it. Check ports 80 and 443. Set up a proxy manually if it is not detected automatically.
Linux	Hand/Headsets	Check that the correct audio device is selected for calls.
	Advanced	Check that the port number for incoming connections is compatible with your network setup; if it isn't, change it. Check ports 80 and 443.
Mac OS X	Audio	Check that the audio-in and audio-out devices are the ones you want to use to make calls.
	Advanced	Check that the port number for incoming connections is compatible with your network setup; if it isn't, change it.
Pocket PC	Options	For Pocket PC there are no audio or network settings you can control.

Call the Skype Call Testing Service (echo123)

To call Skype's automated test service, simply enter "echo123" in Skype's address field and click on the lefthand green button with a picture of a phone handset on it (see Figure 1-3). Once connected, you should hear a prerecorded greeting that explains how the echo123 service works and what you should do next. Follow the verbal instructions and if all goes well you should hear your voice played back to you. When you do, hang up.

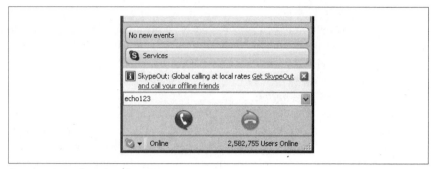

Figure 1-3. Dialing the echo123 service

Hang up

You can hang up a call at any time by clicking on the righthand red button with a picture of a phone handset on it (see Figure 1-4). Congratulations! You've made your first Skype call.

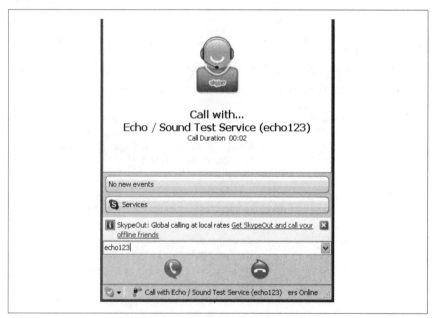

Figure 1-4. Hang up a call at any time by clicking on the righthand red phone button

Troubleshoot

If your call to echo123 worked, great—welcome to Skype! But if it did not, you still have some work to do to make that first call. You're in troubleshooting territory and you should skip ahead to "Troubleshoot Skype" [Hack #12].

Chat Using Skype

If you're new to Skype, this hack will have you chatting online quickly and with a minimum of fuss.

Works with: all versions of Skype.

Skype chat is an implementation of instant messaging, which is an online, real-time interactive communication method that uses simple text to send and receive messages. You and up to 50 (at the time of this writing) other Skype users can simultaneously "chat," sending messages back and forth to each other so that all chat participants can see and participate in the exchange.

Unfortunately, Skype chat does not interoperate with other popular instant messaging systems, such as MSN Messenger, AOL Instant Messenger, and Yahoo!. However, some third-party add-on services are popping up to bridge the gap; for example, Connectotel (*http://www.Connectotel.com/*) demonstrated a Skype to *Short Message Service* (SMS) gateway in early 2005. See Chapter 11 for add-ons, tools, and services that extend Skype.

For this hack, I assume that you already have Skype up and running, you've made your first Skype call with "Make Your First Skype Call" [Hack #1], and you're ready to explore Skype's chat feature. So, if you're ready to chat, let's begin:

Check out how chat works online

Skype provides online visual guides that explain specific Skype features. Before embarking on a chat session, you would do well to get to know Skype's chat features by reviewing the chat visual guide, located at *http://www.skype.com/help/guides/message.html*.

Configure settings

Open Skype and select Tools → Options... (Skype → Preferences... on Mac OS X) to display the configuration settings window. You will find chat settings under the categories listed in Table 1-2. Review chat settings in these categories, make any desired changes, and then save your Skype configuration options.

Start a chat session

As shown in Table 1-3, you can start a one-on-one chat session in a few different ways. You can start a multiperson chat session by using any of the methods listed in Table 1-4. Starting a chat session with one or more other Skype users should open a window that looks like that shown in Figure 1-6. Note that the Pocket PC version of Skype does not currently support multiperson chat sessions.

If you're new to Skype and don't have any contacts with which to chat, you can chat with Skype's automated test service instead. Just enter "echo123" in Skype's address field and start a chat session. It won't be a very interesting chat session, as echo123 will simply repeat back to you the messages you send.

As an added bonus, you can send echo123 the message "callme" (without quotes and with no spaces) and it will call you back to do a voice call test.

Invite more people to join

Starting with a one-on-one or multiperson chat session, as shown in Figure 1-6, you can add more people to the chat session by clicking on either the "Add more users to this chat!" button or the "Add people to this chat" icon (see Figure 1-7).

Chat

Messages exchanged among all chat participants appear in the chat window (see Figure 1-6). You can send your own messages to all participants by entering your message text in the box at the bottom of the window.

Quit chat

You can quit a chat session at any time by clicking on the quit chat icon (see Figure 1-5) in the chat window.

Troubleshoot

If at any point during the preceding steps, chat didn't behave as you expected, or if things have patently gone wrong, you should skip ahead to "Troubleshoot Skype" [Hack #12].

Table 1-2. Skype's chat settings

Platform	Options category	What to look at...
Windows	General	Check that the double-click behavior for contacts is what you want. A double-click can start a chat session or start a call. Decide whether to show emoticons.
	Privacy	Choose what category of contacts to allow chat from. Also decide for how long you want to retain chat histories.
	Notifications	Decide whether you want a pop-up notification when someone starts a chat with you.
	Sounds	Decide whether you want a sound to be played when a chat message arrives.
	Advanced	Check settings for chat style, timestamp display, and whether the chat window should pop up when someone starts a chat with you.

Table 1-2. Skype's chat settings (continued)

Platform	Options category	What to look at...
Linux	General	Check that the double-click behavior for contacts is what you want. A double-click can start a chat session or start a call. Decide whether to show emoticons.
	Privacy	Choose what category of contacts to allow chat from. Also decide for how long you want to retain chat histories.
	Chat Alerts	Decide whether to have pop-up and sound notifications for chat.
Mac OS X	General	Check that the double-click behavior for contacts is what you want. A double-click can start a chat session or start a call.
	Privacy	Choose what category of contacts to allow chat from.
	Events	Choose how instant message events are to be notified.
	Chat	Decide whether to open chats in separate windows. Choose a retention period for chat history, and choose emoticon style.
Pocket PC	Options	Choose what category of contacts to allow chat from.

Table 1-3. Ways of starting a one-on-one chat session in Skype

Action to start a chat session	Windows	Linux	Mac OS X	Pocket PC
In the Contacts tab...				
Select a contact and click on the icon to start a chat session (Figure 1-5).	✔	✔	✔	✔
Select a contact, right-click, and then choose Start Chat...	✔	✔	Contacts → Send Instant Message...	Touch and hold stylus, then choose "Send an Instant Message"
In the Call List tab (the Log tab on Pocket PC)...				
Select a call and then click on the icon to start a chat session (Figure 1-5).	✔	✔	✔	✔
Select a call, right-click, and choose Start Chat....	✔	✔	Contacts → Send Instant Message...	Touch and hold stylus, then choose "Send an Instant Message"

Figure 1-5. Skype icons to start (left) and quit (right) a chat session

Table 1-4. *Ways of starting a multiperson chat session in Skype*

Action to start a chat session	Windows	Linux	Mac OS X
In the Contacts tab...			
Select multiple contacts, and then click on the icon to start a chat session (Figure 1-5).	✔		✔
Select multiple contacts, right-click, and then choose Start Chat...	✔		Contacts → Start Multichat

Figure 1-6. The Skype chat window

Figure 1-7. Button (left) and icon (right) to add more people to an open chat session

HACK #3 Set Up and Make a Conference Call

If you're new to Skype, this hack will help you set up and make a conference call quickly and with a minimum of fuss.

Works with: Windows, Linux, and Mac OS X versions of Skype.

A conference call allows several geographically separated people to talk with each other as though they are sitting in the same conference room. Skype allows you, and up to four others (at the time of this writing), to join together in a conference call.

Before moving on to the mechanics of making a Skype conference call, you should be aware of a number of ground rules and limitations pertaining to Skype conference calls. First, conference participants can't dial-in to your SkypeIn number to join the conference, so you can invite only Skype users and SkypeOut contacts (for which, in the case of the latter, you make the outgoing calls and are billed at the appropriate call rate for each participant's call destination) to join a conference. Conference call participants can, of course, hang up and leave the conference at any time. Second, you, as the conference host, are the only person who can invite more people to join the conference while it is in progress, and you are the only person who can bring the conference to an end. Third, you must have sufficient available bandwidth to host the conference, as your bandwidth needs scale roughly in proportion to the number of conference participants; if you don't, you might want to consider having one of the other conference participants become the conference host, if they have more available bandwidth than you do.

So, you've made your first Skype call ("Make Your First Skype Call" [Hack #1]), you're chatting online ("Chat Using Skype" [Hack #2]) with friends and family as though there's no tomorrow—what's next? Setting up and making a conference call is a snap if you follow these steps:

Check out how conference calls work online
Use Skype's online visual user guide to get to know how conference calls work (*http://www.skype.com/help/guides/conference.html*).

Configure settings
No current version of Skype has any configuration settings specific to making conference calls. However, this may change in the future, so it is always worthwhile to review Skype's settings before moving on to the next step.

Start a conference call
You have quite a few choices when it comes to starting a conference call, as shown in Table 1-5. Note that Skype users on Pocket PCs can participate in conference calls, but they cannot initiate or host conference calls.

Invite more people to join
You can add contacts to a conference call in progress by using any of the methods listed in Table 1-6. There is, however, one small gotcha. If you start a one-on-one call, you cannot convert it into a conference call by adding additional contacts. To be a conference call, a call must start as a conference call! Skype has announced that in some future version of Skype, you will be able to convert a one-to-one call into a conference call without hanging up and starting over.

Talk

The idea behind a conference call is that it's the audio-only equivalent of a group of people gathering around a conference table and talking. So, just talk. Everyone can hear and speak to everyone else.

End the conference call

The easiest way to end your participation in a conference call or the conference call itself if you are its host is to click on the call hang-up button. The hang-up button is the round red button with a picture of a phone on it (this is the same call button you use to hang up one-on-one calls). Alternatively, select Skype → Call → Hang Up from the menu. Lastly, if you're using Skype on Windows with global hotkeys enabled (Skype → Tools → Options → Hotkeys), you can hit the hotkey sequence Alt-PgDn (or whatever hotkey you have chosen for this purpose) to hang up a call or conference call.

Troubleshoot

Can't get conference calling to work? Check out "Troubleshoot Skype" [Hack #12]—it might help.

Table 1-5. Ways of starting a Skype conference call

Action to start a conference call	Windows	Linux	Mac OS X
From the Skype menu bar...			
Select Tools → Create Conference... (or Call → Start Conference Call... on Mac OS X); this will always display the Start a Skype Conference Call window, shown in Figure 1-8.	✔	✔	✔
In the Contacts tab...			
Select multiple contacts and click on the round green call button with a picture of a phone on it (this is the same call button you use to make one-on-one calls).	✔	✔	✔
Select multiple contacts, right-click, and then choose Invite to Conference (Create Conference on Linux).	✔	✔	Contacts → Start Conference
Select multiple contacts and click on the conference call icon, shown in Figure 1-9 (on Mac OS X, instead of initiating a conference call, this will simply display a window similar to that shown in Figure 1-8).	✔	✔	✔
In the Call List tab...			
Click on the conference call icon (Figure 1-9) to open the window to set up and start a conference call (Figure 1-8).	✔	✔	✔

Table 1-5. Ways of starting a Skype conference call (continued)

Action to start a conference call	Windows	Linux	Mac OS X
In the Dial tab...			
Click on the conference call icon (Figure 1-9) to open the window to set up and start a conference call (Figure 1-8).	✔	✔	✔

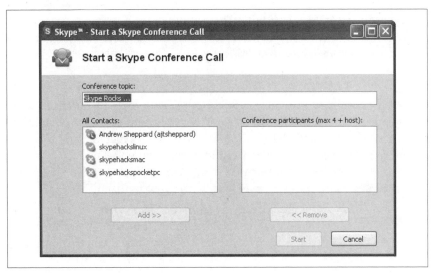

Figure 1-8. Window to set up and start a conference call

Figure 1-9. Icon to invite contacts to a conference call

Table 1-6. Ways of inviting others to join a conference call

Action to invite a contact to a conference call	Windows	Linux	Max OS X
In the Contacts tab...			
Select a contact, right-click, and then choose Invite to Conference.	✔	✔	Contacts → Add to Conference
Select multiple contacts, right-click, and then choose Invite to Conference.	✔	✔	Contacts → Add to Conference
Select a contact and click on the conference call icon (Figure 1-9). This opens the Start a Skype Conference Call window.	✔	✔	✔
Select multiple contacts and click on the conference call icon (Figure 1-9).	✔	✔	✔

Table 1-6. Ways of inviting others to join a conference call (continued)

Action to invite a contact to a conference call	Windows	Linux	Max OS X
In the Call List tab...			
Select a call, and then click on the conference call icon (Figure 1-9). This opens the Start a Skype Conference Call window.	✔	✔	✔

H A C K   Try SkypeOut, Risk Free
#4
Experiment with making calls to regular phones using SkypeOut. Even better, follow the advice in this hack and you can try it for free and without risk.

Works with: all versions of Skype.

There are three easy ways to try SkypeOut. First, you can purchase some SkypeOut credits. Second, you can purchase an item of Skype-compatible hardware bundled with which is a voucher for SkypeOut call minutes. Third, you can use a Skype Gift Certificate that you've been given (visit the web page for Skype Gift Certificates at *http://share.skype.com/blog/products_ and services/we_bring_you..._skype_gift_certificates/* for details).

You can buy SkypeOut credits directly from the Skype web site, *http://www. Skype.com/*, using a variety of payment methods (but see "Avoid Problems Paying for Services" [Hack #15]). With some credits in hand, you can start dialing regular telephone numbers (see "Dial Like a Wizard" [Hack #11]).

Now, here's the risk-free part. If while experimenting with SkypeOut, you keep your calls to less than €1 (about $1.25) in value (this gives you about 58 minutes of call time at SkypeOut's lowest global rate, but see "Avoid Higher SkypeOut Rates" [Hack #17]) and you don't like it, you can simply claim a refund (see "Claim Your Money Back" [Hack #16]) for the *full* amount of the credits you bought. Even if you inadvertently step over the €1 threshold for a full refund, it's not a total loss if you change your mind about SkypeOut, as you can request a refund of the unused balance of your credits. In fact, you can claim a refund at any time on these terms for your last SkypeOut credit purchase, regardless of whether it's your first credit purchase or a subsequent top-up purchase. However, SkypeOut credits do expire, so don't wait too long to request your refund (see "Avoid Forfeiting SkypeOut Credits" [Hack #21]).

An alternative to buying SkypeOut credits is to purchase an item of Skype-compatible hardware that is bundled with a voucher for SkypeOut credits. Skype has partnered with manufacturers of sound headsets and other types of complementary hardware add-ons to encourage you to start using SkypeOut. These vouchers typically offer 30 to 120 minutes of SkypeOut call time based on the lowest SkypeOut global rate, which means that you'll get your full 30 to 120 minutes if you call destinations having the lowest global rate, but possibly far fewer minutes if you call destinations at higher SkypeOut rates. Moreover, in the case of Skype vouchers used to fund Skype services, there is no refund option if you decide you don't like SkypeOut—but, of course, you do get to keep the hardware and use it for other things!

You can find Skype's terms and conditions at *http://www.skype.com/ company/legal/terms/tos_voip.html*. Of particular interest for those who want to try SkypeOut without any risk is "Article 6—REFUND POLICY."

Try Skypeln, Risk Free

#5

Experiment with receiving regular phone calls to a Skypeln dial-in number. Even better, follow the advice in this hack and you can try it for free and without risk.

Works with: all versions of Skype.

SkypeIn is a prepaid subscription service that enables you to have a regular dial-in phone number that routes calls to wherever you are logged onto Skype. This means that a dedicated SkypeIn dial-in phone number can follow you wherever you go—try that with a regular landline!

SkypeIn telephone numbers are available for several countries, and even for regions within those countries. See the Skype web site, *http://www.Skype. com/*, for details and availability.

Regardless of which geographical location you get your dial-in number for, you have the choice of getting a 3-month or 12-month subscription, currently €10 and €30 (about $12.50 and $37.50), respectively. Skype Voicemail (see "Try Skype Voicemail, Risk Free" [Hack #6]) is currently bundled free of charge with SkypeIn. Skype Gift Certificates can also be used to activate the SkypeIn service.

Trying SkypeIn is risk free if you follow this advice. Experiment with SkypeIn for less than 30 days, and then decide whether to keep it. If you decide you don't want SkypeIn, request a refund (see "Claim Your Money Back" [Hack #16]) within 30 days of purchasing a subscription and Skype will refund your money *in full*. Even if you inadvertently step over the 30-day qualifying trial period for a full refund, it's not a total loss if you change your mind about SkypeIn, as you can request a refund of the unused balance, which will be refunded on a pro rata basis. In fact, you can claim a refund on these terms at any time for a SkypeIn subscription, regardless of whether it is a new subscription or a renewal.

You can find Skype's terms and conditions at *http://www.skype.com/ company/legal/terms/tos_voip.html*. Of particular interest for those who want to try SkypeIn without any risk is "Article 6—REFUND POLICY."

Try Skype Voicemail, Risk Free

Experiment with Skype Voicemail. Even better, follow the advice in this hack and you can try it for free and without risk.

Works with: all versions of Skype.

The Skype Voicemail service is for those times when you're already online talking to someone else, or you're otherwise unavailable (for example, offline). Calls are automatically routed to a voicemail account that can have a personalized greeting, and that you can access from wherever you are logged onto Skype. You can keep your voicemails for as long as you want.

Skype Voicemail has a neat feature that allows you to *send* voicemail to any Skype user, regardless of whether *they* are a Skype Voicemail subscriber. Both Skype users and callers that use your SkypeIn number, if you have one (see "Try SkypeIn, Risk Free" [Hack #5]), can leave voicemail messages for you. Indeed, Skype Voicemail is currently bundled for free with a SkypeIn subscription.

If you don't have a SkypeIn account, but nevertheless would like to take advantage of the services provided by Skype Voicemail, a subscription currently costs €5 (about $6.25) for three months and €15 (about $18.75) for one year. Skype Gift Certificates can also be used to activate Skype Voicemail service.

You can try Skype Voicemail for free and without risk if you follow these simple steps. Purchase a three-month or one-year subscription. Experiment with Skype Voicemail for less than 30 days, and if you don't like it, Skype will refund your subscription *in full* upon request (see "Claim Your Money Back" [Hack #16]).

After 30 days, Skype will refund only the unused portion of your last subscription payment on a pro rata basis. In fact, you can claim a refund on these terms at any time for a Skype Voicemail subscription, regardless of whether it is a new subscription or a renewal.

You can find Skype's terms and conditions at *http://www.skype.com/company/legal/terms/tos_voip.html*. Of particular interest for those who want to try Skype Voicemail without any risk is "Article 6—REFUND POLICY."

Roam the World with Skype Zones

Using the Skype Zones service, you can wander the globe and use Skype at any of the 18,000+ wireless hotspots available.

Works with: Windows version of Skype.

Skype has partnered with Boingo, *http://www.boingo.com/*, to provide Skype users with access to wireless hotspots spread around the globe. Using these hotspots, Skype users can make and receive calls, chat, send voicemail, listen to voicemail—in fact, use the whole gamut of Skype services.

Currently available through two different plans, this service may prove ideal for Skype users on the move. The Skype Zones Unlimited plan has a monthly subscription of $7.95 (about €6.35) that allows for unlimited use across the whole Boingo network. The Skype Zones AsYouGo plan has a per-connection fee of $2.95 (about €2.35) that allows access from any single network location for up to two consecutive hours. Clearly, if you roam from point to point on the Boingo network, this second plan can get expensive very quickly!

Skype Zones is different from Skype's other service offerings in two respects. First, the service is priced in U.S. dollars ($) rather than euros (€). Second, trying the service is not risk free in the sense that there is no full refund option should you decide that Skype Zones is not for you. However, on the plus side, there is no long-term contract commitment, and in the case of the Skype Zones Unlimited plan, you can terminate your subscription at any time by notifying Skype and Boingo at least five days before the end of your billing cycle.

You can find full terms and conditions for the Skype Zones service at *http://www.skype.com/products/skypezones/*. You will have to click on the "Sign up for Skype Zones now to get started" link to get to a page with the text of the terms and conditions.

Transfer a File Using Skype

Using Skype, you can transfer files quickly and securely, even while you talk or chat.

Works with: Windows, Linux, and Mac OS X versions of Skype.

You can use Skype to transfer files to other Skype users who have already authorized you. Indeed, it can be an easy way to transfer files among different machines in your own home or business (see "Transfer Files Among Diverse Machines" [Hack #57]).

Skype has several advantages over email attachments when it comes to transferring files. First, it's more secure, because the communications link is encrypted end to end. Second, there's no limit on file size, whereas email attachments, if not limited in size as a policy of the email server, are certainly limited by the size of your mail server inbox. Finally, it can be quicker, as you can transfer a file during a call or while chatting, often with no more effort than that required to drag-and-drop a file.

You can initiate a file transfer in several different ways, as shown in Table 1-7.

Skype file transfer is currently not supported on Pocket PC.

Table 1-7. Ways of initiating a file transfer in Skype

Action to initiate a file transfer	Windows	Linux	Mac OS X
In the Contacts tab…			
Select the contact, right-click, and then choose Send File.	✔	✔	Contacts → Send File
Select the contact and click on the Send File icon (Figure 1-10).	✔	✔	✔
Select multiple contacts, right-click, and then choose Send File.	✔		
Select multiple contacts and click on the Send File icon (Figure 1-10).	✔		
Drag-and-drop the file onto the contact.	✔		✔
In the Call List tab…			
Select the call, right-click, and then choose Send File.	✔	✔	Contacts → Send File
Select the call and click on the Send File icon (Figure 1-10).	✔	✔	✔
In a one-on-one chat…			
Click on the Send File icon (Figure 1-10).	✔	✔	✔
Select the chat participant, right-click, and then choose Send File.	✔	✔	Contacts → Send File
Drag-and-drop the file onto the chat window.	✔		✔
Drag-and-drop the file onto the chat participant.	✔		✔
In a multiperson chat…			
Click on the Send File to All icon (Figure 1-10). This initiates file transfer to all chat participants.	✔	✔	✔
Select an individual chat participant, right-click, and then choose Send File. This initiates file transfer to only that person.	✔	✔	Pull-down menu opposite participant's name → Send File
Drag-and-drop the file onto the chat window. This initiates file transfer to all chat participants.	✔		✔
Drag-and-drop the file onto an individual chat participant. This initiates file transfer to only that person.	✔		Pull-down menu opposite participant's name → Send File

Figure 1-10. Icons for sending a file to one Skype user, or to many at once

You can initiate file transfers at any time, but they will not start until the recipient of a file accepts the transfer (see Figure 1-11). You can carry out several file transfers at the same time, but each will open a new window on the recipient's machine, asking to accept the file transfer. Having to confirm each file transfer can become tiresome very quickly if you have a large number of files to transfer. So, if you have large numbers of files, or whole directories to transfer, you might want to consider "Transfer Folders, Not Just Individual Files" [Hack #84] instead.

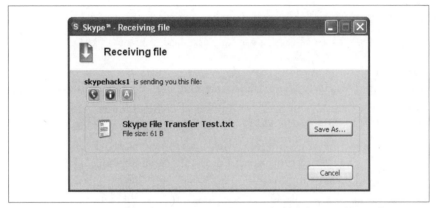

Figure 1-11. A recipient of a file transfer must accept it before the transfer can begin

Like all Skype traffic, file transfers are encrypted end to end, so they are secure while in transit. But remember, once downloaded to your machine, they are again in unencrypted form. Moreover, downloading files even from people you know and trust poses the threat of infecting your machine with a virus, so it's always a good idea to scan all incoming Skype file transfers (see "Scan Files Received via Skype for Viruses" [Hack #75]).

Skype is rather tolerant of a less-than-perfect Internet connection between sender and recipient, and a file transfer will continue even in the face of interruptions and congestion on the Internet. But the speed at which a file will transfer from sender to recipient depends on several factors, not least the lesser of the bandwidths of the sender and recipient and whether you're in a call or otherwise using your Internet connection. Having a Skype-unfriendly connection might also slow file transfers to a crawl (see "Test Your Connection for Skype Friendliness" [Hack #38]). Having a Skype-friendly connection, or reconfiguring your Internet connection to get one, is one of the best ways to improve slow file-transfer speed.

Even though Skype puts no limits on the types or sizes of files you can transfer, bear in mind that extremely large files will take a long time even if you and the recipient have a decent amount of bandwidth, and that a transfer might fail if the destination machine has insufficient disk space.

The great virtues of Skype file transfer are that it's easy, it's secure, it works among different machines running different operating systems, and it will often work behind a firewall/Network Address Translation (NAT)/router and other obstacles when other methods simply won't.

HACK #9   Make Toll-Free Calls

Most regular phone plans don't charge for toll-free numbers you call in your own country, but what about toll-free numbers in other countries? Skype allows you to make free toll-free calls for your own country, and for other countries!!

Works with: all versions of Skype.

Many VoIP plans charge for what would otherwise be toll-free calls (1-800 and the like in the U.S. and other numbers elsewhere) under a regular phone plan. Indeed, until recently, Skype also charged for these types of calls.

Now, many toll-free calls are free when made using Skype. Even better, you don't have to be a SkypeOut subscriber to take advantage of making toll-free calls without paying a penny.

Regular phone plans normally don't charge for calling toll-free numbers in your own country, but that is not usually the case for toll-free numbers in other countries. In fact, such numbers might simply be blocked. With Skype toll-free calling, there is no such restriction.

Support for all types of toll-free numbers in all countries is not yet available. Skype currently supports the following countries and number prefixes:

France
+33-800, +33-805, +33-809

Poland
+48-800

United Kingdom
+44-500, +44-800, +44-808

United States and Canada
+1-800, +1-866, +1-877, +1-888

You can obtain toll-free directory assistance for some U.S. toll-free numbers by calling +1-800-555-1212. The service is free, but not all U.S. toll-free numbers are listed—only those for subscribers that choose to list them.

Some toll-free numbers in the U.S. are geographically restricted in the sense that calls to that number will be accepted only if they originate from a caller in a known geographic region. Because you can make SkypeOut calls from anywhere, these restricted numbers cannot determine your location and therefore may block the call.

As already mentioned, you don't have to be a current SkypeOut subscriber to dial these toll-free numbers from *anywhere*. Just enter in Skype's address bar one of the prefixes listed earlier, along with the rest of the toll-free number, and click the big green call button—you'll be connected for free. If you call certain toll-free numbers on a regular basis, you might want to consider adding them to your Contacts list.

Lastly, if you've connected to a toll-free number and you have problems navigating an automated phone system using Skype's keypad (the "press 4 to get your account balance" sort of thing), "Avoid Problems with Interactive Telephone Services" [Hack #79] should help you.

Forward Calls

Have your calls follow you around! Skype's call-forwarding feature can forward your calls when you're on the move.

Works with: Windows version of Skype.

Skype gives you the option to forward incoming calls to up to three alternative Skype accounts (or regular phone numbers if you're a SkypeOut subscriber). This works whether the incoming call is from another Skype user or, if you have a SkypeIn number, from a regular phone. However, how quickly calls are forwarded depends on your online status, as shown in Table 1-8.

Table 1-8. Typical delay before a call is forwarded

Online status	Call forwarded
Skype not running	Immediately
Online	Between three to five rings
Offline	Immediately
Skype Me	Between three to five rings
Away	Between three to five rings
Not available	Between three to five rings
Do not disturb	Between three to five rings
Invisible	Between three to five rings

To forward calls you must first specify the forwarding Skype names or regular phone numbers (select Skype → Tools → Options... → Call Forwarding & Voicemail), as shown in Figure 1-12. To activate call forwarding you must put a checkmark in the checkbox opposite "Forward calls when I'm not on Skype."

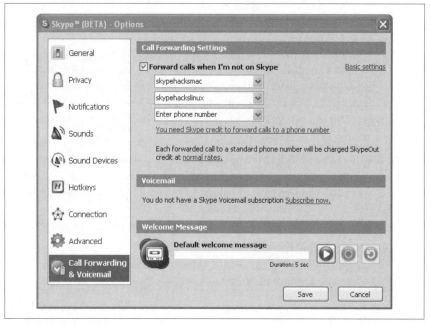

Figure 1-12. Call-forwarding Options dialog

Skype call forwarding enables you to redirect incoming Skype calls to another Skype name, mobile phone, or landline number. If none of the forwarding contacts is available (for example, they're offline), or none of them picks up the call, the caller will either get a message indicating that the call could not be completed, or be directed to voicemail (if you are a Skype voicemail subscriber).

Dial Like a Wizard

HACK
#11

Use Skype's Dialing Wizard to find the correct dial number format and call rate.

Works with: all versions of Skype.

Dialing the wrong number using SkypeOut can be costly in terms of both time and money. You can waste time as you fumble to find the right sequence of digits to make the call, and you can waste money because connecting to the wrong number can be costly, as some SkypeOut rates are more than €1 per minute, and all calls are rounded up to whole minutes.

You can dial a telephone number with Skype in many ways. You can enter digits directly from your computer keyboard into Skype's address bar, use Skype's keypad (on the Dial tab), double-click on an entry in the your Contacts list (Skype can also be set up so that double-click starts a chat), use an advanced USB handset, click on a link in your web browser (see "Make Calls from Your Web Browser" **[Hack #43]**), or access a shortcut on your desktop (see "Add Fast-Dial Shortcuts to Your Menu or Desktop" **[Hack #49]**), among other options. Regardless of what method you use to dial a number, all will be for naught if you don't get the format right.

> To enter the prefix + using the keypad on Skype's Dial tab, click and hold down your left mouse button over the button with 0+ on it for 2 seconds.

Skype Dialing Wizard

Perhaps the least error-prone method of finding the right digit sequence to call is to use the Skype Dialing Wizard (see Figure 1-13), which you can find at *http://www.skype.com/products/skypeout/rates/dialing.html*.

This wizard also has the added advantage of giving you the per-minute call rate for the number you want to dial. And if your web browser is configured properly (see "Make Calls from Your Web Browser" **[Hack #43]**), you can dial the number directly from your browser with just one click.

Skype's Dialing Wizard quotes call rates in euros. Knowing the exchange rate between euros and your home currency will allow you to make a quick mental calculation to convert the call rate into something more meaningful. Alternatively, if you don't know the current exchange rate or you simply don't trust your mental arithmetic, visit the Skype rates page, *http://www.skype.com/products/skypeout/rates/all_rates.html*, and select your home currency from the drop-down list at the top of the page.

After making the call, you can add the number to your Contacts list if it's a number you are likely to call often in the future. For the Windows version of Skype, you can do this by navigating to the Call List tab, right-clicking on a call entry, and selecting Add to Contacts. For the Pocket PC version of Skype, navigate to the Log tab, stylus touch and hold on a call entry, and select Add to Contacts.

Figure 1-13. The Skype Dialing Wizard

  Skype's reporting of errors is sometimes less than user friendly. For instance, try entering a nonsense number such as +12035551212127865273648929. After failing to connect, Skype will report, "Service unavailable—try again."

Alternatively, you might be presented with a numeric error code. Errors #1040 and #1050 in Skype for Mac OS X, for example, typically mean that the SkypeOut number you entered is invalid, even though they are displayed like this: "Internal Error, please try again (#1040)" and "Internal Error, please try again (#1050)." Moreover, Skype's error codes are not consistent across platforms, as the error codes corresponding to #1040 and #1050 on Mac OS X are #10404 and #10503 on Windows. Unfortunately, at the time of this writing, no single resource lists all error codes for all platforms, so you must search for your specific error code in the Skype knowledgebase or in Skype's online forums.

Skype Widget

If you use Skype on Mac OS X, you needn't even go to the trouble of open-ing a browser to have functionality equivalent to Skype's Dialing Wizard. Skype has produced a widget for the Mac OS X dashboard that basically replicates the functionality of the Dialing Wizard in a nifty and quickly accessible tool (see Figure 1-14).

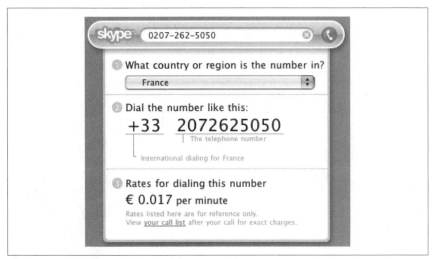

Figure 1-14. The Skype Widget for the Mac OS X dashboard

Troubleshoot Skype

H A C K
#12

Is Skype refusing to play ball? Use these resources and tips to troubleshoot problems with Skype.

Works with: all versions of Skype.

No piece of software is error free or even problem free, so when things go wrong you can either give up, or troubleshoot the problem. If you are an O'Reilly book reader, that puts you most definitely into the category of someone who is willing to troubleshoot!

This hack provides places to look for information and seek help, and some things to try for some of Skype's more-common problems.

Online Information and Help

These online sources of information and help are both useful and free! When researching a problem, you should visit these information sources in the sequence presented in the following list.

User guides

Skype has put together a number of visual guides for its software, located at *http://www.skype.com/help/guides/*. These visual guides are very good, as they break each Skype activity into small, easy-to-follow steps. Often, a quick review of your actions for a particular Skype activity using one of these guides will pinpoint where, and sometimes how, things went wrong.

Troubleshooter

Skype's interactive troubleshooter, *http://support.skype.com/?_a=troubleshooter*, leads you through a step-by-step diagnosis of your problem, and presents suggestions for how you might fix it.

Sound setup guide

If you think that you have a sound setup problem, which is where most users new to Skype come to grief, read one of Skype's sound setup guides, located at *http://www.skype.com/help/guides/soundsetup.html*.

Knowledgebase

Search Skype's knowledgebase at *http://support.skype.com/?_a=knowledgebase* using keywords that best describe the problem or its principal symptoms. The knowledgebase can answer a lot of common questions, and not just on technical matters.

Community forums

Search the Skype community forums at *http://forum.skype.com/search.php* using keywords that best describe the problem or its principal symptoms. Odds are that if someone else has experienced your problem, some kind soul has found a fix for it and has posted a reply to the forums. If you don't find anything useful on the forums that addresses your particular problem, feel free to post the problem to the forums and ask the Skype community for help. Expect some sort of response within 24 hours.

Support request

Frankly, if you've made it to this step, you must be desperate. In my experience, making a support request to Skype is a lot like putting a message into a bottle and tossing the bottle into the sea. Again, in my experience, not only are support requests ignored, they aren't even acknowledged! Let's all hope that Skype puts more emphasis on responding to support requests in the future. However, if you're desperate enough to try, you can send your proverbial message in a bottle from here: *http://support.skype.com/?_a=tickets&_m=submit*.

Troubleshoot

Having trawled through Skype's knowledgebase and online forums, these appear to be the most common problems, and fixes.

General.

Out-of-date version of Skype and old device drivers
 Error number: N/A

 Most likely cause: using older versions of Skype and out-of-date drivers for your computer hardware (particularly for the sound and network devices in your computer, and the firmware in your router) not only can be the direct cause of problems, but also can exacerbate other problems indirectly.

 How to fix: 1) Update the version of Skype you are running to the latest version. 2) Update your drivers and firmware by downloading updates from the web sites of the manufacturers for your devices.

Skype login failed
 Error number: 1101, 1102, or 1103 (Skype was unable to connect to the Skype P2P network).

 Most likely cause: the Internet connection is down or misconfigured, or you are being blocked. Another possible cause is a conflict with your *Data Execution Prevention* (DEP) setting.

 How to fix: 1) Open a web browser and check that your Internet connection is up and working. If it's temporarily offline, that may explain why Skype can't connect to its network. 2) Check your firewall settings; specifically, check that (ideally) port 80, port 443, and those ports above 1024 are open. 3) If you use a proxy, you may have to set up Skype manually to use it (you can do this only on Windows, by selecting Skype → Tools → Options... → Connection). 4) I discuss how to correct conflicts with your DEP setting shortly under the heading "Skype crashes or hangs."

SkypeOut call failed
 Error number: 9504 (failed to connect to Skype server, transient problem); 6503, 6504, 10500, or 10503 (Skype network is temporarily overloaded); 10404 or 10503 (1040 or 1050 on Mac OS X, number is invalid or has been entered incorrectly); 10403 (number not supported or is forbidden); 9403, 9407, or 9408 (there's a problem with your Skype account and you've been suspended temporarily from making SkypeOut calls).

 Most likely cause: you have entered the number incorrectly or the Skype network is temporarily overloaded.

How to fix: 1) Check the format of the number you are trying to dial, and then try again (perhaps try using the Skype Dialing Wizard, *http://www.skype.com/products/skypeout/rates/dialing.html*). 2) Wait 10 to 15 minutes for network congestion to pass and then try again. 3) Check your SkypeOut credit balance. You may have no credits left! 4) If calls to echo123 work, as do calls to other Skype users, but problems with making SkypeOut calls persist, the most likely cause lies with Skype's PSTN gateway providers. Report each incident of a failed SkypeOut call to *pstn-feedback@skype.net*, stating your location, the time at which you attempted to place the call, the number you were calling, and what specifically happened. 5) Submit a problem ticket to Skype.

Skype dial keys don't work with phone systems having interactive menus
Error number: N/A

Most likely cause: this is a highly unpredictable problem, as the dial keys work like a charm for some Skype users, but not at all for others. They can also work one day, but not the next. No one seems to know the cause, but it is a persistent complaint on the Skype forums, regardless of platform.

How to fix: 1) Keep trying and be very careful with your key presses. 2) Try again later or on another day. 3) Use an add-on tool, such as Khaos-Dial (*http://www.khaoslabs.com/khaosdial.php*).

Windows.

Can't hear yourself and/or others
Error number: 6101 (problem with sound-out device) or 6102 (problem with sound-in device).

Most likely cause: a problem with your sound card, or a conflict between your sound card and another application you are running.

How to fix: 1) Check that the correct sound device is selected in Skype (choose Skype → Tools → Options... → Sound Devices). It is always a good idea to specify your audio-in and audio-out devices for Skype explicitly instead of relying on the Windows default sound device (which can change when a new sound device is installed, or when a sound device is plugged in or unplugged). 2) Temporarily disable any applications (for example, TotalRecorder) that may also be using your sound card and see if the problem goes away. 3) Update to the latest drivers for your sound device.

Skype crashes or hangs
Error number: 1101 or 1102 (but, obviously, no error number is reported if Skype crashes or hangs when it first tries to run).

Most likely cause: a conflict with the DEP setting. This is a problem that is specific to Windows XP (SP2) and Windows Server 2000 (SP1).

How to fix: disable DEP. Select Start → Control Panel → System, and in the System Properties window navigate to the Advanced tab. Under the Performance category, click on the Settings button. This will open the Performance Options dialog. Navigate to the Data Execution Prevention tab and click on the second radio button, "Turn on DEP for all programs and services except those I select." Click the Add... button and add *Skype.exe* to the list of those programs for which DEP won't be enforced. Click Apply and then OK.

High CPU usage by Skype
Error number: N/A

Most likely cause: a conflict with another application you are running, a conflicting BIOS setting, a high task priority for Skype, or a high CPU temperature.

How to fix: 1) Try running Skype on its own and see if the problem goes away. If it does go away, try running Skype alongside other applications one by one until the problem reappears. These following applications sometimes cause CPU usage to become excessive: Norton AntiVirus, TotalRecorder, ZoneAlarm, NetLimiter, Steganos Internet Anonymizer, SpySweeper, and other P2P VoIP softphones similar to Skype. 2) Intel's SpeedStep technology can sometimes cause this problem. Try disabling it in your machine's BIOS. 3) Lower Skype's task priority. Press Ctrl-Alt-Delete, which will open the Windows Task Manager. Navigate to the Processes tab and right-click on *Skype.exe*, choose Set Priority, and try lowering Skype's current task priority level. 4) A high CPU temperature can have many causes, but the most obvious cause is an obstruction to the flow of air that is cooling your CPU. If there is an obstruction—for example, air vents are blocked or covered—clear things so that air flows freely once again. To check your CPU temperature you can use a free utility called SpeedFan, which you can download at *http://www. computerbase.de/downloads/software/systemueberwachung/speedfan/*.

Linux.

Skype won't work with your sound device
Error number: N/A

Most likely cause: you have an *Advanced Linux Sound Architecture* (ALSA) sound device for Linux, but you have not enabled *Open Sound System* (OSS) emulation.

How to fix: at present, Skype works only with OSS sound on Linux machines. If you have an ALSA sound device, you must enable its OSS emulation layer for Skype to use it.

Sound is stuttering

Error number: N/A

Most likely cause: you have an ALSA sound device, but Skype is trying to use an OSS driver rather than OSS emulation for ALSA.

How to fix: enable the OSS emulation layer for your ALSA device. Remove or disable the OSS driver.

Skype won't run on 64-bit Linux

Error number: N/A

Most likely cause: you are running 64-bit Linux and don't have 32-bit versions of the Qt and other runtime libraries installed on your machine.

How to fix: as Skype for Linux is a 32-bit application, it will run on 64-bit Linux only if you have the right 32-bit libraries installed.

Save Money with Skype
Hacks 13–24

For some people, Skype might be a sufficiently interesting application of VoIP technology to justify playing with it. For most people, however, the motivation for bringing Skype into their life will be based on simple economics. Skype has the potential to save you money; in fact, quite a lot of money!

In this chapter, I will help you get a handle on whether Skype will save you money and, specifically, how much money. Given the wide range of telephone services that Skype can potentially replace, or complement, I cannot cover every scenario. But this chapter does provide some ways of looking at the potential savings and some tools to quantify those savings. Your goal is to estimate these savings with a sufficient margin for error so that you will feel confident enough to make a decision: switch to Skype, or stick with what you've got.

Switching to Skype is not an all-or-nothing proposition. You may choose to use Skype merely as an adjunct to your existing phone services. Alternatively, you may choose to run Skype in parallel with your existing setup for a while before switching fully to Skype. If you're bold, you may leap right in and make Skype a full-blown replacement to your existing telephone system. Whatever approach you take, when figuring savings your focus will necessarily be on the long-term savings of your telephone system as it will look sometime in the future. For this reason, and as an aid for comparisons, I will express savings on an annual basis.

When thinking about savings that stretch far into the future, it is necessary to think like an economist to gauge your true lifetime savings. Savings from using Skype are likely to persist long into the future, so a $100 annual savings is $100 saved this year, next year, and every year beyond that. Such a series of cash savings stretching as far as the eye—or at least the imagination—can see is termed a *perpetuity*. A $100 perpetuity is clearly worth much more than just $100, as it is really $100 stacked on top of $100, on top of another $100, and so on, as the years pass by. For example, if you figure that by switching to Skype you will save $500 per year, just imagine having twenty-five $20 bills counted into the palm of your hand at the end of the first year, and then again at the end of the second year, and then again and again year after year.

H A C K   Back-of-the-Envelope Estimate of Skype Savings
#13

Follow this simple method to get a rough idea of your potential savings from switching to Skype.

Works with: all versions of Skype.

On the *Skype Hacks* web site, you will find a hack—"Save Money with Skype"—that leads you through a rather complete explanation of how to determine how much you'll save by switching to Skype. However, if you simply want to get a rough idea of your potential savings, you can do so with nothing more than a pencil, a calculator, and a blank sheet of paper (or an envelope).

If you look at your current telephone bill, you can logically divide it into two parts: variable calls, and fixed charges and taxes. It is not uncommon for the latter, fixed charges and taxes, to comprise the major part of your phone bill. Indeed, they represented fully 56% of my old phone bill!

You can use Skype to attack both parts to reduce your overall bill for phone services. Bear in mind that adopting Skype does not mean you have to get rid of your existing phone service. You can mix-and-match regular telephone services with Skype, or with other VoIP services (see "Get the Best Deal for VoIP Telephony" [Hack #22]).

Estimate Your Cost-of-Call Savings

Each time you make a phone call, the cost of that call is determined by three pieces of information. The first is the duration of the call; for example, 3 minutes, 12 seconds. The second is the call rate, usually expressed as the price for 1 minute of call time; for example, $0.10 per minute. The third is the call-rounding interval, usually expressed in seconds and rounded upward; for example, calls that are rounded up in 6-second intervals will cost $0.10 × 6/60 (= $0.01) per unit interval, while calls that are rounded up in 60-second (full-minute) intervals will cost $0.10 per unit interval.

Basically, the per-unit rate for anything other than 1-minute rounding is the per-minute call rate (in your home currency), times the rounding interval measured in seconds, and divided by 60 seconds. Shorter call-rounding intervals are to your advantage, so you should know that SkypeOut calls are

---

rounded to the full minute. To understand more about call rounding, you may want to look at "Round Call Time to Your Advantage" [Hack #23].

Table 2-1 shows some examples of call rounding.

Table 2-1. Examples of call rounding

Call duration (mm:ss)	Call units for 6s rounding	Call units for 60s rounding
0:17	3	1
0:50	9	1
1:12	12	2
1:54	19	2
3:04	31	4
16:17	163	17

This rounding can have quite a pronounced effect, particularly if you make lots of short-duration calls. Suppose, just for a moment, that you can make regular calls at the same per-minute cost as you can by using SkypeOut, but with 1-second rounding. Clearly, in this case, SkypeOut is at a disadvantage, but how much of a disadvantage? Table 2-2 gives the answer.

Table 2-2. Unused call time due to rounding up to the whole minute

Typical call duration	Average unused call time (approx.)
15 seconds–1 minute	38%
15 seconds–3 minutes	22%
15 seconds–10 minutes	9%
15 seconds–15 minutes	6%
15 seconds–30 minutes	3%

Table 2-2 shows that if your current phone plan rounds to 1-second intervals (and some plans do), by comparison, when using SkypeOut for short-duration calls, you effectively pay 38% more simply because you are paying for call time you did not use (all those fractions of unused full minutes that mount up). As your average call duration increases, this "call-rounding effect" gradually becomes less and less significant.

This is all rather ugly detail, to be sure; but it is simply a reflection of the fact that phone bills—like taxes—are rather complex. And it puts you in a position to find out whether switching to SkypeOut for some or all of your calls will save you money, and if so, how much money.

For the calls for which you'd like to consider using SkypeOut, estimate their average duration, their monthly total, and their average call rate (in your home currency per minute). You can estimate these averages by reviewing one or more past telephone bills, or if you don't hang on to old bills, by guessing your average call duration and your total call minutes per month and getting an average call rate from your phone company's web site. Let me remind you that for this back-of-the-envelope hack, we're not striving for absolute accuracy, only numbers with which you feel comfortable. Remember, you can always come back later with new numbers and redo the analysis. Enter your estimates in Table 2-3.

Table 2-3. Estimates from your existing phone bill

Average call duration	15 sec–1 min	❒
(check only one)	15 sec–3 min	❒
	15 sec–10 min	❒
	15 sec–15 min	❒
	15 sec–30 min	❒
Average call rate cost	_____	per minute
Typical cost of calls	_____	per month

A worked example, Table 2-4, should make things clear.

Table 2-4. Estimates from your existing phone bill

Average call duration	15 sec–1 min	❒
(check only one)	15 sec–3 min	✔
	15 sec–10 min	❒
	15 sec–15 min	❒
	15 sec–30 min	❒
Average call rate cost	$0.05	per minute
Typical cost of calls	$45	per month

Now go to the Skype web site and find an equivalent call rate (or an average of call rates) that matches your existing call destination(s). For example, if most of your calls are to regular U.S. phones, use the SkypeOut rate for the U.S. You can find SkypeOut rates for all call destinations at *http://www.skype.com/products/skypeout/rates/all_rates.html*.

At the top of the SkypeOut rates web page is a pull-down list from which you can choose to have the rates quoted in your home currency. Enter your estimate for the average SkypeOut rate in terms of your home currency in Table 2-5.

Table 2-5. Calculating your effective SkypeOut rate based on expected level of unused call time

Average SkypeOut rate	_____ _	per minute
Adjustment factor	_____ _	from Table 2-2
Effective SkypeOut rate	_____ _	per minute

Again, a worked example, Table 2-6, makes it all clear.

Table 2-6. Calculation of the effective SkypeOut rate

Average SkypeOut rate	$0.021	per minute
Adjustment factor	+22%	from Table 2-2
Effective SkypeOut rate	$0.026	per minute

The effective SkypeOut rate is simply the average SkypeOut rate adjusted upward by the factor for the call-rounding effect.

Now you are in a position to estimate your phone call savings should you switch to using SkypeOut. In Table 2-7, per-minute call savings are obtained simply by subtracting the effective SkypeOut rate (Table 2-5) from your average current regular phone call rate (Table 2-3). To turn this number into a percentage, divide it by your average current call rate. Monthly call savings are obtained by multiplying your current typical monthly cost of calls (Table 2-3) by 1, minus the effective SkypeOut rate (Table 2-5), and dividing that by your average current call rate (Table 2-3); that is, by (1 – effective SkypeOut rate/average current call rate). Your annual savings are, of course, just 12 times your monthly savings.

Table 2-7. Estimating your phone call savings

Call savings	_____	per minute
...as a %	_____	per minute
Monthly call savings	_____	per month
Annual call savings	_____	per year

Table 2-8 shows a worked example.

Table 2-8. Estimated phone call savings

Call savings	$0.024	per minute
...as a %	48%	per minute
Monthly call savings	$21.60	per month
Annual call savings	$259.20	per year

Estimate Your Fixed Charges and Taxes Savings

In terms of fixed charges and taxes, your phone bill is a veritable minefield of complexity. You could be forgiven for thinking that it is a conspiracy concocted by your telephone company (usually a government-regulated monopoly) and the government to get from you as much money as possible before you even lift the handset to make a call! Not lifting the handset from its cradle for a month might reduce the cost of your calls to zero, but it will likely have very little impact on your fixed charges and taxes. For that reason, I will assume that your fixed charges and taxes scale in proportion to the number of telephone lines you have. Remember, this hack is a back-of-the-envelope estimate and this is just an assumption. If you don't like it, simply change it and work through the details of your new assumption. To carry out a more thorough analysis, see the web extra hack "Save Money with Skype" (you'll find more details on this at the end of this hack).

In Table 2-9, enter your estimate for current monthly fixed charges and taxes.

Table 2-9. Estimating your fixed charges and taxes

Typical monthly charges	_____	per month
Number of phone lines	_____	

Table 2-10 is a worked example.

Table 2-10. Estimated fixed charges and taxes

Typical monthly charges	$80	per month
Number of phone lines	2	

Given the assumption that fixed charges and taxes scale in proportion to the number of phone lines, you will start to save money on fixed charges and taxes only if you can eliminate regular phone lines. Before providing an entry for Table 2-11, you might want to quickly skip ahead and skim parts of Chapter 3, as that chapter has several configurations for Skype that eliminate some—in some cases all—regular phone lines.

Table 2-11. Eliminating existing phone lines

Number of phone lines to eliminate	_____

For the worked example, Table 2-12, assume you can eliminate one of your two regular phone lines.

Table 2-12. Number of eliminated phone lines

Number of phone lines to eliminate	1

To calculate your savings of fixed charges and taxes by eliminating existing phone lines (Table 2-13), take your existing fixed monthly charges and taxes (Table 2-9) and divide it by your existing number of phone lines (Table 2-9), and then multiply the result by the number of phone lines you intend to eliminate (Table 2-11). You obtain your savings, expressed as a percentage of your existing fixed charges and taxes, by dividing your estimated savings by your current charges and taxes. To convert your estimated monthly savings to an annual basis, simply multiply them by 12.

Table 2-13. Estimating fixed charges and taxes savings

Fixed charges and taxes savings	_____	per month
...as a %	_____	per month
Annual charges and taxes savings	_____	per year

A worked example, Table 2-14, makes the necessary calculations clear.

Table 2-14. Estimated fixed charges and taxes savings

Fixed charges and taxes savings	$40	per month
...as a %	50%	per month
Annual charges and taxes savings	$480	per year

Estimate Your Total Savings

Now you're at the easy part, because you've done all the hard work.

First, copy your previous entries and results into Table 2-15. Your total current phone bill is simply the sum of your cost of calls and your fixed charges and taxes. Likewise, your total estimated savings are the sum of your estimated call savings and fixed charges and taxes savings. To express your total savings as a percentage, divide them by your total current phone bill. Total estimated savings on an annual basis are 12 times your total monthly savings.

Table 2-15. Estimating total savings

Typical current cost of calls	_____	per month	Table 2-3
Typical current charges and taxes	_____	per month	Table 2-9
Total current phone bill	_____	per month	

Table 2-15. Estimating total savings (continued)

Cost of call savings	_____	per month	Table 2-7
Fixed charges and taxes savings	_____	per month	Table 2-13
Total estimated savings	_____	per month	
...as a %	_____	per month	
Total annual savings	_____	per year	

At last, our worked example, Table 2-16, is complete.

Table 2-16. Estimated total savings

Typical current cost of calls	$45	per month	Table 2-4
Typical current charges and taxes	$80	per month	Table 2-10
Total current phone bill	$125	per month	
Cost of call savings	$21.60	per month	Table 2-8
Fixed charges and taxes savings	$40	per month	Table 2-14
Total estimated savings	$61.60	per month	
...as a %	49%	per month	
Total annual savings	$739.20	per year	

Making Adjustments and Decisions

The foregoing analysis is meant only as a rough and ready analysis of your potential savings from adopting Skype, in one form or another, for phone services. It made several assumptions, not the least of which was that your existing phone plan rounds calls in increments of 6 seconds (or less) and that no other out-of-pocket expenses arise from adopting Skype. In the latter category, things such as a USB box to interface your existing phone system to Skype and the need to keep a PC running all the time if you want Skype available 24/7 are items that you should include in your analysis. How you choose to configure Skype will affect both how you can use Skype and how much money this might save you. I discuss how to configure Skype in many interesting and different ways in Chapter 3.

When making a decision, you should also factor in some margin for error to cover the possibility that your back-of-the-envelope analysis is wide of the mark. Clearly, the more uncertain your data, the more margin for error you should allow in your decision making. Of course, another option is to improve your savings estimate by doing a more thorough analysis.

What is certain is that before you switch to Skype, some due diligence in terms of analyzing the potential savings and weighing the pros and cons of features gained versus features foregone is required. This book provides some tools and ways of thinking about the issues. But in the final analysis, it's your decision.

See Also

- The "Save Money with Skype" web extras hack, which you can download from the book's web site at *http://www.oreilly.com/catalog/ SkypeHacks/index.html*. The "Save Money with Skype" hack does a much more thorough analysis of your potential Skype savings.

- This hack's back-of-the-envelope analysis is also available in the form of a convenient and easy-to-use Excel spreadsheet, also downloadable from the book's web site. This "Skype Savings Estimator" spreadsheet replicates—in a quick and easy-to-use format—the analyses provided by this hack and the more thorough web extra hack, "Save Money with Skype."

HACK #14 Avoid Falling Foul of the Taxman

Pay the proper Sales and Use taxes and Value Added Taxes (VAT) to avoid the wrath of the taxman. Some people may even qualify to claim back VAT!

Works with: all versions of Skype.

A shockingly large proportion of most regular telephone bills comprise fixed charges and taxes. In my case, before switching to Skype, fixed charges and taxes represented fully 56% of my total bill. Fixed charges seem to guarantee that your telephone company, often a state-run entity or regulated monopoly, will make a profit before you even lift the handset to make a call. At the same time, the taxes on your phone bill have become the means by which government funds new, and wasteful, crackpot schemes. Well, no more.

By switching to Skype, you can easily and legitimately sidestep many of the fixed charges and fees. Also, you can legally avoid many, but alas not all, of the taxes.

Over the years, your regular telephone bill has accumulated quite a few "special" taxes, similar to the way in which barnacles accumulate over time on the hull of a ship. Neither can be said to be particularly advantageous to forward motion. Some of these "special" taxes were introduced long ago as only a "temporary measure" but, surprisingly, are still with us today. You can sidestep these "special" taxes if they are specific to your regular telephone bill and to the regulatory environment within which your telephone company operates.

What you cannot avoid are the "consumption" taxes that are applicable to all products and services you consume, including those from Skype. In the U.S., these consumption taxes are typically known as Sales and Use taxes, and may be levied at the state and local level. In the *European Union* (EU), they are known as Value Added Tax, or more simply, VAT. Similar taxes apply the world over, though under different names.

Often, these taxes are collected at the source and are folded into the price of the product or service and collected on behalf of the taxman by the vendor. However, when they are not so collected, your obligation to pay them does not go away.

All this talk about taxes might be somewhat stupefying. But the good news is that even after applying a Sales and Use tax or VAT to Skype's incredibly low rates, your overall tax burden for your telephone service will almost certainly be much less than before. And casting off all those "temporary" and "special" taxes specific to your regular telephone bill sure feels good—and is beneficial to your wallet!

U.S. Sales and Use Tax

Typically, Skype does not charge VAT or any other tax on its services if you reside outside the EU. That means U.S. buyers of Skype services are not charged any tax.

In the U.S., each state has its own Sales and Use tax rate (for some states, the rate is 0%). If this tax is not collected (as a sales tax) by the vendor of a product or service you buy, you are still liable for it (as a use tax) and must remit the tax owed. You have, in effect, been nominated by your state as your own tax collector. Individuals usually remit this tax as part of their individual state annual tax return, and businesses usually remit specific Sales and Use tax forms and payments quarterly. In addition, your local tax jurisdiction (town, city, county, or borough) may also levy a Sales and Use tax. Visit your state and local tax authority's web sites for more details.

European VAT

The mechanics of VAT are such that it is a tax on the "value added" during each stage of production of a product or service. As such, if you are a business, you typically charge VAT to your customers, but you can also claim back the VAT you paid for the materials and services used in the production of your product or service. The difference between what you collect in VAT on behalf of the taxman and what you claim back in VAT is then the tax on the "value added" by your company in the production chain that ultimately leads to a final consumer.

Even if you have paid VAT on Skype services, you may be somewhat surprised to find that the credit remaining in your account and the costs of your calls are listed without VAT. So, if you were to sum your call costs and add your remaining credit, this would be less than your total payments, the difference being the VAT you paid.

You can find a complete list of SkypeOut calling rates (with and without VAT, and quoted in a currency of your choice using online conversion rates) at *http://www.skype.com/products/skypeout/rates/all_rates.html*.

Claim back VAT. If you are a business, your telephone bill is usually an expense that qualifies for VAT-exempt or VAT-claimback status. As such, you may be able to claim back any VAT that Skype charged when you bought Skype credits and any other services. At the time of this writing, Skype did not offer the option of VAT exemption for qualifying entities.

If your billing address is within the EU, Skype will automatically charge you VAT. Now, the process by which you claim VAT back (or get a VAT credit) from your member country tax authority might be tortuous and painful (you will, after all, be dealing with your government's bureaucracy), but there is usually a well-defined process by which you can claim your VAT back.

To smooth the VAT claim-back process you can obtain a VAT-compliant invoice by going to your Skype account page and printing a copy, or by downloading it as a *.csv* (comma-separated value) file for import into a spreadsheet or into your accounting system. To obtain your call history as a *.csv* file, from Skype select Tools → Go to My Account Page, sign in and click on Call List, and then click on Export.

At the time of this writing, the 25 EU member states were: Austria, Belgium, Cyprus (the Greek part), the Czech Republic, Denmark, Estonia, Finland, France, Germany, Greece, Hungary, Ireland, Italy, Latvia, Lithuania, Luxembourg, Malta, the Netherlands, Poland, Portugal, Slovakia, Slovenia, Spain, Sweden, and the United Kingdom of Great Britain and Northern Ireland. Skype is a Luxembourg company and so charges the Luxembourg VAT rate, currently 15%. This rate is below that of most, but not all, EU localities (the Canary Islands, Madeira, the UK Channel islands, and the Isle of Man all have a lower rate).

As with all taxes, VAT is a veritable minefield of complexity. A useful jumping-off point for beginning your journey into this complexity is the document "VAT in the European Community," which you can find at *http://europa.eu.int/comm/ taxation_customs/resources/documents/vat_ec_lu-en.pdf*.

Avoid Problems Paying for Services

HACK #15

Avoid problems and additional charges when paying for Skype services.

Works with: all versions of Skype.

Paying for Skype services is seemingly so fraught with problems and difficulties that it merits its own discussion forum on *www.Skype.com*: Payments and Billing. Likewise, Skype's knowledgebase contains a Payments and Billing category, and it is a good resource for answering many questions you have on billing.

What follows are some tips and guidelines on how to avoid much of the aggravation associated with paying for Skype services.

Payment Methods

There are several ways of paying for services: Visa, MasterCard/Eurocard, DinersClub, PayPal, Moneybookers, Rabo Direct Betalen (the Netherlands only), Hansabank online (Estonia only), eNETS (Singapore only), ELBA Payments (Austria only), eBetalning (Sweden only), and Offline Bank Transfer (Japan, Germany, Austria, Belgium, Denmark, Spain, Finland, France, the UK, Italy, Luxembourg, the Netherlands, Norway, and Sweden). As indicated, not all payment options are available in all countries. Check the Skype web site for the payment options currently available to you.

A more indirect way of paying for Skype services is by means of vouchers and Skype Points, and Skype Gift Certificates.

Business users of Skype can pay for Skype services by means of Skype Groups, which allows a group administrator to purchase and mange Skype Credits, SkypeIn numbers, and Voicemail for all members of the group. For mor details, go to *http://www.skype.com/products/skypegroups/*. Skype Groups is not discussed further in this hack..

Vouchers used to promote Skype are provided by companies with which Skype has partnered (makers of headsets and other Skype accessories). Each voucher has a monetary value printed on it together with an equivalent number of SkypeOut call minutes based on Skype's global rate, currently €0.017 per minute. You can redeem vouchers at *https://secure.skype.com/store/voucher/redeem.html*.

You can earn Skype Points only by referring people to Skype. Presently, you cannot use these points for anything; they just accrue. However, Skype intends to allow points to be exchanged in payment for Skype services sometime in the future. For details, see *http://share.skype.com/tools_for_sharing/tools_for_sharing/skype_points_faq/*.

Skype Gift Certificates can be used to pay for Skype credits, SkypeIn numbers, and Voicemail. See *http://share.skype.com/products_and_services/we_bring_you..._skype_gift_certificates/* for more details.

Avoid Problems

What follows is advice that is specific primarily to U.S. buyers of Skype services. Payment options available to U.S. buyers, at the time of this writing, are Visa, MasterCard/Eurocard, PayPal, and Moneybookers.

Verification. Before you can make any Skype purchases, you must go through a process of verifying your email address, during which you must also explicitly agree to Skype's Terms of Service.

One, and only one, Skype account per payment account. The very first thing you should be aware of is that there is a one-to-one relationship between a specific credit card or a specific online payment account and a Skype account name. You cannot use the same payment account to fund several different Skype accounts.

This is enforced as part of Skype's antifraud efforts. What it means, in effect, is that if you have more than one Skype account, you must use a different credit card or online payment account (PayPal or Moneybookers) for each of them. Obtaining multiple credit cards just to fund multiple Skype accounts might involve a lot of paperwork and hassle. Moneybookers allows only one account per person, so you won't have any luck there. With PayPal, however, you can set up multiple accounts (all you need is a unique email address for each) and fund them independently, and pay for different Skype accounts that way.

You can avoid some of the hassle associated with funding and managing multiple Skype accounts by signing up for the Skype Groups service, details for which can be found at *http://www.skype.com/products/skypegroups/*.

Initial €10 limit. When you first buy Skype credits you are limited to buying only €10 worth. Subsequently, you can buy credits in increments of €10 and €25.

No transfer of credits. You cannot transfer any remaining Skype credits or balances to another Skype user. Either you must use the credits yourself, transfer the account to another person (give your Skype username and password to someone you trust), or forfeit them.

Payments from anonymous proxies will be rejected. Skype will reject any attempt to pay for Skype services, by any payment method, if you use an anonymous proxy that hides your *Internet Protocol* (IP) address. Again, this is part of Skype's antifraud effort.

Delays. Payments not made by credit card (for example, payments made via eCheck) may take several days to clear. Until your payment clears, Skype will mark its status as "pending," and the funds will not be added to your Skype account balance until payment is complete, nor will they be available for use.

Minimize money transfer fees. At the time of this writing, Moneybookers charged 1%, up to a maximum of €0.5, to transfer money. Currently, you can buy SkypeOut credits in blocks of €10 and €25. To minimize money transfer costs, as a percentage of the whole, you might want to consider buying credits in blocks of €25 (€0.5 is 2% of €25) rather than €10 (€0.5 is 5% of €10). That way, you'll top up your account less often and spend less money on transfer fees.

Exchange rate fees. If your online payment account (PayPal or Moneybookers) or credit card is not denominated in euros, you will be billed in your home currency based on some exchange rate. The final exchange rate you get for credit card transactions is typically set by Visa or MasterCard in conjunction with your issuing bank, and is typically 2% in their favor, but may be much more. Read your account terms and conditions very carefully because foreign currency transactions should be described there in detail.

VAT. If the address of your online payment account (PayPal or Money-bookers), or that associated with your credit card or its issuing bank, is located within the EU, Skype may automatically charge you VAT on any Skype purchases you make. Conversely, if the address is outside the EU, you will most likely not be charged VAT. At the time of this writing, Skype's VAT rate was 15%.

Claim Your Money Back

HACK #16

Under certain circumstances, Skype will refund your money for missing credits and hiccups with other services.

Works with: all versions of Skype.

Even when you do everything you can to smooth the process of paying for Skype services and use them in a reasonable way, things can go wrong.

To claim a refund, you basically have three options.

The No-Quibble Refund

If at any time and for any reason, you are unhappy with any Skype service—SkypeOut, SkypeIn, or Voicemail—you can request a refund of your last subscription payment.

For SkypeOut, if you have spent less than €1 of your last subscription payment, Skype will refund the whole amount of that payment. If you have spent more than €1, Skype will refund only the balance left.

For SkypeIn and Voicemail, if you ask for a refund within 30 days of your last payment, Skype will refund the whole amount of that payment. After more than 30 days, Skype will refund only the amount remaining for your subscription on a pro rata basis.

These types of refunds take five to seven business days to appear in your online financial statements.

The Quibble Refund

If you are generally happy with the services provided by Skype, but there are specific issues for which you want redress, you can request a refund on a case-by-case basis. You should address such a refund by gathering your facts and presenting them clearly to Skype in the form of a support request posted at the Skype web site. If your facts are correct and your request is reasonable, Skype may very well refund your money.

In the Submit a Support Request form at *www.Skype.com*, you are given the option of directing your request to a specific department. Clearly, directing your request to the right department will speed up a reply. To claim your money back, you should direct your request to one of these departments, as appropriate: Refund Request, Fraudulent Charges, Incorrect Charges, or Billing.

For completeness, here is a list of Skype support departments: Billing, Error 9403, Error 9407, Error 9408, Forgotten Username, Fraudulent Charges, General, Incorrect Charges, Payment Cancelled, Payment Refused, Refund Request, SkypeIn, Suggestions, and Technical Problems.

I cannot overemphasize the importance of getting your facts straight and making only reasonable requests. If the problem is a recurring one, keep a notebook and jot down things as they happen. That way, the facts will be at your fingertips when you need them. Reasonableness is a rather squishier concept, as one person's reasonable claim is another person's outrageous imposition. However, if you were to imagine your request being read aloud in a court of law without gasps of indignation or too many raised eyebrows, you've probably struck the right tone.

Again, if your request is granted, this type of refund will take five to seven business days to appear in your online financial statements. If your request is not granted, and you still think you're in the right, you can report the problem to your credit card or online payment processing company.

Requesting a Charge Back

If you paid for Skype services using PayPal or a credit card and Skype has refused to refund your money, you have the option of initiating a *charge back* (a charge back occurs when you, the customer, try to recover your money from your financial institution, which will then, in turn, try to recover the money from Skype).

To request a charge back, someone has to have screwed up. Moreover, you must demonstrate with reasonable certainty that it wasn't you who screwed up!

Before making a charge-back request, you typically must show that you have made a good-faith effort to resolve the issue with the merchant—in this case, Skype. Keep a good paper trail and be sure to do things in a timely fashion as your option to initiate a charge back might be time limited (you must typically dispute a charge within 60 days of receiving the statement on which the charge appears).

In the U.S., credit card purchases are protected under the Fair Credit Billing Act, which you can find at *http://www.ftc.gov/os/statutes/fcb/fcb.pdf*. You can find a consumer-friendly summary at *http://www.ftc.gov/bcp/conline/pubs/credit/fcb.htm*.

For a charge back to work, you must prove that Skype has breached some contractual terms, acted in blatant bad faith, or been so outrageous that the vast majority of people would find their behavior reprehensible. Basically, you must persuade your financial institution that you are right and Skype is wrong.

This can be rather messy and can take a lot of time, in terms of both the time you waste filling out forms, making calls, and following up on things, and the time between initiating a charge back and its final conclusion. You should not enter into a charge back lightly.

To initiate a charge back you must phone or write to your financial institution and make the request. In the case of PayPal, you can initiate the charge-back process online; just log in to your PayPal account, go to the Resolution Center, and follow the instructions for filing a claim.

HACK #17 Avoid Higher SkypeOut Rates

SkypeOut rates can vary depending on the number called. Don't be caught out by higher rates.

Works with: all versions of Skype.

SkypeOut rates vary by call destination—where you are calling to, not where you are calling from. A call to your next-door neighbor is charged the same SkypeOut rate whether you are calling from your home or from a vacation hotel thousands of miles away. Moreover, SkypeOut rates do not depend on the time of day or anything like that.

Not only do SkypeOut rates vary from country to country, rates can also be very different for different categories of phone number within the same country. If SkypeOut rates were determined solely by the country calling code (for example, +44 for the UK and +34 for Spain), life would be a lot simpler. Sadly, life isn't so simple.

It would also be nice if SkypeOut rates were chiseled in stone and so would remain unchanged forever. But, again, life is not so simple and SkypeOut rates do change from time to time.

Currently there is no easy way to determine a SkypeOut rate before making a call. All SkypeOut rates are published at *http://www.skype.com/products/skypeout/rates/all_rates.html*. Another option is to use the Skype Dialing Wizard, which you can find at *http://www.skype.com/products/skypeout/rates/dialing.html*.

For calls made to the same country code, SkypeOut rates can vary based on whether the recipient of the call is a mobile phone, has a certain area or region code, or is a *shared cost* number (shared cost numbers are premium numbers often used by businesses and other institutions).

SkypeOut rates for mobile phones vary not just by destination country, but also by mobile network carrier. So, for example, the SkypeOut rate for calls to mobile phones in Belgium might depend on which mobile carrier is the provider for the call recipient.

Shared cost numbers in the UK have the area codes 0844, 0845, 0870, or 0871. Calls to these numbers are billed at a substantially higher rate than regular calls to the UK.

Higher-Rate Avoidance Strategies

Obviously, as Skype-to-Skype calls are always free, one way of avoiding higher SkypeOut rates completely is to convert friends, family, and others to Skype. From Skype's menu bar, just select Tools → Share Skype with a Friend (Contacts → Share Skype with a Friend… on Mac OS X; the option is not available on Pocket PC), and follow the instructions. It's as simple as that.

Clearly, if you can't convert others to Skype, another obvious way to avoid SkypeOut rates for calls that are higher than their lowest global rate is not to make such calls! This might seem a rather fatuous piece of advice, were it not for the fact that it is easy to call a higher rate number inadvertently (for example, a mobile phone or UK shared cost number).

In an ideal world, Skype would tell you if it will bill for the number you are dialing at a rate higher than its global rate, and ask you whether you want to proceed before placing the call. Alas, we live in a less-than-ideal world.

Before making the call, you can either look up the rate on the Skype web site, or place the call through Skype's Dialing Wizard (or through the Skype Widget on Mac OS X; see "Dial Like a Wizard" **[Hack #11]**). However, doing this for every call would be overkill, so you might want to consider doing this only when you are calling a number you have not called before, or if you are simply unsure.

If you have a regular telephone service in addition to Skype, you might want to check out its rates and compare them with Skype's. There's no doubt that Skype's rates are among the lowest around, but they are not always the best deal (see "Get the Best Deal for VoIP Telephony" [Hack #22]). Obviously, if you want to save money, you should always use the lowest rate available to you, from whatever source.

Similarly, some prepaid calling cards can beat Skype's rates for some destinations. Google on "prepaid phone card" and you'll be overwhelmed by choices.

When shopping around for the very lowest rates, you may want to trade off some potential savings against the cost in terms of your time spent hunting down the very best deal. Once you are down into single-digit euro cent rates (€0.01 to €0.09), unless your call volume is exceedingly high, shopping around is most distinctly an activity of diminishing returns.

HACK #18 Avoid Additional Mobile Phone Charges

The rate charged for both the Skype caller and a mobile phone recipient can vary depending on what mobile phone is called and where it is geographically located.

Works with: all versions of Skype.

SkypeOut call rates vary by destination and by the type of receiving device—regular phone or mobile (see "Avoid Higher SkypeOut Rates" [Hack #17]).

Often, the rate charged to a mobile phone depends on its location, both when dialing out *and* when receiving calls. When a mobile phone is outside its designated home network, it is charged additional roaming fees for outgoing and (possibly) incoming calls. So, you can inadvertently cost your call recipient a lot of money by calling him at the wrong time and place. How are you to know when he is outside his regular network (for example, when he is traveling)? This is where a little forward planning by the person who is traveling pays dividends. Ask him to tell you and others in advance when he'll be traveling and suggest that he make his place of doing business or his hotel his alternative contact number. And, on his Skype or regular phone voicemail greeting, have him leave a message telling people where he is and how best to contact him.

Obviously, if you use a mobile phone and Skype, this works in reverse when you are traveling, therefore saving you money. Think ahead and save money.

As an alternative to calling someone's mobile phone, if your message is short, you might want to send a *Short Message Service* (SMS) message instead. SMS messages are typically far cheaper than voice calls.

Make Money with Skype

#19 Join the Skype Affiliate Program and have Skype pay you!

Works with: all versions of Skype.

If you have your own web site or blog, you can refer people to Skype and get paid for it under Skype's Affiliate Program. You get paid a percentage of the money spent by those people whom you refer to Skype via your web site or blog, and who subsequently buy Skype services within 90 days of being referred. Here's how it works:

1. Join Skype affiliates by completing the short application form on Skype's web site.
2. Sign in to your new affiliate account.
3. Choose the links to place on your web site or blog.
4. Sit back and wait for the money to roll in!

You can join the Skype Affiliate Program by visiting *http://www.skype.com/partners/affiliate/*.

So, how much can you expect to make? This rather depends on how successful you are at driving people to Skype and whether they buy Skype services. The program is set up to reward success in converting people to Skype services; the more people you convert, the more money you make. Table 2-17 shows the commission rates in effect at the time of this writing.

Table 2-17. Skype affiliate commission rates

Monthly converts	SkypeOut	SkypeIn	Skype Voicemail
1–unlimited	5%	10%	10%

Skype will track who buys, how much they buy, and when they buy. Every customer who clicks through to Skype from your web site is counted, even if he visits Skype's web site directly later on. Provided he purchases Skype services within 90 days from clicking through from your site, you will get a piece of the action.

Before investing the time and effort to sign up for the Skype Affiliate Program and modifying your web site or blog—all of which, incidentally, took me less than 15 minutes—you might want to do some simple money calculations.

Consider this what-if scenario. Suppose that with just a little effort promoting your web site, and Skype services specifically, you judge that 3,000 referrals per month and a 10% conversion rate are not unrealistic. That means 300 converts to Skype services per month. Furthermore, of these converts, suppose 250 buy €10 of SkypeOut credits, 100 of those also buy a one-year subscription to SkypeIn, and 50 buy voicemail only. Crunching the numbers, here's what we get:

Monthly income = 250 × €10× 5% + 100 × €30 × 10% + 50 × €15 × 10% = €500 (about $625)

Not bad for a little upfront effort to set up and a little ongoing effort to promote your web site and Skype services. And, of course, there's nothing stopping you from doing this on all your web sites, or on those you set up just for this purpose.

For those who want to look at different scenarios and how they might profit from the Skype Affiliate Program, a Skype Affiliate Income Estimator spreadsheet is available from this book's web site at *http://www.oreilly.com/catalog/SkypeHacks/index.html*.

Skype Points

An alternative to the Skype Affiliate Program, you can make money (points to be used as Skype credit, actually) through the Skype Points program.

You can accrue Skype Points only by referring people to Skype. Presently, you cannot use points for anything; they just accrue. However, Skype intends to allow points to be exchanged in payment for Skype services sometime in the future. For details, see *http://share.skype.com/tools_for_sharing/tools_for_sharing/skype_points_faq/*.

Make Money with the Skype API

You can make money using the Skype Application Programming Interface (API), if you have programming skills.

Works with: all versions of Skype that support the API.

Skype has an API that allows those with programming skills to extend Skype's functionality in new and interesting ways. There is a burgeoning market for software and hardware add-ons for Skype (see Chapter 11) that use the Skype API.

Programming using the Skype API is not difficult, and there are some free components that allow you to call the API from different languages. For those too intimidated by the Skype API, an alternative is scripting languages for extending Skype's functionality. Or, you can use scripting in conjunction with the API, which is dealt with in Chapter 12.

All it takes to make a useful add-on for Skype is a good idea and the wherewithal to carry it through.

You can make money using the Skype API in three ways: through bounties, by developing add-ons that you can sell, and by working as a Skype programmer.

Bounties are offered by companies and open source projects for Skype add-ons that enhance their products or services. For example, at the time of this writing, there is an open bounty of $1,500 to extend Asterisk (a popular open source *Private Branch Exchange* (PBX) system: *http://www.asterisk.org/*) to work with Skype.

The bounty for Asterisk-Skype integration (and other bounties) is listed at *http://www.opensourcexperts.com/*.

Bear in mind, the trend of offering bounties in both commercial and open source communities is a growing; just Google on "Skype (bounty OR bounties)" to find out more.

Many Skype add-ons are free, but many are also being sold. Obviously, add-ons with "must have" functionality are more likely to sell. To get some idea of what sorts of add-ons for Skype already exist and how they are being sold, see Chapter 11.

At the time of this writing, Skype was growing at a phenomenal rate and had been acquired by eBay. Job and work-for-hire offers occasionally crop up on the Skype forums. Searching job search web sites (for example, *http://www.monster.com/*) using the search term "Skype" will produce a handful of job openings; a handful now, but many more in the future, to be sure. And, if you're really, really, really good, there's always the option of getting a job with the big boys. Skype maintains its list of job openings at *http://www.skype.com/company/jobs/*.

H A C K
#21   Avoid Forfeiting SkypeOut Credits

You must continue to use your SkypeOut account so that you don't lose your SkypeOut credits.

Works with: all versions of Skype.

You will lose your SkypeOut credits only if you are an infrequent SkypeOut user. If you keep a SkypeOut balance only for emergencies, travel, or whatever, you must make the occasional call just to avoid forfeiting your remaining SkypeOut balance. As the Skype "Terms of Service" (May 2005) states:

> 6.5 A credit balance for SkypeOut service expires 180 days after last chargeable usage of SkypeOut service. Credit balances not used within said 180 day period will be lost.

You can find complete details at *http://www.skype.com/company/legal/terms/tos_voip.html*.

Make at least one call every 180 days and keep your SkypeOut credits safe.

Get the Best Deal for VoIP Telephony

Skype is not your only option for VoIP telephony. You may want to consider other providers instead of or as a complement to Skype, based on your needs.

Works with: all versions of Skype.

Skype offers free Skype-to-Skype calls and some of the lowest rates available for calls to regular phones. However, other VoIP providers offer rates lower than Skype for some call destinations. Some even offer free calling to destinations for which Skype charges. Moreover, there might be other services (for example, 911 emergency service) that Skype does not provide and which are important to you.

Of course, nothing is stopping you from having as many VoIP providers as you want. You have a great deal of choice nowadays, and you can pick and choose as though from a menu. It's certainly worth hunting down the best deal by keeping an eye on what's out there. For example, Finarea SA's Voip-Buster service (*http://www.voipbuster.com/*) offers *free* calls to regular telephones in some countries. Even Skype can't beat that!

> At the time of this writing, Finarea SA was offering free calls (with some restrictions) to Australia, Austria, Belgium, Canada, China, the Czech Republic, Denmark, Finland, France, Germany, Greece, Hungary, Ireland, Israel, Italy, Luxembourg, the Netherlands, Norway, Poland, Portugal, Russia, Spain, Sweden, Switzerland, Taiwan, the United Kingdom, and the United States.
>
> For details, visit *http://www.voipbuster.com*.

You should consider many factors (such as voice quality, reliability, and usability) when deciding on the best choice for you, based on your calling habits. Even if you are a Skype fan, you can still choose to complement Skype with other VoIP offerings or, indeed, with regular phone and mobile phone offerings. Choice is a wonderful thing!

You can find plenty of VoIP alternatives to Skype by Googling on "VoIP phone service." But to get you started so that you have a sense of what's out there, Table 2-18 lists a grab bag of suggestions for where to start looking for the best VoIP deals.

Table 2-18. A grab bag of alternative VoIP providers

http://www.vonage.com/	http://www.voipbuster.com/
http://www.sipphone.com/	http://www.sipgate.de and .co.uk/
http://www.voipgate.com/	http://www.ineen.com/
http://www.gizmoproject.com/	http://www.lingo.com/
http://www.freeworlddialup.com/	http://www.packet8.net/
http://www.wavigo.com/	http://www.dialpad.com/
http://www.woize.com/	http://www.sunrocket.com/
http://www.jajah.com/	

Many of these are "me too" services that have sprouted up in the wake of Skype's success. None of them comes with any sort of testimonial or recommendation from the author or publisher.

HACK #23 Round Call Time to Your Advantage

By understanding how Skype figures the cost of your call, you can save money.

Works with: all versions of Skype.

Over the long run, the way in which call times are rounded can make a big difference. This is particularly true if your call volume is large, as it might be for medium to large organizations that use SkypeOut.

To illustrate why, consider this example. Ten thousand calls are made with a random duration of between 15 and 60 seconds. First, calls are rounded up to the next 6-second interval, and then calls are rounded up to the whole minute. Using just one set of randomly generated data, you should get results similar to these: 6-second rounding → 66,240 (approx.) billing units, and 1-minute rounding → 10,000 (exact) billing units. Furthermore, suppose calls are uniformly priced at $0.10 per minute (that's $0.01 per 6-second interval). Clearly, 1-minute rounding will result in a total bill of $1,000. However, by contrast, 6-second rounding will bring the total bill down to about $660. That's a big difference. Remember, the per-minute call rate is the same in both cases; rounding alone accounts for the difference.

When calls are rounded not to the next second, but up to some other time interval, for some fraction of your calls that fall short of the next full time increment, you are effectively paying for call time that you don't use. To see the significance of this effect, let's again look at some results from making 10,000 random calls based on a minimum and maximum time limit for the calls (see Table 2-19).

Table 2-19. Call-rounding effect: call time paid for but unused (approx.)

Call time not less than (seconds)	Call time not more than (minutes)	6-second rounding	60-second rounding
15	1	6%	38%
15	3	2.5%	22%
15	10	1%	9%
15	15	0.5%	6%
15	30	0.3%	3%

Even though SkypeOut rates are some of the lowest there are, the downside is that Skype rounds calls to the nearest minute. So, a call between 5 seconds (not 1 second, for reasons discussed shortly) and 60 seconds will be rounded up to 1 whole minute for billing purposes. Likewise, a call of *N* minutes plus 1 to 60 seconds will be rounded up to *N* + 1 minutes and billed accordingly.

Round Calls and Save Money

SkypeOut calls of 4 seconds or less are free (the clock starts running once you are connected). So, one way to save money is not to hang around if your call recipient's answer machine kicks in. Skype displays call duration in real time, so a careful watch and bailout before the first 4 seconds are up will save you a whole minute's worth of billing. Of course, if you do need to leave a message, you must sacrifice at least 1 minute of SkypeOut credit. But keep the message short, and you'll do yourself—and no doubt the recipient—a favor.

Pay special attention to the fact that only the first 4 seconds of a call are free. Once a call is 5 seconds or longer you will be billed for a full minute. Thereafter, all fractions of a minute—from 1 second to 60 seconds—are rounded to a whole minute for billing purposes. So, for example, a call lasting 6 minutes, 1 second will be billed as a 7-minute call.

Skype's Terms of Service agreement, which you can find at *http://www. skype.com/company/legal/terms/tos_voip.html*, spells out all of this.

What the 4-second rule effectively allows you to do is round down the first minute to zero for calls lasting 4 seconds or less. This will be the *only* time you have the opportunity to round down, so make the most of it.

At 5 seconds and thereafter, when the minute mark rolls over into the next, a bite is taken out of your SkypeOut credit every time; therefore, you may want to force calls to be prematurely rounded. Whether your call is short or long, keep a close eye on the call timer. When the next minute mark is approaching, consider bringing the call to a close before you roll into the next minute. Ka-ching! Another minute's worth of credit saved.

A minute saved here and a minute saved there, and pretty soon you're into some serious savings. Just remember, the systematic application of these rules for call rounding will save you plenty in the long run.

For those readers who would like to analyze the economic effects of call rounding in more detail, perhaps in comparison with an existing call plan, a Skype Call Minutes Rounding Estimator spreadsheet is available from the book's web site at *http://www.oreilly.com/catalog/SkypeHacks/index.html*.

HACK #24 Manage Bandwidth Costs

The costs of running Skype can mount up if you pay for Internet traffic by the megabyte.

Works with: all versions of Skype.

Even when not making a call, Skype consumes about 0.5 kilobytes per second of bandwidth. If your machine has been designated a super node (incidentally, being a super node in the Skype network isn't really something over which you have any explicit control—either you are one, or you aren't), bandwidth consumption can jump tenfold to 5 kilobytes per second. Obviously, bandwidth consumption jumps considerably above these levels when making a call. However, the bandwidth consumed when Skype is idle can mount up.

Taking the worst-case scenario, suppose your machine lives in an almost permanent state of being a super node and that your call volume is a negligible proportion of the bandwidth consumed. Five kilobytes per second translates into about 13 gigabytes of data transfer per month.

In Europe, a monthly cap of 4 gigabytes on Internet traffic is not uncommon, and busting this cap can be expensive. If your PC is running constantly, and you use your Internet connection for other things besides Skype, it's not inconceivable—though it is perhaps unlikely, given that we're looking at the worst case—that Skype may push you over your cap.

Now, if your Internet is unmetered, this should not be a problem. However, if you pay for your Internet traffic by the megabyte or gigabyte, the costs of having Skype running continuously can mount up. People who connect to the Internet via satellite, for example, often have a comparatively low monthly data-transfer allowance and are charged a punitive rate for going over their limit.

Companies that deploy Skype to a large number of users—for example, a call center—will certainly want to keep an eye on how much bandwidth Skype consumes, especially if their call volume is high. Additional bandwidth costs effectively increase the cost of using Skype, so you should factor this into your decision to use Skype.

There are two parts to managing Skype's bandwidth costs: monitoring and metering.

Monitoring

Medium to large companies will no doubt have network monitoring tools already in place. For small companies and individuals, several commercial and free applications are available that will help you get a handle on your Internet connection usage patterns.

Google on "free network monitor" and you'll be presented with a long list of software tools, many of which are free.

If after an extensive period of monitoring—say, a month—you determine that Skype is a problem, you should perhaps meter its use of your Internet connection.

Of course, if you've deemed that Skype bandwidth consumption is not a problem, you're free to move on to other things while enjoying Skype.

Metering

Metering bandwidth has two aspects.

Large organizations may choose to meter Internet bandwidth usage to allocate the costs of its use to departments in some proportion to its consumption. The biggest users of bandwidth get to pay most of the costs, and the smallest users pay a small proportion of the costs. This is a common approach in large organizations.

For small organizations and for individuals, metering is normally a means by which to throttle or choke off bandwidth. In this sense, metering is used to ration bandwidth consumption.

We will look at metering as a means of rationing bandwidth.

Run Skype only when needed. Perhaps the simplest method of controlling Skype's consumption of bandwidth is to run it only when you need to make a call. If Skype isn't running, it isn't consuming bandwidth. It's as simple as that. Bear in mind, however, that you won't be able to receive any calls when Skype isn't running.

Run Skype for only a limited part of the day. If you need Skype for only a limited part of the day—say, 9 a.m. to 5 p.m., or whatever your business hours are—you can start and stop Skype based on the time of day (see "Run Skype Based on Time of Day" [Hack #41]). That way, Skype will be running for only that part of the day for which you need it.

Ration bandwidth as part of a QoS plan. *Quality of Service* (QoS) not only allows you to ration available bandwidth to Skype's advantage to improve its voice quality, but you can also use it to ration bandwidth consumption to manage costs (see "Improve Service Quality" [Hack #59]).

## CHAPTER THREE

Configure Skype
Hacks 25–42

Skype has gone to great efforts to make installing and configuring its software as easy and problem free as possible. Sadly, it isn't there yet. And, one could argue, these procedures can never be truly problem free given the sheer variety of computer hardware already out there and the rapid pace at which new hardware is introduced. Similarly, software in the form of sound device drivers, Skype add-ons, and operating system services are so intertwined with Skype that a problem for one of those almost inevitably is a problem for Skype.

Some end-user configuration will almost certainly be needed. However, configuration really falls into two distinct categories. The first is configuration to get Skype to simply work, and this chapter helps a little in that respect. The second is configuration to get Skype to work the way you want; that is, improving performance and customization. The focus of this chapter is most distinctly on the second category—a focus that is further maintained and expanded in Chapter 4. For the first category—getting Skype installed and up and running—refer to Skype's own troubleshooting and other resources at *http://www.skype.com/*, though "Troubleshoot Skype" [Hack #12] may be of some help, too.

An often-overlooked simple prerequisite to using any software is to check that your hardware and operating system meet the minimum requirements. This simple step is too often brushed aside in the headlong rush to get the application installed, only later to find yourself wasting a lot of time tinkering with it and wondering why it doesn't work, or doesn't work very well. To help you *not* to make that mistake, I've provided Skype's minimum hardware requirements at the time of this writing in Table P-1 in the Preface.

Internet Connections

Nowadays, you can connect to the Internet in a multitude of ways: through dial-up, cable, Digital Subscriber Lines (DSL), wireless hotspots (WiFi and Bluetooth), mobile phones (General Packet Radio Service, or GPRS), and even satellites! Business users have even more choices. So, almost by necessity, this chapter will narrow its scope in terms of the Internet connection technologies it will cover.

Unless stated otherwise, this chapter will assume that you have a broadband connection that is provided through cable, your phone line (typically some flavor of DSL), or a WiFi or Bluetooth wireless link. Note that while it is possible to use Skype over a dial-up connection, call quality in that case is such a hit-or-miss affair that it won't be considered a viable option in this chapter.

Moreover, bear in mind while you read the hacks in this chapter that your Internet connection sometimes determines how you can and cannot configure Skype the way you want. For example, if you obtain your Internet connection through some flavor of DSL, you will almost certainly have to retain at least one regular phone line no matter what. The same may also be true if you get your Internet connection through satellite because many satellite Internet services use a dial-up connection for sending data and a satellite dish for receiving data (which, of course, is highly asymmetric and not good for VoIP).

A flavor of DSL, called *Dry DSL*, does not require the telephone line on which it operates to be "active." That is, it can connect you to the Internet without requiring a number and a phone service on the line over which it operates. However, this type of DSL is still rare, so I won't cover it here. But it is something to bear in mind—and perhaps research—as you read the hacks in this chapter.

Ways to Configure Skype

How you configure Skype determines, in large part, what you will get out of Skype. Presented in this chapter are hacks that range from simply making Skype calls while sitting at your computer, to effectively using your existing home phone system with Skype as a replacement for regular phone service. Typically, the more you push the envelope with Skype, the more money you can save. However, none of the Skype configurations presented in this chapter is an all-or-nothing proposition. You can mix and match options and run the old in parallel with the new until you are confident that the new will work the way you want!

In terms of configuring Skype, in many ways you really are limited only by your imagination. But to get you started, Figure 3-1 shows you a number of configuration options that are linked to hacks describing how you can configure Skype in different ways to use the whole range of Skype hardware at your disposal.

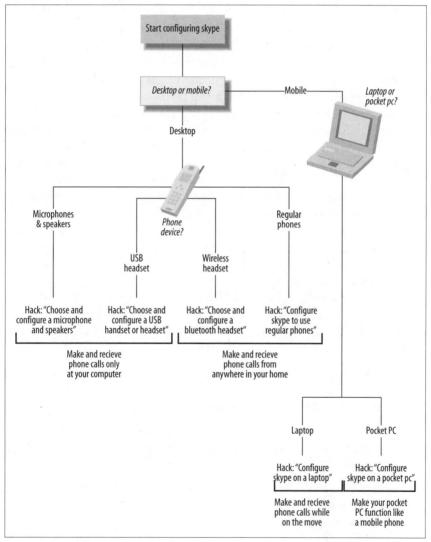

Figure 3-1. Configuration choices for Skype

Figure 3-1 shows that your first choice is whether you are primarily interested in using Skype while on the move (mobile), or from the comfort of your home or office (desktop).

Mobile users of Skype have two additional choices: laptop or Pocket PC. I cover how to configure Skype for these choices in "Configure Skype on a Laptop" [Hack #31] and "Configure Skype on a Pocket PC" [Hack #32], respectively.

Home and office users of Skype really have to decide first whether they only want to make and receive calls while they're sitting at their computer, or whether they want the same flexibility that their current phone system affords. Your choice of sound device will dictate into which of these two categories of Skype users you will fall. Sound devices that tie you to your computer are ones that plug into your machine and provide only one voice channel; and, as these devices typically connect to your computer by means of a cable, your freedom of movement during a call is necessarily constrained to the length of that cable. "Choose and Configure a Microphone and Speakers" [Hack #27] and "Choose and Configure a USB Handset or Headset" [Hack #28] discuss configurations of this kind. Sound devices based on Bluetooth or that interface to existing phone equipment spread throughout your home or office do not tie you to your computer. Such devices provide functionality that more closely resembles a regular phone system; namely, limited mobility within the confines of your home or office. "Choose and Configure a Bluetooth Headset" [Hack #29] describes a hands-free way of making and receiving calls while walking about, and "Configure Skype to Use Regular Phones" [Hack #30] describes a configuration that can, if you take it to the limit of its possibilities, result in a phone system driven by Skype that is almost indistinguishable from your existing phone system.

It's your choice!

Connecting Hardware to Your Computer

This chapter includes hacks that will have you playing around with hardware and possibly tinkering with your existing phone system and wiring. Therefore, a few guidelines are in order.

When plugging and unplugging hardware for your computer, you should follow this procedure to avoid any unnecessary aggravation:

1. Power off—not just your computer, but other peripherals too.
2. Connect new hardware and/or remove old hardware.
3. Power on peripherals and new hardware.
4. Power up your computer.

Even though some device connection methods (for example, USB) are what's known as *hot pluggable* (meaning that you can insert and remove the connector without powering off), I've experienced fewer problems when following the preceding procedure.

As shown in Figure 3-2, you can attach sound devices to your computer using a number of common connection methods. Each connector is typically associated with these types of sound devices:

3.5mm plug
> Associated with microphones (handheld, clip-on, and desktop), speakers, earphones, and headsets (earphones with a boom microphone, which in this case has two 3.5mm plugs). Often, 3.5mm plugs and the sockets on your computer they plug into are color-coded: pink for microphones, and green for speakers and earphones. Normally, the sockets on your computer have small pictures of a microphone and earphones next to them to clarify their purpose.

USB plug
> Associated with desktop microphones, array microphones, earphones, handsets, headsets, and Skype-to-phone adapter boxes.

Bluetooth dongle
> This dongle plugs into a USB port, but it communicates with the sound device—typically a Bluetooth headset—over Bluetooth wireless. If your computer has Bluetooth built in (and more and more of the newer ones do), you won't need one of these.

RJ11 phone plug
> This the most common type of phone connector (at least in the U.S.) for regular phone handsets, desktop phones, wireless phone base stations, and Skype-to-phone adapter boxes.

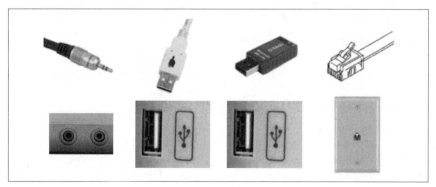

Figure 3-2. Sound hardware connectors, left to right: 3.5mm plug, USB plug, Bluetooth dongle, and RJ11 phone plug (sockets are shown beneath the plugs)

Setting the Sound Devices Used by Skype

Once your sound hardware is connected, tested, and shown to be working (see "Test Your Sound System" [Hack #25]), just configure Skype to use it:

Windows
> Select Skype → Tools → Options... → Sound Devices.

Linux
> Select Skype → Tools → Options... → Hand/Headsets.

Mac OS X
> Select Skype → Preferences... → Audio.

Pocket PC
> Normally, the sound-in and sound-out devices are intrinsically part of the device and are configured at the factory, so Skype itself has no configuration options for sound devices on Pocket PC. Of course, you can use a Bluetooth headset with Skype on Pocket PC, provided it is Bluetooth enabled (see "Configure Skype on a Pocket PC" [Hack #32]).

My experience has been that it always pays to specify explicitly the sound devices that Skype uses. Nowhere is this truer than for USB devices, as oftentimes the last USB sound device to be plugged into your computer seems to assume it has a God-given right to become your default sound device. This sometimes also means that it will become your default sound device for Skype regardless of whether that was what you wanted. This is especially the case if your computer has several sound devices of various types connected to it.

Safely Cutting Your Phone Lines

To cut your incoming phone wires safely you will need a pair of wire cutters (or sharp scissors) with insulated handles and a roll of electrical insulation tape, and you will need to follow a simple procedure to do the actual cutting, as shown in Figure 3-3.

The telephone company provides power to your phone wires; that's why your regular telephone works during a power cut. Now, even if you've had the phone company "disconnect" you, your phone wires may or may not still have electrical power. Consequently, you must be careful not to short the wires when cutting them. Even a momentary short can be bad news. This can happen if you cut two or more wires at the same time, Step 1. The solution is simple: cut only one wire at a time, Step 2. As you cut wires, you should insulate their exposed ends with electrical tape, Step 3.

Now, if this activity looks to be beyond your comfort zone, you always have the option of calling the phone company and having them send a technician

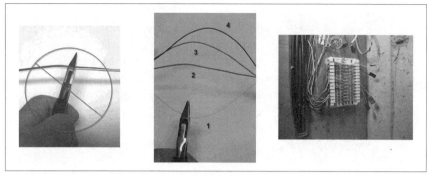

Figure 3-3. Steps for cutting your phone lines. Step 1: don't cut all the wires at once; Step 2: cut wires one by one; and Step 3: insulate the ends of cut wires as you go

to do the job for you. Even after paying for this to be done, your Skype savings will most likely recoup the cost in very little time.

> If you have a home alarm system that is monitored through your phone line, you may want to contact your alarm monitoring service first. Depending on how your alarm is wired into your phone line, even if you have cancelled your regular phone service, just cutting your phone line may trip your alarm system and have the police on your doorstep—both in short order! A little research, organization, and preparation should keep you out of trouble.

HACK #25 Test Your Sound System

Sound is perhaps the number-one problem for Skype users. Some quick-and-dirty tests should help isolate sound problems: is it your sound system or Skype?

Works with: Windows, Linux, and Mac OS X versions of Skype.

Before attacking a problem, you must isolate the problem. Just as for a rabid dog, it helps to have the thing cornered before you kill it!

If you experience sound problems when using Skype, the first thing to determine is whether the problem lies with your sound system or with Skype. By testing your sound system independently of Skype, you'll have a better chance of isolating the problem. These simple tests should help:

Windows

General

Skype uses the sound devices installed and configured under Windows. If you have set up Skype to use the Windows default device

(Skype → Tools → Options... → Sound Devices), which is also the default for a new Skype installation, and you subsequently add new sound devices—for example, by plugging in a USB speaker system—your Windows default device and that used by Skype may now be the newly installed device and not the phone device you want. To avoid sound device selection issues, it's always best to specify explicitly the audio-in and audio-out devices within Skype. Skype provides a user guide specifically for Windows XP sound setup, at *http://www.skype.com/help/guides/soundsetup_xp.html*.

Sound-out

Open Windows' Sound Recorder application (Start → All Programs → Accessories → Entertainment → Sound Recorder). Within Sound Recorder, select File → Open and then navigate to *C:\Windows\ Media*. Open any *.wav* file you find there and click the Play button. If you hear a sound, the sound-out component of your sound system is working.

Sound-in

In Windows' Sound Recorder, click on the Record button and speak into your sound-in device for a few seconds. Click the Stop button and then click Play. If you hear your voice played back, the sound-in component of your sound system is working.

Sound-in and sound-out

An alternative method for checking your voice input and output devices in a single test is to use the Windows Sound Hardware Test Wizard (Start → Control Panel → Sounds and Audio Devices → Voice → Test hardware...).

Linux

General

Skype works with the *Open Sound System* (OSS) on Linux, for which its sound input and output are associated with the device /dev/dsp. Skype also works with the *Advanced Linux Sound Architecture* (ALSA) on Linux, but only using ALSA's OSS emulation layer. Check that your Linux system supports one of these two sound standards and, if you have ALSA, that the OSS emulation layer is installed and enabled. Also check that Skype is set up to use /dev/dsp as its audio device for calls (Skype → Tools → Options... → Hand/Headsets). Skype provides a user guide specifically for Linux sound setup; see *http://www.skype.com/help/guides/soundsetup_linux.html*.

Sound-out

> On Linux, there are usually several audio playback applications (see *http://linux-sound.org/* for a complete list of Linux sound software). In your favorite file browser, search for some sound files to play. Try looking for audio files with these extensions: *.mp3*, *.wav*, *.ra*, . *aiff*, or *.m4a*. Once you have found some sound files click on one of them and it should play in the default player for that extension. If you can hear a sound, the sound-out component of your sound system is working.

Sound-in

> Use your favorite sound recording utility (mine is krecord, which is part of the KDE desktop) to record your voice. While using the same utility, play back your voice recording to yourself. If you can hear your own voice, the sound-in component of your sound system is working.

Mac OS X

General

> Mac OS X sound, like most of Mac OS X, is so well thought out that sound is comparatively problem free on the Mac. This statement is supported by the fact that Skype has no user guide dedicated to sound setup for Mac OS X. Even so, it is always a good idea to specify explicitly the sound devices to be used by Skype (Skype → Preferences... → Audio).

Sound-out

> Start the Apple QuickTime application and navigate to a folder that has some sound files (QuickTime Player → File → Open File..., and then navigate to */System/Library/Sounds*), pick a sound, and play it. If you hear the sound, your sound-out device is working.

Sound-in

> Start the Apple iMovie HD application and create an arbitrarily named movie file—say, *test_sound_in*. Click on the Audio button. Above the Audio button will appear a Microphone label, a horizontal sound level meter, and a round record button with a red dot in the middle. Click on the record button and speak into your sound-in device. While you speak, you should see some response from the sound meter. After a few seconds, click on the record button again to stop recording. Now, drag the scrollbar at the bottom of the iMovie window all the way over to the left, and then click on your recording, which will be labeled something like Voice 01. Click on the Play button and you should hear your own voice played back to you. If you do, your sound-in device is working.

If you can hear sounds when an audio file is played or when your voice recording is played back to you, but not at the level you desire, go to the sound control panel (select Start → Control Panel → Control Panel → Sounds and Audio Devices on Windows, System Preferences → Sound on Mac OS X, and whatever is your preferred sound hardware configuration tool on Linux) and make any necessary adjustments.

If your sound system works properly independently of Skype and you are experiencing sound problems when using Skype, it's a good bet that your sound problem is caused by Skype.

Test Call Sound Quality (echo123)

HACK
#26 Use the echo service provided by Skype to test your transmit and receive voice quality.

Works with: all versions of Skype.

If you have just installed Skype and want to give it a try, or if you're having problems with your sound system or sound quality, there is no better way to test Skype than to use its echo service.

> echo123 is an English-speaking service; echo-chinese is a similar service, but in Chinese (dialect Mandarin, Taiwan); soundtestjapanese is for Japanese speakers; and testyuyin is another voice test service for Chinese (dialect Mandarin, mainland China).

echo123 is nothing more than a Skype username set up by Skype and linked to an automatic sound recording and playback system. Enter "echo123" (or one of its other language variants) in the Skype address bar and start a call. A voice on the other end will guide you through the process of recording your own voice and then playing it back to you. If you can hear the automated announcement and your own voice when it is played back to you, you will know that your sound input and sound output devices work properly. As a further test, you can have Skype call you! Open a chat session with echo123 and send the text message "callme" (enter it without any whitespace and without any quotes), and Skype's echo service will call you back for a voice test. It's as simple as that.

Fix Sound-Quality Problems

If your echo123 test doesn't work, you have a problem. While it is impossible—given the sheer variety of hardware available—to give specific advice on how to repair or configure your sound system, there are some general guidelines that, if followed, are likely to fix the problem with the least pain (see "Troubleshoot Skype" [Hack #12]).

Choose and Configure a Microphone and Speakers

#27 Choose and set up a microphone and speaker system for your PC or Mac and configure them to work with Skype.

Works with: Windows, Linux, and Mac OS X versions of Skype.

Microphone options are shown in Figure 3-4 and speaker options in Figure 3-5.

Figure 3-4. Microphone choices, left to right: handheld microphone, clip-on lapel microphone, desktop microphone, and array microphone

Figure 3-5. Speaker choices, left to right: desktop speakers (separate power supply, 3.5mm plug), and portable speakers (USB plug and powered from USB port)

Given the not-very-high demands placed on sound equipment in terms of fidelity for voice communication, almost any microphone and speaker system will do the job. Your decision will be driven, at least in part, by what sound input and output ports you have available on your computer.

Nevertheless, what follows are some general guidelines that will help you make a choice that best meets your needs and your budget. If your computer has a speaker system (as most now do), but you must buy a microphone, you basically have these choices.

Handheld or clip-on microphone

These are often quite cheap (less than $10) and usually plug into your sound card using a 3.5mm plug. However, you may quickly tire of having to hold a microphone to speak, while a clip-on microphone can make you feel like you are on a leash held by your computer!

Desktop or array microphone

A desktop microphone is simply a microphone with a stand. This type of microphone typically plugs into your sound card using a 3.5mm plug, but the more modern types plug into a USB port. Good desktop microphones can be had for $30 or less. Array microphones stand on your desk, but have directionality, a high level of ambient noise rejection, and oftentimes echo cancellation built in. If you live or work in a noisy environment, an array microphone is a far superior choice to any other microphone. Connection options are the same as for desktop microphones, but expect to pay $50 or more for an array microphone.

If you don't have a speaker system and you must buy one, almost any speaker will do, as the demands for voice communication are quite low. Bear in mind that you don't speak in stereo, so a mono speaker is perfectly adequate to make and receive calls with Skype. Perhaps of more concern is how you want to connect a speaker to your computer. A 3.5mm plug is the most common way to connect to a sound card. But if you don't have a sound card and you do have a spare USB port, speakers are available that plug into a USB port and are self-configuring (as a sound-out device), and may indeed be powered only by the port itself (needing one less main power socket).

Using a microphone and speaker with Skype will mean setting up a configuration like one of those shown in Figure 3-6.

Each configuration option shown in Figure 3-6 has its pros and cons:

Option 1 and option 2

Usage

Skype used as an enhancement to your existing phone system.

Pros

You can save money off your phone bill. Simple to set up and configure. Often uses existing hardware, so reduces the costs of experimenting with Skype.

Cons

You can make and receive calls only while sitting at your computer. More likely to suffer echo problems in comparison with other sound devices.

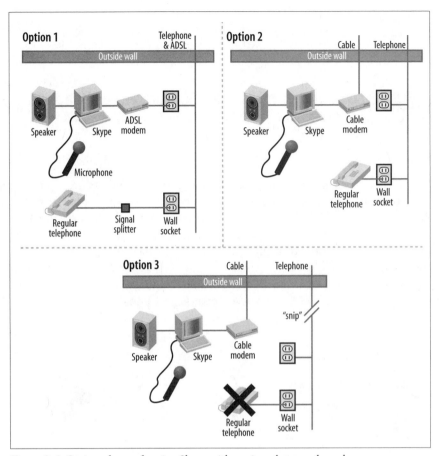

Figure 3-6. Options for configuring Skype with a microphone and speaker

Option 3

Usage

Skype used as a replacement for your existing phone system.

Pros

You can save *a lot* of money off your phone bill. Simple to set up and configure. Often uses existing hardware.

Cons

You can make and receive calls only while sitting at your computer. More likely to suffer echo problems in comparison with other sound devices. No 911 emergency service. No 411 directory service. No support for a regular fax machine. Clearly, as this option eliminates your existing phone service, you'd have to be fairly dedicated to Skype or saving money, or both, to choose this option. But it is a choice!

The "Snip" shown in option 3 is only a metaphorical "snip," as all you really need to do is cancel your existing phone service.

HACK #28 Choose and Configure a USB Handset or Headset

A guide to choosing and setting up a USB handset or headset for your PC or Mac with a minimum of fuss.

Works with: Windows, Linux, and Mac OS X versions of Skype.

USB handsets can be either basic or advanced. Basic handsets are really just a microphone and speaker in the convenient form factor of a phone-shaped handset, whereas advanced handsets also have a keypad and sometimes an LCD readout. Don't underestimate the importance to many people of the familiarity and comfort of using a handset, particularly those who have not been bitten by the "geek" or "techie" bugs. For many "ordinary" people, calls made from a handset are simply more familiar and therefore more pleasant, if not in a quantitative sense, certainly in a qualitative sense.

Your handset and headset choices are shown in Figure 3-7.

Figure 3-7. USB handset and headset choices, left to right: basic handset, advanced handset, wired headset, wireless headset and USB base station, and desktop speakerphone

In terms of choosing a handset or headset for use with Skype, you may find the following guidelines of help:

Basic handset
  This type of handset is the simplest to configure because it is usually a self-configuring USB sound device that requires no additional software. Also, it is very cheap; some cost less than $20. However, as these handsets lack a keypad, all interaction with Skype has to be done using your mouse and keyboard; that is, you can't make, or pick up, a call using only this type of handset.

Advanced handset
  By adding a keypad to a basic handset, you gain extra features and control over how Skype works, all from the handset itself. However, to take

advantage of these you must install software that enables the phone to interact with Skype. Normally, this type of handset allows you to make and pick up a call using only the handset. In addition, you may get additional features, such as call memory and speed dial (separate from what Skype itself provides in this respect). As an added bonus, most advanced handsets have built-in echo correction. Expect to pay $30 and up for an advanced handset.

Headset

The key thing here is comfort. Pay particular care to comfort issues if you wear glasses. If you make frequent calls or long calls, or both, you'll need to choose a headset that's comfortable for you. Otherwise, after a surprisingly short while, you may be forgiven for thinking your head is held in a vice! Also, if you like to get up and stretch occasionally, or reach for things close by, you might want to get a headset with a 10-foot (3-meter) cable, or use a USB extension cord. That way, you'll have limited mobility around your desk. A headset that is uncomfortable is worthless at any price, so don't skimp on this one; good, comfortable headsets start at around $40.

Wireless headset

A wireless headset gives you mobility. In fact, sometimes quite a bit, as some wireless headsets have a range of up to a few hundred feet. However, mobility costs, and you should expect to pay something well north of $100 for a good wireless headset (plus base station). Comfort is again an issue if you intend to wear the headset for prolonged periods. And, for those of you who wear glasses, make sure that damn thing will stay on your ear with your glasses on!

Desktop phone

If having the familiarity of a desktop phone that can make and receive calls using Skype is important to you, expect to pay for the privilege. Desktop USB phones that are compatible with Skype cost $40 and up; and, just as for advanced handsets, you may have to install and configure additional software to exploit its advanced features fully.

When configuring Skype to use a USB headset or USB handset, you have a number of choices based on your type of Internet connection, as shown in Figure 3-8.

Each configuration option shown in Figure 3-8 has its pros and cons:

Option 1 and option 2

Usage

Skype used as an enhancement to your existing phone system.

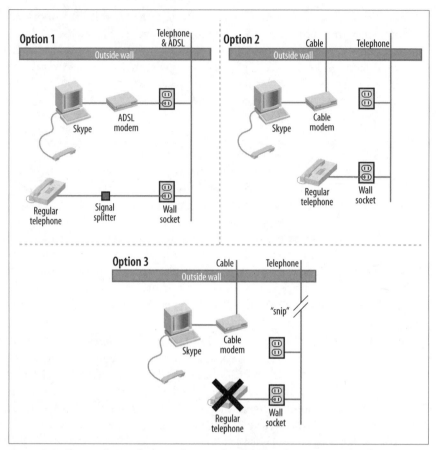

Figure 3-8. Options for configuring Skype with a USB handset or a USB headset (in this figure a USB handset is shown but the configuration is the same if you substitute a USB headset)

Pros

You can save money off your phone bill. Simple to set up and configure; oftentimes USB devices are self-configuring. USB handsets and USB headsets are comparatively cheap (good ones can be had for between $20 and $50). Hands-free operation in the case of a USB headset, and the comfort and familiarity of holding what feels like a phone in the case of a USB handset.

Cons

You can make and receive calls only while sitting at your computer, unless you're using a device that connects wirelessly to a USB base station. Headsets can become uncomfortable if worn for prolonged periods; this is particularly true if you wear glasses (as the hooks over the ears are squeezed between your ears and skull).

Option 3

Usage

Skype used as a replacement for your existing phone system.

Pros

You can save *a lot* of money off your phone bill. Simple to set up and configure; oftentimes USB devices are self-configuring. USB handsets and USB headsets are comparatively cheap (good ones can be had for between $20 and $50). Hands-free operation in the case of a USB headset, and the comfort and familiarity of holding what feels like a phone in the case of a USB handset.

Cons

You can make and receive calls only while sitting at your computer, unless you're using a device that connects wirelessly to a USB base station. Headsets can become uncomfortable if worn for prolonged periods; this is particularly true if you wear glasses (as the hooks over the ears are squeezed between your ears and skull). No 911 emergency service. No 411 directory service. No support for a regular fax machine. Clearly, as this option eliminates your existing phone service, you'd have to be fairly dedicated to Skype or saving money, or both, to choose this option. But it is a choice!

The "Snip" shown in option 3 is only a metaphorical "snip," as all you really need to do is cancel your existing phone service.

HACK #29 Choose and Configure a Bluetooth Headset

A guide to choosing and setting up a Bluetooth headset for your PC, Mac, or Pocket PC, with a minimum of fuss.

Works with: all versions of Skype.

Bluetooth is a wireless technology that allows for ad hoc connection of all sorts of electronic gadgets. Configuring Bluetooth devices is comparatively easy, but the range is limited to about 32 feet (about 10 meters) or less, though some more-modern Bluetooth devices boast ranges substantially greater than 32 feet. The benefits of Bluetooth are that it provides hands-free operation of gadgets, together with some limited mobility, combined with a standardized wireless technology that simplifies device setup and configuration.

One very popular such gadget is the Bluetooth headset, shown in Figure 3-9. Bluetooth headsets normally clip over one ear so that a microphone boom points to your mouth. As always, anything that has to do with your ear can be a real problem if you wear glasses or a hearing aid of some sort. Even if you can get the thing to hang on your ear without a problem, there's the issue of comfort, as presumably you'll wear the headset for prolonged periods. Battery life may also be an issue if you make frequent or long calls, or both; so, always check the manufacturer's specifications before buying (talk time is rarely less than 3 hours and may be as much as 10 hours, and standby time can sometimes be 100 hours or more). Bluetooth headsets start at $30 and the more advanced models can cost well more than $100. The more advanced models have more than pick up and hang up as features, but these are unlikely to work with Skype unless the device comes bundled with software to properly interface to Skype (through the Skype Application Programming Interface, or API).

Figure 3-9. Bluetooth headsets

Many of the more-modern computers are already Bluetooth enabled, which is also true of handheld devices running Pocket PC. However, if you want to use a Bluetooth headset but your computer or handheld is not Bluetooth enabled, you will first have to invest in a Bluetooth dongle (which plugs into a USB port on your computer) or a Bluetooth card for your handheld. Once your computer or handheld is Bluetooth ready, you typically follow this procedure to make Skype work with a Bluetooth headset:

1. Launch the Bluetooth configuration utility that came with your computer or handheld device, or the utility that came with your Bluetooth dongle or card. Set your Bluetooth device to discover other Bluetooth devices that are in range.

2. Put your Bluetooth headset into "pairing mode." If your computer or handheld detects your headset, you will be requested to enter a "passkey," which is a numeric key used to identify your headset and should

be provided by the headset user guide. If you can't easily find the proper passkey, entering "0000" is always worth a try!

3. Once your headset and computer or handheld are "paired" put your headset in normal operating mode.

4. Explicitly configure Skype to use the headset as your sound-in and sound-out device for Skype (Skype → Tools → Options... → Sound Devices on Windows, Skype → Tools → Options... → Hand/Headsets on Linux, or Skype → Preferences... → Audio on Mac OS X).

5. Read the user guide that came with your headset to find out how to pick up and hang up calls by pressing buttons on the headset.

6. Try a test call to echo123. If you want to practice picking up calls using your headset, send the chat message "callme" to echo123 and the echo service will call you back.

7. If you're having problems making your headset work, try obtaining help from the manufacturer. Failing that, you can go to the Skype web site (*http://www.skype.com/*) and take advantage of its troubleshooting resources and community forums. However, before doing that, it's always worth checking that your Bluetooth headset isn't switched off or in low battery mode, and a repeat of the "pairing" process often fixes things.

Once your Bluetooth headset is working with Skype, it's always a good idea to do a test call and explore the limits of your mobility without losing signal. After a minute or two of walking around your office or home, you'll have a pretty good idea of where you can and cannot make and receive Skype calls using your headset.

See Also

- A Bluetooth-specific thread for Windows XP (SP2) on the Skype forums, at *http://forum.skype.com/viewtopic.php?t=10822&highlight=800.*

Configure Skype to Use Regular Phones

By making your existing phones work with Skype, you not only eliminate the expense of buying new ones, but you also end up with a phone system that largely looks and feels the same as before.

Works with: Windows and Linux versions of Skype.

Connecting your existing phones to Skype is easy. Using this hack, you can hack around with your existing phone system in a variety of interesting ways, from simply having the convenience and familiarity of a regular phone next to your computer for making and receiving Skype calls, to driving all the existing copper wiring throughout your house using Skype in what is basically a replacement of your regular phone service. If all this sounds somewhat daunting, don't worry, as even the most advanced hacking requires little more than a pair of wire cutters, a roll of electrical insulation tape, and a little common sense!

Configuring Skype to work with a regular phone requires a Skype-to-phone adapter box, shown in Figure 3-10, and some associated software. Skype-to-phone adapter boxes cost $50 or less (though more-expensive and feature-rich units are hitting the market as I write) and are interfaced through and sometimes powered by your computer's USB interface.

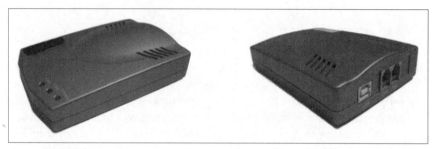

Figure 3-10. Skype-to-phone adapter, front and back

Normally, getting a Skype-to-phone adapter up and working is simplicity itself. Plug one end of a USB cable into the back of the adapter, and the other end into an available USB port on your computer. Install the software and drivers, give the new software access to Skype (Skype will prompt you to give your permission), and then simply plug a regular phone into the adapter using an RJ11 connector.

If you want to be able to switch between a regular phone line and Skype, there's usually a "line" socket on the adapter that you can connect to a phone socket in the wall using a regular RJ11 cable (RJ11 plugs on both ends). Double-check that your Skype sound-in and sound-out devices are set to your new adapter (Skype → Tools → Options... → Sound Devices on Windows, Skype → Tools Options... → Hand/Headsets on Linux, and Skype → Preferences... → Audio on Mac OS X), and that's it! You're ready to make Skype calls with a regular phone—or, indeed, regular calls through a regular phone line (if you still need one, read on).

Skype-to-phone adapters are clearly designed with the idea of driving a single regular phone in mind. However, some of the configuration options in this hack drive multiple phones from a single adapter. I have had no problems doing this, as fairly modern phones draw little power to operate. But, if you have older phones or clunkers that draw a lot of power, you might overload your Skype-to-phone adapter, especially if your adapter is powered solely by your computer's USB port. Anyway, a little experimentation with more than one phone attached to your adapter should give you some answers, and some practical operating guidelines.

Options for configuring Skype with regular phones run the whole gamut from simply using a regular phone handset while sitting at your computer, to driving your home phone system with Skype (see Figure 3-11). Look at the available choices and how you would like to use Skype with your existing phone infrastructure. And, as perhaps a key part of your decision making, consider how much money you want to shave off your current phone bill. Characteristically, the more you do with Skype and the less you use the services of your regular phone company, the more money you can save. Lastly, bear in mind that Figure 3-11 and Figure 3-13 merely show some of the configuration options you might want to try; don't be afraid to experiment and let your imagination run free, as Skype and its underlying technologies are almost begging to be hacked!

The first thing to notice about the options illustrated in Figure 3-11 and Figure 3-12 is that you can completely convert your existing phone infrastructure to Skype only if you obtain your broadband Internet connection through cable or something other than DSL.

Here are the relative merits of the configuration options:

Option 1, option 2, option 4, and option 5

> *Usage*
>> Skype used as an enhancement to your existing phone system.

> *Pros*
>> Shaves money off your phone bill. Looks and feels like a regular phone system. Easy to set up. Uses existing phone infrastructure and equipment. Retains 911 emergency service and 411 directory assistance (or equivalents outside the U.S.). Works with regular fax machines (attached to a regular phone line). Remote monitoring of your home alarm system continues uninterrupted (provided you cut only the phone lines *not* used by your alarm monitoring service).

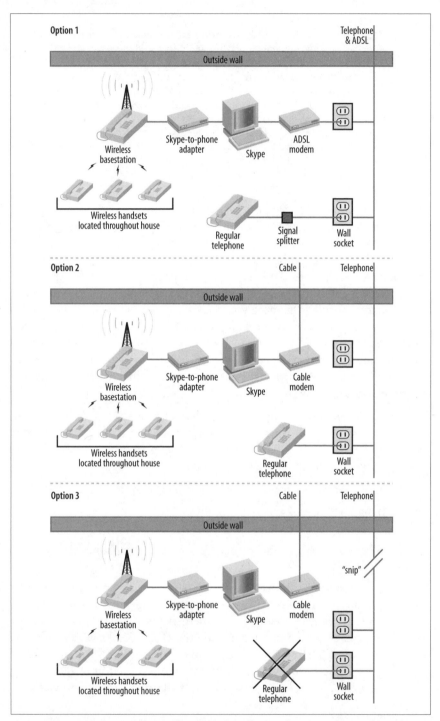

Figure 3-11. Options to configure Skype (regular phone and existing phone infrastructure)

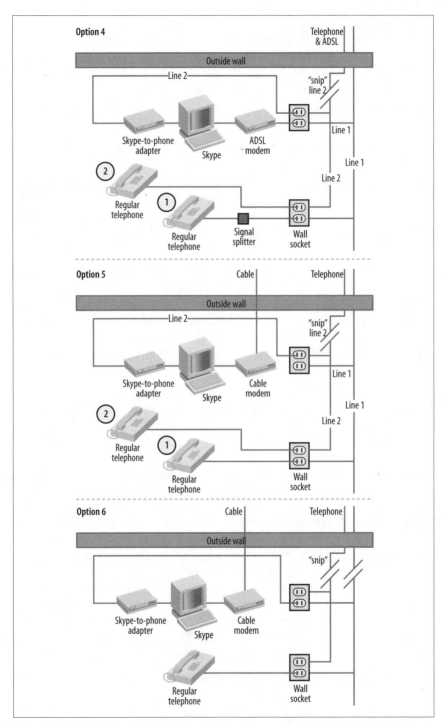

Figure 3-12. Options to configure Skype (regular phone and existing phone infrastructure)

Cons

Can make and receive Skype calls only while your computer is powered up and Skype is running. In addition, options 4 and 5 require a
modest amount of hacking around (DIY skills) with your existing
phone line wiring.

Option 3 and option 6

Usage

Skype used as replacement for your existing phone system.

Pros

Can save *alot* of money, perhaps as much as 80% or more off your
current phone bill (my savings, for comparison, are 82%). Looks
and feels like a regular phone system. Uses existing phone infrastructure and equipment.

Cons

Can make and receive calls only while your computer is powered up
and Skype is running. Requires a modest amount of hacking around
(DIY skills) with your existing phone line wiring. No 911 emergency service and no 411 directory assistance (or equivalents outside the U.S.). Doesn't work with regular fax machines. Requires
careful thought and planning to retain uninterrupted remote home
alarm system monitoring.

> The "Snip" shown in option 3 is only a metaphorical
> "snip," as all you really need to do is cancel your existing
> phone service.

Adapting your existing phone infrastructure to work with Skype, in whole or
only in part, can be a challenge. But then again, the payoff can make the
effort worthwhile. Indeed, with a little planning, some small expenditures
on new equipment (which you recoup through your savings within a matter
of months), and a willingness to experiment, you can in large measure replicate your existing phone system and services, but at a fraction of what you
pay now. I describe my Skype phone system in "Build a Skype Server" **[Hack
#35]**; my estimated savings using this system are a little shy of $700 per year.
That's $700 this year, next year, the year after that, and in subsequent
years—big savings! Moreover, with a little ingenuity, there are workarounds
for most of Skype's "limitations"—911, 411, fax, and so forth—and I
present these workarounds as hacks in Chapter 10.

So, pick a configuration option and get hacking! (And saving!)

Configure Skype on a Laptop
Configuration tips to make Skype ready for the road.

Works with: Windows, Linux, and Mac OS X versions of Skype.

Laptops have advanced in features and power so much in recent years that, in terms of performance and features, the newer ones differ little from desktop machines. Even so, there are a number of things to bear in mind, and things to try, when you're configuring Skype on your laptop.

Copy Your Skype Data

Much, but not all, of your Skype data is now stored on the Skype network. Examples of the stuff you leave behind are voicemail history, chat history, and your call list.

So, if when you next log onto Skype on your laptop, you want to see exactly what you last saw on your desktop, synchronize the *Skypename* folders on the two machines:

Windows
> C:\Documents and Settings*Username*\Application Data\Skype*Skypename*

Linux
> /home/*Username*/.Skype/*Skypename*

Mac OS X
> /Users/*Username*/Library/Application Support/Skype/*Skypename*

Username is your login name for the machine and *Skypename* is the name you use to log in to Skype.

> Skype has surprisingly good forward and backward compatibility in terms of its data. However, there are limits, and you will have fewer issues if you only transfer data between machines that run the same version of Skype.

Echo and Sound Quality

Given the necessarily fixed close proximity of a laptop's built-in speakers and microphone, you can't fix a problem with echo by simply moving the microphone further away from the speakers, which is typically the first thing to try. Frankly, even though a laptop's built-in speakers and microphone might do in a pinch, you will save yourself a lot of pain and frustration if you simply get a good headset (a combination of earphones and a microphone on a boom), or a USB handset.

In terms of headsets, if your laptop has both USB ports and a 3.5mm audio jack, you have a choice. For example, you might choose a headphone with a 3.5mm plug to conserve USB ports. If you don't have an audio jack, you pretty much have to go with a USB headset, unless your laptop is Bluetooth enabled, in which case using a Bluetooth headset is an option.

Whatever type of headset you finally adopt, your evaluation criteria when considering what type and style of headset to get should be the following, in order of importance:

Comfort

> Given that you may end up wearing a headset for prolonged periods, you may find the effect of an uncomfortable headset somewhat akin to Chinese water torture: a minor irritation to start with and excruciating pain in the long run! Comfort issues are important for everyone. But if you wear glasses, comfort becomes doubly important, as the headset's earphones compress the arms of your glasses between your ears and skull. Any time you spend on choosing a headset in terms of assessing its comfort is time well spent.

Size

> As you'll be traveling with these things, get the smallest pair you can find—with the proviso that comfort still comes first.

Cost

> Voice communication does not put great demands on audio quality or fidelity. Therefore, unless you intend to use the earphones of the headset to listen to high-quality music as well, buy the cheapest set that meets your criteria of comfort and size.

Internet Connection

Laptops connect to the Internet in one of the following ways: wireless (WiFi and Bluetooth), Ethernet, or modem.

Wireless provides the greatest flexibility in terms of making a connection to the Internet using a laptop. If your laptop is wireless enabled, you have the opportunity to connect to an ever-growing choice of free and fee-based wireless access points (see "Make Free Calls While on the Move" **[Hack #64]**). Moreover, if your laptop has both WiFi and Bluetooth wireless, as more and more machines do nowadays, your choices for wireless connection points are greater still.

Ethernet is such an established networking technology that there is little to say, other than don't forget to carry a patch cable! Even if your primary connection is wireless, having a patch cable is good backup.

A modem is doable, but not recommended.

Avoid Being a Super Node

Most laptops probably need as much bandwidth and available resources as they can get. However, if your machine is nominated by the Skype network to become a super node, this can put a strain on your laptop, which could cause Skype call quality to suffer.

Skype has not made public the rules by which particular machines become super nodes. However, if you disable Skype's use of ports 80 and 443, you certainly lower the probability that your machine will become a super node. To disable ports 80 and 443, select Skype → Tools → Options... → Connection on Windows and uncheck the "Use port 80 and 443 as alternatives for incoming connections" box (select Skype → Tools → Options... → Advanced on Linux; the option is not available on Mac OS X).

Configure Skype on a Pocket PC

Configure Skype on your Pocket PC so that it has features similar to those of a mobile phone—but without the three-year contract, or recurring monthly charges!

Works with: Pocket PC version of Skype.

Most Pocket PC devices have both sound devices and networking built in. For those that don't, simply adding an expansion card can rectify the situation.

Skype gives you relatively few configuration options on Pocket PC because the sound and network devices are far more integrated with the device and under more direct control of the Pocket PC operating system. To configure both you should use the configuration facilities of Pocket PC (Start → Settings → System → Microphone enables you to set the microphone's gain and enable automatic gain control, and Start → Settings → Connections usually provides utilities to configure both Bluetooth and WiFi). Two Skype-specific configuration options always worth playing with to get the behavior you want are "Prevent device standby mode when online" and "Echo cancellation ON," both of which you can find under Skype → Tools → Options.

One option that is really useful, but not available on all Pocket PC devices, is the ability to disable touch-screen input during a call. Otherwise, when you hold the device next to your head to talk and listen during a call, there's a chance that a stray finger or other body part that touches the screen might be mistaken for the stylus, and you run the risk of inadvertently disconnecting the call. My Dell Axim X50v has a slide-switch on the side that you can conveniently push up and down with your thumb to disable/enable all touch-screen input during a Skype call. Yours might have a similar feature.

WiFi Versus Bluetooth

Many Pocket PC devices have both WiFi (802.11) and Bluetooth. You can connect to the Internet using either, if a suitable wireless access point is in range. For WiFi, that usually means an Internet-ready wireless router is in range, and for Bluetooth, it usually means that a Bluetooth-enabled computer with Internet access is in range and can be used as a gateway to the Internet.

The tradeoff is that WiFi has greater range, perhaps as much as a few hundred feet, compared to Bluetooth's 32 feet, but it consumes a lot more power than Bluetooth. On a handheld device, this can make a big difference to the battery life and therefore impacts how long you can talk with Skype. Bluetooth power consumption in talk mode is typically one-fifth that of WiFi and in standby mode it can be as little as one one-hundredth. Clearly, if you have a choice and range is not an issue, disable WiFi and use Bluetooth to connect to the Internet to use Skype for a considerably longer period.

Using Your Pocket PC as a Mobile Phone

Your Pocket PC can effectively act like a mobile phone once it's in range of a wireless access point that gives it access to the Internet.

More and more public places have some form of free wireless access (for example, public libraries and coffee shops), and others have paid wireless access (for example, Skype's own Skype Zones service). Most workplaces have some form of wireless connectivity to the Internet, and the same is true of many homes.

Many readers will no doubt spend most of their waking hours within range of one form of wireless Internet connection or another. Heck, if you're really desperate to use Skype, you can even use a wireless modem to connect to the Internet using the cellular network; though, in that case, bandwidth restrictions will limit you to Skype chat only.

The point is that given the pervasiveness of wireless connectivity nowadays, it takes only a little ingenuity, planning, and organization to turn your Pocket PC running Skype into a close substitute for a mobile phone. Think about it. The cost savings might make the effort worthwhile.

Hacking the Hack

If you have a Bluetooth-enabled Pocket PC device, you can try a few more, neat configuration hacks.

You can pair it with a Bluetooth headset to make it a hands-free phone (see "Choose and Configure a Bluetooth Headset" **[Hack #29]**).

Or you can pair your Pocket PC with a Bluetooth-enabled desktop computer and configure it so that it acts as a wireless handset for Skype running on the desktop, which is nice if you want to move around during a call. In this mode, your Pocket PC is operating as an audio gateway so that your handheld device's built-in microphone and speaker, in effect, act as the sound devices for Skype running on the desktop.

HACK #33   Test Your Internet Connection Bandwidth

Test to make sure Skype's bandwidth needs are met.

Works with: all versions of Skype.

What is bandwidth and why is it important? Bandwidth is a measure of the rate at which your computer can exchange data with the Internet. Its most obvious manifestation is how quickly web pages load in your browser: low bandwidth means slow loads, and high bandwidth means fast loads, all other things being equal. Bandwidth, like money, is something of which having more is generally better than having less. Even though Skype's bandwidth needs are surprisingly low to have high-quality conversations over the Internet, your Skype experience will definitely improve with increased bandwidth (see also "Test Your Internet Connection Latency" **[Hack #34]**).

Bandwidth is typically measured in units of kilobits per second (Kbps), where 1 Kbps = 1,000 bits per second, or megabits per second (Mbps), where 1 Mbps = 1,000,000 bits per second. The more bits per second your Internet connection supports, the faster you can exchange data over the Internet. If you connect to the Internet through a regular telephone using a modem, your bandwidth will be measured in Kbps, whereas broadband Internet connection speeds are typically measured in Mbps (or in multiples of 100 Kbps). One last wrinkle for bandwidth measurement is that your data exchange rate might not be symmetrical (that is, it might be asymmetric), so your upload bandwidth might be different from your download bandwidth. If your broadband connection is asymmetric, prudence dictates that you should use the lower of the two numbers when making decisions.

> Skype prefers to publish its bandwidth usage numbers in kilobytes per second, where 8 bits = 1 byte. Here are some useful conversion factors between kilobytes and kilobits: 0.5 kilobytes per second = 4 Kbps, 3 kilobytes per second = 24 Kbps, and 16 kilobytes per second = 128 Kbps.

Skype's Bandwidth Needs

According to Skype, on average, a single conversation consumes between 3 and 16 kilobytes per second (24–128 Kbps) of bandwidth. When Skype is idle, it typically consumes 0.5 kilobytes per second (4 Kbps). Actual bandwidth usage depends on so many factors that you should think of these numbers as guidelines rather than as something set in stone. As with all uncertain data, it makes sense to build in some margin for error when making your decision.

The very best dial-up modems have a (symmetrical) speed of 56 Kbps. Many Skype users report that sound quality at this data rate is quite good, and is still usable down to about 20 Kbps. But clearly, dial-up voice quality is much more of a hit-or-miss affair, and will degrade rapidly with reducing bandwidth. At what point Skype becomes unusable is rather subjective; but you probably should consider Skype's lower boundary of 24 Kbps as the absolute bare minimum.

> Users of Pocket PC-enabled phones and PDAs that connect to the Internet using a mobile phone wireless Internet connection (for example, GPRS) have reported making calls using Skype even at bandwidths of less than 24 Kbps. However, such reports are rather sketchy about voice quality and call reliability.
>
> Of course, having too little bandwidth to make a voice call does not stop you from using Skype. You can always use Skype-to-Skype chat.

If you intend to use Skype not just for one-on-one conversations, but also for conference calls, your bandwidth requirements will necessarily increase. Skype currently supports conference calls among up to five parties (you included) and chat among up to 50 other Skype users. Clearly, if you want to use these Skype features, your bandwidth needs will increase proportionately. Conference calls and multi-user chat mean that you must have a broadband connection rather than a dial-up connection. Moreover, such a broadband connection should ideally have a bandwidth of greater than 250 Kbps.

One last thing to remember about Skype's bandwidth needs is that it shares whatever bandwidth you have with other services and applications running on your machine. If you have only a dial-up connection, you should refrain from doing anything else that might rob Skype of bandwidth—for example, browsing the Internet. A broadband connection might allow you to do other things while you talk on Skype, but if you detect that sound quality is deteriorating, the first thing you should do is stop anything you're doing that might be consuming bandwidth.

Measure Your Connection Bandwidth

The easiest way to get a handle on your Internet connection bandwidth is to use an online measurement tool. Ideally, use one that measures both upload and download bandwidth, because where Skype is concerned, you should use the lower of the two numbers when deciding whether your connection will serve Skype's bandwidth needs.

Many web sites offer to measure your Internet connection speed free of charge. Googling on "measure Internet connection bandwidth" will produce a long list of such sites. One of the more comprehensive, and free, services is available at *http://www.numion.com/*. This service measures the upload and the download speeds of your Internet connection and, as an added bonus, measures your connection's latency (see Figure 3-13).

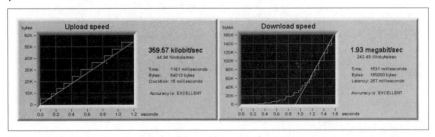

Figure 3-13. Measuring the bandwidth and latency of your Internet connection

 The MaxSpeed test at *http://www.numion.com/* requires that you have the Java 2 Platform, Standard Edition (J2SE) installed on your machine. J2SE is free, and you can download it at *http://java.sun.com/*.

Test Your Internet Connection Latency
#34 Test to make sure Skype's latency needs are met.

Works with: all versions of Skype.

From Skype's point of view, latency is a measure of the delay that occurs between the moment you speak and the moment your recipient hears what you said. During face-to-face conversations, the delay is obviously not noticeable because the distance your voice has to travel is so short.

However, as this delay lengthens, conversation becomes more and more stuttering and broken, and the likelihood of the call participants talking over each other increases.

> The Apollo moon landings provided a dramatic demonstration of latency. The moon orbits Earth at an average distance of 238,900 miles and the speed of light is 186,000 miles per second. This meant that there was a minimum round-trip delay of about 2.6 seconds between someone in ground control asking a question and his receiving an answer from an astronaut standing on the moon. This meant that conversations between ground control and the astronauts on the moon were necessarily made more difficult by the long pauses caused by latency.
>
> Similarly, people who get their Internet connection via satellite (specifically, geostationary satellite) face a minimum 0. 24-second round-trip delay between transmission and receipt of data because of the long signal path through space. Electronics and cabling along the end-to-end path between sender and recipient simply add to this delay. Some Skype users talk over a satellite link—if you live somewhere really remote, it might be your only option to connect to the Internet—and they report that even though the sound quality might be good, the link latency is noticeable and makes for difficult conversation.

Skype's Latency Needs

Skype works by connecting one machine to another over great distances, sometimes on opposite sides of the globe. Between the two machines is the Internet. Not surprisingly, depending on the speed of your Internet connection and how data is routed over the Internet, end-to-end or one-way latency (between caller and recipient) can grow quite long. Anything over 0.3 seconds will make your conversation more and more forced, in the sense that you will have to pause to know with certainty that the speaker has stopped speaking, or risk talking over one another. A latency of between 0.15 and 0. 3 seconds is noticeable, but can be accommodated fairly easily provided the callers cooperate; this is especially true if the callers know each other, as each will be somewhat familiar with the other's speaking habits. Anything below 0.15-second latency and your conversation will be little different from a good landline connection.

All of these latency rules of thumb are derived from my experience. If you want a more objective source of guidelines for the impact of latency on voice-call quality, you should consult the International Telecommunication Union (ITU) at *http://www.itu.int/* and get a copy of "Recommendation G. 114: One-way transmission time." At the time of this writing, the cost was 25 Swiss francs. For the curious, here are some summary numbers:

- Latency less than 0.15 seconds: mostly acceptable.
- Latency between 0.15 and 0.4 seconds: acceptable (maybe).
- Latency more than 0.4 seconds: unacceptable.
- And for comparison, here are some typical numbers for regular telephones and mobile phones:
- Long-distance telephone: less than 0.05-second latency.
- International telephone: about 0.1-second latency.
- Telephone to mobile phone: about 0.15-second latency.
- Mobile phone to mobile phone: between 0.3- and 0.4-second latency.

Measure Your Connection Latency

The easiest way to get a handle on your one-way and round-trip Internet connection latency is to use an online measurement tool. One such tool is the MaxSpeed test, which you can find at *http://www.numion.com/* (refer back to Figure 3-13).

HACK #35 Build a Skype Server

Skype needs to be running to place and receive calls. Set up a stripped-down PC to act as a Skype server that will provide 24/7 operation.

Works with: Windows and Linux versions of Skype.

One irritating feature of Skype is that it must be running on a computer for you to make and receive calls with it. That is, when your computer is off, Skype doesn't work. Moreover, when you run Skype on the computer you use day in and day out, Skype's performance (call quality, reliability, and so forth) can suffer if you are doing other things that rob Skype or otherwise deprive it of the runtime resources it needs. This is particularly true if your day-to-day computer is barely above Skype's minimum hardware requirements.

Presumably, sometime in the future we'll see Skype-enabled phones and devices with Skype embedded and running on its own processor; a "plug it in and it'll just work" sort of thing. Until then, you can use this hack, which describes how to build a "Skype server" that provides 24/7 phone service with a minimum of hassle and fuss.

You have two choices when building a Skype server: build one, or convert an old machine you have conveniently at hand. Whichever route you take, there are a number of checkpoints worth addressing first:

1. Are Skype's minimum hardware requirements met? See Table P-1 in this book's Preface for Skype's minimum hardware requirements at the time of this writing.

2. If your hardware isn't up to snuff, do you have parts at hand to bring it up to specification, or can you buy the parts to do so? This essentially reduces you to a choice between upgrading your old machine or building a new machine from scratch. Building a new machine doesn't have to be cost prohibitive, as my Skype server cost a little more than $250, and that included *two* Skype-to-phone adapters (see Table 3-1). Remember, a Skype server needs no mouse, keyboard, monitor, CD-ROM drive, or floppy drive—other than at the time of its configuration.

3. Where are you going to locate your Skype server? Ideally, it should be somewhere with access to power, good ventilation, an Internet connection, your regular phone lines (RJ11 sockets in the U.S.), and—depending on how house-proud you happen to be—out of sight. My choice was to install my Skype server in my basement (see Figure 3-14), which is possibly the ideal location, but not necessarily one open to everybody. If your choices are more limited, that's all the more reason to think long and hard about where to put your Skype server once it's built.

4. You should factor in the cost of building and running a Skype server into your savings analysis (see "Back-of-the-Envelope Estimate of Skype Savings" [Hack #13]). Running costs will depend on the machine that you choose to convert to, or build, to run Skype 24/7. An old clunker of a machine may consume so much power that it would be worthwhile building a new machine in the long run. As always, run the numbers and make some decisions.

Let's look at the cost of running a Skype server 24 hours a day, 365 days a year. Without a monitor and other peripherals to guzzle power, a small modern computer typically consumes between 50W and 100W. If your cost of electricity is $0.10 per kWh, the annual cost of running your Skype server is between $44 and $88. These are just ballpark numbers and you'll no doubt come up with your own, but it does show that the cost of running a Skype server 24/7 is not insignificant. (Cost = power consumed in kW × 365 days × 24 hours × cost per kWh. 50W is 0.05 kW and 100W is 0.1 kW.)

Table 3-1. Typical cost of building a new Skype server from scratch (author's actual costs of building a server)

Component	Cost
IN-WIN BT610P.180BFU2 Black steel MicroATX computer case 180W power supply	$39.99
BIOSTAR M7VIG400 Micro ATX motherboard with AMD Duron 800 mobile CPU	$69
OCZ value series 512MB (2 x 256MB) 184-Pin DDR SDRAM unbuffered DDR 333 (PC 2700) dual-channel kit system memory	$43.75
10GB hard-disk drive (used)	$12.95
Skype-to-phone USB adapter (two at $43.90 each)	$87.80
Linux operating system	Free
Total	$253.49

Figure 3-14. Skype server to provide 24/7 phone service; server is at the top of the photo, cable modem and wireless router are to the left, and patch board for household phone wires is to the right (the large cabinet for household power distribution in the center of the photo is not part of the Skype server configuration)

Building and installing a Skype server for your home is fairly easy and requires only a modicum of technical skills. If you can install hardware and software on a computer and are willing to wield a screwdriver and a pair of wire cutters, you already have the skills to do this.

Here's a step-by-step guide to getting your Skype server up and running:

1. Order any new hardware you'll need. At a minimum, this will most likely mean that you'll need to order a Skype-to-phone adapter. We'll assume you'll get two adapters to drive two separate telephone lines.

2. Build a new computer, or reconfigure an old computer to meet Skype's hardware requirements.

3. Borrow a CD-ROM, floppy disk, mouse, keyboard, and monitor from another system to configure your Skype server.

4. Install and configure some flavor ("distro") of Linux. For a Skype server you won't need a lot of services that run by default, so trim the list of services started at boot time to only those needed to make Skype work. Also, disable the screensaver (after all, there isn't any screen to "save") and power standby features, as these may interfere with Skype.

5. Download and install Skype. Create two Skype user accounts—for example, SkypeUser1 and SkypeUser2. Configure Linux to start two instances of Skype at boot time automatically, under two Linux logon names—say, SkypeLinux1 and SkypeLinux2. Configure the settings for Skype; for example, for 24/7 operation you may want to have your Skype status as permanently "Online." Setting up Linux to run multiple instances of Skype is somewhat involved. To keep this hack to a manageable length, I provide the details in a technical note available from this book's web site, *http://www.oreilly.com/catalog/SkypeHacks/index.html*.

6. Connect your Skype-to-phone adapters to USB ports on your Skype server and install any necessary software. Have SkypeUser1 use one USB adapter and SkypeUser2 use the other as its sound-in and sound-out device. Connect regular phone handsets and test Skype on both adapters.

7. Sign up your new Skype accounts for SkypeIn and SkypeOut service as needed. If you already have Skype accounts configured and ready to go, simply move these to the Skype server (in which case, change the Linux and Skype usernames as appropriate).

8. Cancel your regular phone service.

9. Cut your incoming phone lines.

10. Connect the adapters to your home phone lines via the RJ11 sockets in your wall (in the U.S.; other countries use different socket types). Test Skype again using phones plugged in throughout your house.

11. Remove the borrowed CD-ROM, floppy drive, mouse, keyboard, and monitor and move the server to its new location. Plug in all the cables and connectors, and then power it on. Test Skype once more.

12. If all has gone well, you now have 24/7 phone service on two phone lines—all provided by Skype. You'll never receive a phone bill from your regular phone company again—now ain't that something!

Incidentally, the preceding step-by-step guide is not some theoretical musing on how to set up and configure a Skype server. Quite the contrary, it's the procedure I used to replace my existing home phone system completely with Skype (see Figure 3-15).

Hacking the Hack

For those readers who are security conscious and don't trust Skype yet, building a Skype server has an added advantage. By placing the Skype server on your Internet connection *outside* your firewall, you gain the piece of mind that should a hacker break into your server or compromise Skype somehow, as the server interfaces with nothing more than copper phone lines beyond the firewall, any damage will necessarily be contained and limited to the Skype server *outside* the firewall. The worst case is that you'll need to do a reinstall on your Skype server—and, perhaps, a better job of locking it down from a security point of view so that it can protect itself. Indeed, if your firewall is sufficiently restrictive that Skype won't work on the inside, placing your Skype server outside your firewall is the only way in which you can take advantage of Skype's phone services.

Make Skype Work with Personal Firewalls

Skype is rather good at working with firewalls without the need for any additional configuration, but sometimes it needs some help.

Works with: all versions of Skype.

Many VoIP applications simply don't work from behind a firewall or Network Address Translation (NAT) device. And many, if not most, broadband Internet users operate from behind one or the other, or both!

Skype does a good job of transcending these barriers to communication, mostly without any additional configuration, but Skype is not foolproof in this respect. This hack will help you if you're having problems getting Skype to work from behind a firewall.

Firewall problems are most often signaled by Skype error #1102, "Skype cannot be started;" though #1101, "No connection," and #1103, "No

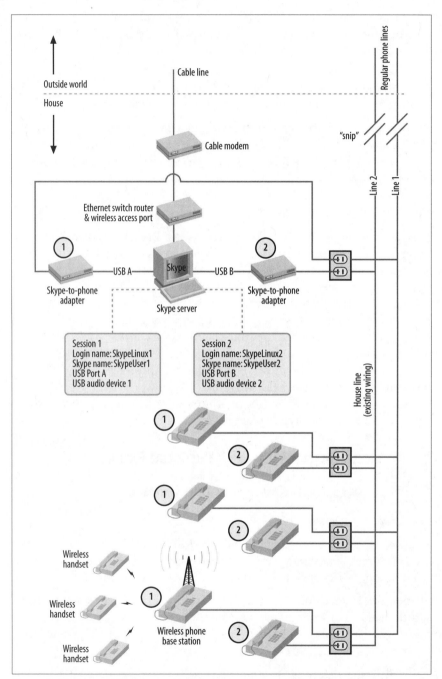

Figure 3-15. Using a Skype server to replace two existing regular phone lines

connection," are also common. These errors mean that your Internet connection is down or misconfigured, you are behind a restrictive firewall or proxy that is blocking Skype's access to the Internet, or your network or Internet service provider is somehow blocking Skype.

To learn more about the nature of your Internet connection, and how it might be blocking Skype, you can try these tests:

Other Peer-to-Peer (P2P) applications
> Are other P2P-type applications also blocked? If the answer is yes, it's more likely that your firewall is blocking all P2P-type traffic, including Skype. Otherwise, it is more likely that the problem is a network problem specific to Skype.

Telnet
> From a command or shell prompt, enter "telnet -ex yahoo.com 80". If the screen goes blank, enter "x", and you should be greeted with a telnet prompt (see Figure 3-16). If you are, you likely have a Skype-specific Internet connection problem.

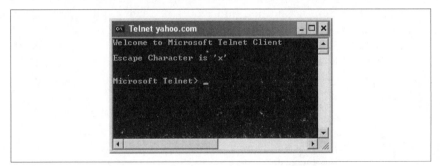

Figure 3-16. Telnet prompt

Broadly speaking, there are two types of firewall: those implemented in software and which run on your desktop machine, and those implemented as part of some piece of network hardware (router, proxy, etc.). First, I'll discuss the general requirements for all types of firewall needed for Skype to work, and then I'll discuss software firewalls and hardware firewalls in turn.

At a minimum, Skype requires unrestricted access to outgoing *Transmission Control Protocol* (TCP) ports above 1024, or to ports 80 and 443 specifically. Skype prefers the former, but can live with the latter. Skype's voice quality and functionality will be improved if, in addition, your firewall is open for two-way *User Datagram Protocol* (UDP) traffic on all ports above 1024. These are the first things you should check.

Whether Skype should try to use TCP ports 80 and 443 is controlled through its options. For Windows, select Skype → Tools → Options... → Connection; for Linux, select Skype → Tools → Options... → Advanced. Neither Mac OS X nor Pocket PC versions of Skype provide for explicit use of ports 80 and 443.

When Skype is installed, it randomly chooses a port above 1024 on which to listen for incoming traffic. You can inspect the port Skype has chosen on your machine by selecting Tools → Options... → Connection on Windows; Tools → Options... → Advanced on Linux; and Skype → Preferences... → Advanced on Mac OS X (this information is not available for Pocket PC). If you don't want to open up all ports above 1024 for Skype, you can open only the specific port Skype has chosen for TCP and/or UDP traffic.

Software firewalls run on your machine and monitor incoming and outgoing Internet traffic for malicious activity. Moreover, applications that connect to the Internet from your machine are also monitored and, indeed, are usually blocked from connecting until you give them explicit permission. Windows XP (SP2) and Mac OS X come with their own firewalls that are turned on by default. Most Linux distributions have a firewall included, though it may not be enabled by default. Moreover, several firewall applications are available from independent vendors and from open source projects.

 When you upgrade Skype to a newer version, this may be detected by your firewall and you may be prompted to give permission again for Skype to access the Internet.

Skype has a number of user guides for configuring the following popular software-only firewalls that run on Windows:

- Windows XP SP2 Firewall
- Norton Personal Firewall
- ZoneAlarm Pro
- McAfee Firewall Pro

You can find these guides at *http://www.skype.com/help/guides/firewall.html*.

Giving advice on configuring hardware-based firewalls is problematic because of the sheer variety of equipment in existence. Really, the advice comes down to opening the correct ports for Skype to use and making sure that port 80, if used, is not set to pass *HyperText Transport Protocol* (HTTP) only. Skype doesn't use HTTP. For the specifics of how to open ports and filter protocols, you will have to refer to the documentation for your firewall hardware.

Another known issue arises when your machine becomes a Skype super node, which is something over which you have no control. Super nodes are regular Skype clients that change their behavior, and in the process consume more network resources, to make Skype's global network work properly. Without super nodes, Skype would not work as well as it does, or perhaps not at all. But this may be of little comfort if *you* are one of the super nodes! The problem arises when a super node has so many incoming network requests—specifically, large numbers of TCP connections—that your router/firewall is overwhelmed. This is particularly true if your hardware has fairly minimal onboard processing power.

See Also

- Additional guidance on router/firewall configuration is available at *http://www.skype.com/security/guide-for-network-admins.pdf*.

HACK #37 Set Up Multiple Phone Lines

You can have multiple Skype phone lines by running multiple instances of Skype on the same machine.

Works with: Windows version of Skype.

To have several phone lines you must have several instances of Skype running. These instances can run on different machines, or on a single machine. For this to work, each instance of Skype must run independently from the others. This hack gives some suggestions on how to set up and configure multiple phone lines using Skype.

First, a word of caution. If all the running instances of Skype (whether on the same machine or spread across machines) share the same Internet connection, setting up multiple phone lines is an idea that can be taken too far, because too many instances of Skype sharing the same connection might, at some point, overwhelm it to the degree that call quality is universally degraded.

Multiple Machines

The simplest way to obtain multiple phone lines using Skype is to run Skype on multiple machines, each with its own sound device and/or phone hardware attached. This is very easy to set up and configure, as each is independent of the other.

For a small office, or a home with multiple computers (Dad has a PC, Mom has a Mac, and Junior has a Linux box, for instance), this might be the best option.

Multiple Instances of Skype on the Same Machine

You can have multiple phone lines through a single machine, but it will require a little bit of forward planning, setup, and configuration. Here's the procedure:

1. Multiple phone lines cannot use the same sound device—well, not without a lot of confused calls. So, you must install and configure a separate sound device for each phone line (running instance of Skype) you want. This might be as simple as having a number of different USB handsets, all the way up to multiple USB Skype-to-phone adapters driving the phone wires of your home (see "Build a Skype Server" [Hack #35]).

2. Nothing is stopping you from running several instances of Skype using the *same* Skype name. Indeed, there are some advantages—for instance, all lines will ring for the same incoming call. However, for illustration purposes, I will assume that you have created two new Skype accounts for the purpose of having two separate and distinct phone lines. Let's call these two accounts SkypeUser1 and SkypeUser2.

3. Configure your machine to run multiple instances of Skype, each using a different logon name; namely, SkypeUser1 and SkypeUser2. For two phone lines, log on to SkypeUser1, start Skype, and configure it to use a sound device—say, USB Handset 1. Similarly, switch to SkypeUser2 (Start → Log Off → Switch User) and log on, and then do the same for what we'll call USB Handset 2. Now, incoming calls to SkypeUser1 will be handled by USB Handset 1. Similarly, incoming calls to SkypeUser2 will be handled by USB Handset 2. It's as simple as that! There is, however, one small gotcha to this setup. As only one user session is visible at a time on your monitor, you can effectively make outgoing calls only from the active session; unless, of course, your sound hardware can initiate Skype calls, which is the case for some of the more advanced Skype-compatible sound devices (such as USB handsets with keypads and Skype-to-phone adapters).

4. Be sure to configure each separate instance of Skype to use a separate sound device.

Some Skype hardware that uses the Skype API won't work if you have two identical devices attached, even if the two instances of Skype associated with the devices are running in separate user sessions. Check with the manufacturer before you buy.

Multiple Virtual Machines

This is really only for serious techies!

When I set up my Skype Test Lab for this book, I was confronted with the difficulty of testing Skype on a variety of platforms and, in the case of Linux, on a variety of distros (SuSE, Fedora Core 4, Gentoo, Debian, and others). To solve this problem I simultaneously ran different operating systems in different virtual machines (Windows) on my computer using VMware Workstation (*http://www.VMWare.com/*). In each virtual machine there was a different instance of Skype, and with some jiggery-pokery with sound devices, you can make each instance of Skype in each virtual machine have a different sound device, which amounts to having several independent phone lines, all provided by a single machine!

You can do the same on Linux using open source machine-virtualization software, such as Xen (*http://www.xensource.com/*) and User-mode Linux Kernel Port (*http://sourceforge.net/projects/user-mode-linux/*).

Test Your Connection for Skype Friendliness

Skype's performance depends somewhat on how P2P friendly your network is. Find out with these tools.

Works with: all versions of Skype.

Before testing your Internet connection for Skype friendliness, it's worth summarizing what an ideal P2P-friendly connection should look like:

- Outgoing TCP connections should be allowed for remote ports 80, 443, and 1024 and above.
- Outgoing UDP packets should be allowed for remote ports 1024 and above.
- NAT should retain "state," which means that translations should be remembered for a period so that other packets can reuse them. Ideally, state should be kept for an hour or more, but even maintaining state for 30 seconds will improve things.
- Multiple ports (both TCP and UDP) can be used in parallel.

UDP packets are the preferred method of communication for most P2P applications, including Skype, because they are fast and less demanding (than, say, TCP) on network resources. Skype can work without using UDP, but call quality suffers.

A quick and easy way to test the P2P friendliness of your network connection is to use a neat little tool called NAT Check, which is freely available for Windows, Linux, and Mac OS X from *http://midcom-p2p.sourceforge.net/*. NAT Check gives a summary of useful information, which is indicative of the friendliness, or unfriendliness, of your network connection to P2P applications in general, and to Skype in particular. Here's an example of output from NAT Check:

```
TCP RESULTS:
TCP consistent translation:           YES (GOOD for peer-to-peer)
TCP simultaneous open:                YES (GOOD for peer-to-peer)
TCP loopback translation:             NO  (BAD for P2P over Twice-NAT)
TCP unsolicited connections filtered: YES (GOOD for security)
UDP RESULTS:
UDP consistent translation:           YES (GOOD for peer-to-peer)
UDP loopback translation:             NO  (BAD for P2P over Twice-NAT)
UDP unsolicited messages filtered:    YES (GOOD for security)
```

The preceding output was generated on Windows by running the command natcheck > p2p_test.txt in a command prompt window. After the command has finished running, you can find the results of the test in the file *p2p_test.txt*.

As a mini-guide to interpreting the output from NAT Check these notes may be of some help:

Consistent translation

Tells you if state is maintained. If "YES," input and output ports are the same for consecutive packets, thereby reducing network overhead.

Simultaneous open

P2P applications, Skype included, typically perform better if they can operate over several ports at once. A "YES" here tells you that multiple ports can be used without a problem.

Loop-back translation

In twice-NAT, both the source and destination addresses are subject to translation as packets traverse NAT in either direction. A "NO" here means that your machine cannot communicate with other hosts on the same private network using public (translated) port bindings assigned by the NAT.

Unsolicited messages filtered

> This tells you whether packets originating from an unknown source are discarded. A "YES" here is good from a security point of view (errant packets are blocked) and in terms of network performance (discarded packets no longer consume network resources).

An alternative to running NAT Check on your machine is to look up on the Web whether your firewall/router/NAT is P2P friendly from a list maintained at *http://bgp.lcs.mit.edu/~dga/view.cgi*. This is an inferior method to running an actual test on your machine, but it might provide some quick answers. If your device is listed, look at the entry in the UDP Consistent Translation column, as a "yes" here will most likely mean that your network connection is P2P friendly.

Lastly, it's preferable for your network hardware to support packet fragmentation and reassemble. Though not essential, this feature will improve call quality.

HACK #39 Eliminate Echo and Noise

Improve Skype's voice quality with these tips for echo cancellation and noise reduction.

Works with: all versions of Skype.

Echo and noise are such common problems for Skype users that I would be remiss not to provide a hack that addresses the problem. While the symptoms of echo and noise during a conversation are all too apparent, their causes and remedies are often quite the opposite. The tips in this hack should help you not only track down the cause, but also fix the problem.

A lot of the more up-to-date sound hardware has built-in echo cancellation and noise reduction, often implemented through *digital signal processing* (DSP). This is particularly true for array microphones. Having decent sound hardware is always a good investment for the Skype user. So, depending on your budget, upgrading your sound hardware in the face of persistent and incurable echo and noise is a worthwhile consideration, particularly if the remainder of this hack doesn't cure the problem.

Also worthy of some research on your part is whether your operating system, or sound card, or other sound hardware has echo cancellation and noise reduction built in. If it does, it may, or may not, be enabled by default.

As for any problem, you should first try to isolate it. Test your sound system outside of Skype (see "Test Your Sound System" [Hack #25]). If you still have echo and/or noise problems outside of Skype, there's something wrong with your sound setup. Otherwise, you know the problem is with Skype.

If the problem is with Skype, try some of these suggestions of what to do to fix things:

Symptom: echo

> Fix: if you experience echo problems during a call, before hanging up tell the other party to test his setup by calling the echo123 service. After hanging up, you should likewise test your setup by calling echo123. This way, you can find out who actually has the echo problem: you or the other party. If both you and the other party have no echo problems when calling echo123, the next thing to do is to call a different Skype contact for which you know you've not had echo problems in the past. If echo is still a problem for you, try turning down your speaker volume and/or moving the microphone further away from the speaker. On laptops, the proximity of the built-in microphone to the built-in speaker is fixed, so in that case, you might want to try a headset instead. One cause of echo not related to your sound setup is data packet loss associated with your Internet connection. Beyond trying to call at different times (when Internet traffic congestion might be less of a problem), there's not much you can do about this. A tool such as PingPlotter (*http://www.pingplotter.com/*) may help isolate this cause of echo. Activity on your computer that consumes Internet bandwidth and resources may also be a cause of echo. If you are web browsing, listening to streaming music, downloading a file—basically, doing anything that consumes bandwidth—and you're calling with Skype at the same time, try stopping the non-Skype activities and see if that improves the echo problem. The least likely cause of echo is the way in which Skype routes your calls. You can force Skype to route your calls differently by deleting the Skype super-node list it maintains in *shared.xml*. You can do this by stopping Skype from running, deleting *shared.xml*, and then restarting Skype. On restarting, Skype will build a new *shared.xml* file with a different super-node list.

Symptom: distorted sound and/or echo

> Fix: Skype can sometimes overcompensate for your volume control as part of its effort to set your sound system's gain automatically. In *config.xml*, find the automatic gain control tag, `<AGC>` (there are two entries, one under the parent tag `<Call>` and the other under `<General>`), and set its value to 0—that is, set both entries to `<AGC>0</AGC>`. With `<AGC>` set to 0 you must adjust your sound volume levels manually to obtain the best sound quality. Also, try toggling the automatic echo control tag, `<AEC>`, between 0 and 1 to see if that brings any improvement—that is, toggle back and forth between `<AEC>0</AEC>` and `<AEC>1</AEC>`.

Before making any changes to *config.xml*, stop Skype from running. Make the changes you want to *config.xml*, save your changes, and then restart Skype. Failure to follow this procedure will most likely result in your changes being ignored.

See Also

- For guidance on how to edit Skype's configuration file safely, and for some additional tweaks to try, see "Tweak Skype by Editing config.xml" [Hack #45].

Reset Your Skype Configuration

Roll back your configuration to plain-vanilla defaults without having to do an uninstall and reinstall.

Works with: all versions of Skype.

Configuration settings for Skype are mostly controlled from a file, named *config.xml*, which resides on your machine.

Here's where you can find it:

Windows
C:\Documents and Settings*Username*\Application Data\Skype*Skypename*\
config.xml

Linux
/home/*Username*/.Skype/*Skypename*/config.xml

Mac OS X
/Users/*Username*/Library/Application Support/Skype/*Skypename*/config.xml

Pocket PC
\Application Data\Skype*Skypename*\config.xml

Username is your login name for the machine and *Skypename* is the name you use to log in to Skype.

Sometimes, if Skype is misbehaving, it is advantageous to reset your configuration as close as possible to the factory defaults. Uninstalling Skype and wiping out all user data will surely do the job. But before taking such Draconian measures, try this instead.

Stop Skype from running, delete or rename your existing *config.xml* file (it always pays to make a backup of the file, just in case; you'll get this automatically if you simply rename *config.xml*), and restart Skype. Skype will rebuild the *config.xml* file with many plain-vanilla defaults. This might improve Skype's behavior, but without the heartache and aggravation of an uninstall/reinstall.

After using this technique to reset your configuration, you should go through Skype's options (Skype → Tools → Options…) one by one and set them to the way you want. For example, you might find that Skype now uses the default audio in/out devices rather than your previously set up and preferred devices.

Hacking the Hack

Skype uses a second configuration file, *shared.xml*, which you usually can find here (where *Username* is the username under which you log on to your computer):

Windows (version 1.3 and before)
`C:\Documents and Settings\All Users\Application Data\Skype\shared.xml`

Windows (version 1.4 and after)
`C:\Documents and Settings\`*Username*`\Application Data\Skype\shared.xml`

Linux
`/home/`*Username*`/.Skype/shared.xml`

Mac OS X
`/Users/`*Username*`/Library/Application Support/Skype/shared.xml`

Pocket PC
`\Application Data\Skype\shared.xml`

You also can reset the *shared.xml* file by stopping Skype from running, renaming or deleting the file, and then restarting Skype. When Skype restarts, it will build *shared.xml* with new data and this may improve things if Skype is behaving unexpectedly or if it's suffering from poor voice quality and/or slow file transfers.

HACK #41 Run Skype Based on Time of Day

Control when Skype starts and stops to ration bandwidth usage, or to regain explicit control over when you are available online.

Works with: Windows, Linux, and Mac OS X versions of Skype.

By controlling when Skype runs, you can ration the amount of Internet bandwidth your machine uses, and therefore cumulative Internet traffic, which is important if you pay for Internet connectivity by the megabyte or even gigabyte. Also, at the same time, you regain explicit control over when you are available online, which may be important if you want to be available only from, say, 9 a.m. to 5 p.m., Monday through Friday.

Here's how you can start and, almost as importantly, stop Skype based on the day of the week and time of the day:

Windows

Start Windows' task scheduler (Start → All Programs → Accessories → System Tools → Scheduled Tasks). Click on Add Scheduled Task, name the task Skype Start, and follow the instructions in the Scheduled Task Wizard to run (start) Skype.exe on your chosen days and times. Next, click on Add Scheduled Task again, name this task Skype Stop, and again follow the instructions in the Scheduled Task Wizard—but this time, before you click the Finish button, check the "Open advanced properties for this task when I click Finish" checkbox. This will open a properties window, into which you should add the command-line option `Skype.exe /shutdown` for Skype to stop running on your chosen days and times.

Linux

Edit your *crontabs* file using the command `crontabs -e` (this will create a new *crontabs* file if one doesn't already exist), and add these entries to run Skype between 9 a.m. and 5 p.m., Monday through Friday only:

```
DISPLAY=:0
0 9 * * 1-5 /usr/bin/skype
0 17 * * 1-5 killall skype
```

Note that if you omit `DISPLAY=:0`, you will likely find that Skype won't be displayed on your screen.

Mac OS X

This also uses *crontabs*, but these are the entries you must add:

```
0 9 * * 1-5 open -a /Applications/Skype.app/Contents/MacOS/Skype
0 17 * * 1-5 killall Skype
```

Note that if you don't use open -a as shown earlier, Skype will prompt you for your Skype name and password regardless of whether you have checked the "Remember my name and password on this computer" checkbox. In this case, if you are not there when cron starts Skype, Skype will be running, but you won't be logged on!

Pay particular attention to spelling for Linux and Mac OS X, as they're both case sensitive. On Linux, the Skype executable is skype (all lowercase), and on Mac OS X it is Skype (first letter capitalized).

HACK
#42
Schedule When Skype Runs the Mac Way

Use iCal and a little AppleScript to schedule when Skype runs, and when it does not.

Works with: Mac OS X version of Skype.

For Mac users who shun the command line, or simply don't know what *crontabs* is—and don't want to know—there is a simple way to have Skype start and stop on the days and at the times you choose. That way, you can control when you are available to receive calls and, at the same time, ration Skype's consumption of Internet bandwidth, which may be important if you need it for other things or if you pay for your Internet traffic by the megabyte or gigabyte.

iCal, Apple Computer's desktop calendar, has a really neat feature that allows you to associate an AppleScript with an event in your calendar. That event can be a one-off event, or it can be a recurring event that you specify— for example, Monday through Friday, at 9 a.m. By defining two events—one for when you want Skype to start running, and another for when you want Skype to stop running—and attaching scripts to those events, you can control when Skype runs and, almost as important, when it does not. The start event you define runs the *skype_start.scpt* AppleScript and the stop event you define runs *skype_stop.scpt*. Between these two bracketing events, Skype will run. At all other times, Skype won't run (unless you have set Skype to start when you start your machine and you reboot during the period of time outside the two bracketing events).

```
-- File: skype_start.scpt

do shell script "open -a /Applications/Skype.app/Contents/MacOS/Skype"
```

```
-- File: skype_stop.scpt

do shell script "killall Skype"
```

For example, to run Skype only from 9 a.m. to 5 p.m. each day, open iCal and define a new event (iCal → File → New Event). Set the event for 9 a.m. and make it repeat every day. Set the alarm for this event to run the script *skype_start.scpt* "on date" at exactly 9 a.m. Set a similar event for 5 p.m. and associate it with *skype_stop.scpt*. Your calendar should now have two events that bracket the period for which you want Skype to run, and it should look something like Figure 3-17.

Each day the start script will awake at 9 a.m. to start running Skype (which you should set up so that it automatically logs you onto your Skype account). Then, at 5 p.m., the stop script will run and will shut down Skype. Now you're available to take Skype calls only between 9 a.m. and 5 p.m., with the added advantage that outside that time period, Skype is consuming neither Internet bandwidth, nor machine resources (CPU and memory). As the saying goes, "If you don't need it, don't run it!"

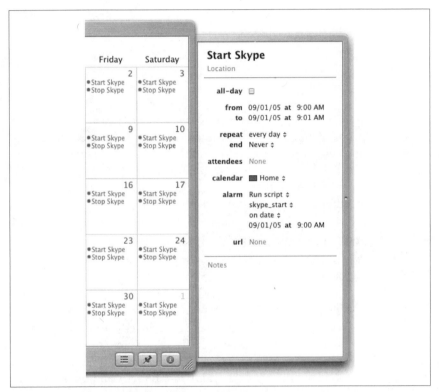

Figure 3-17. Schedule when Skype starts running, and when it stops running, using iCal

## CHAPTER FOUR

Tweak and Tune Skype

Hacks 43–51

In many ways, this chapter builds on the previous one. However, the emphasis here is even more on making Skype do the things you want—that is, on tweaking and tuning Skype in interesting ways. Indeed, sometimes tweaking it in ways—it must be said—that the engineers at Skype probably never intended! Think of it this way. This chapter's goal is not only to make Skype work in interesting and novel ways, but also to stimulate your imagination and encourage *you* to experiment with Skype.

HACK #43 Make Calls from Your Web Browser

Configure Internet Explorer so that you can make calls directly from a web page or from the browser toolbar.

Works with: Windows version of Skype.

There are three ways in which you can make calls directly from within a web browser. The first method uses the URL prefix *skype:* (note the missing //, as this method won't work if you include //) to control Skype from within a browser. The second method uses the *callto://* URL prefix and can be used in a number of ways to make calls, including from your browser's address bar or from a link embedded in a web page. The third method uses the Skype Toolbar, which is an add-on application for Internet Explorer (and is available for Microsoft Outlook as well) that you can download at *http://www. skype.com/products/skypetoolbars/*.

skype:

You're probably familiar with URLs such as *http://www.oreilly.com/*. Now Skype has added its own type of URL, which looks like this: *skype:echo123*. Entering "skype:echo123" in a browser's address bar will open Skype and call the Skype sound-test service.

The syntax of the *skype:* URL is somewhat intimidating, but it is not as difficult to use as the following syntax diagram might make it seem, as you will soon see when we try some examples:

```
Skype URL   = "skype:" [targets] ["?" query ] ["#" fragment ]

targets     = 1* (target / ";" )
target      = identity / PSTN
identity    = skypename / alias
skypename   = 1*(ALPHA / DIGIT / "." / "," )
skypenames  =  1*( skypename / ";")
alias       =  ... ; see ["TechGroup/DataFormats"]
                  ; unicode chars are in UTF-8 and % encoded
                  ; see RFC3987 uchar mapping
PSTN        = "+" (DIGIT / ALPHA ) *(DIGIT / ALPHA / "-" )
                  ; PSTN supports +800-FLOWERS
query       = action [ *( "?" term "=" conditon ) ]
term        = 1*ALPHA
condition   = 1*unserved  ; to be clarified by Skype
fragment    = 1*unserved  ; to be clarified by Skype
```

> Note that *skype:* won't work with speed-dial numbers. For example, *skype:7?call*, where 7 is an existing speed-dial number, won't work.

skype: is quite powerful—and quite simple in practice—as the examples in Table 4-1 show. To try these examples, open a browser window and enter them in the address bar, then press Return.

Table 4-1. Examples of how to use skype: from a web browser

skype: URL	What it does
skype:echo123	Calls or chats with Skype's sound-test service (it does one or the other depending on what you have set double-click to do)
skype:echo123?call	Calls Skype's sound-test service
skype:+442075551212?call	Calls a regular phone number (you must be a SkypeOut subscriber for this to work)
skype:echo123?chat	Chats with Skype's sound-test service
skype:skypehackslinux?voicemail	Leaves voicemail for Skype user skypehackslinux
skype:skypehackslinux?add	Adds skypehackslinux to your Contacts list
skype:skypehackslinux?sendfile	Opens the File Send dialog to select a file to send to skypehackslinux
skype:skypehackslinux?userinfo	Shows a profile for skypehackslinux

Table 4-1. Examples of how to use skype: from a web browser (continued)

skype: URL	What it does
skype:?chat& *id=2005-09-02T12:00:00TZ*	Opens an existing chat session having the ID specified (YYYY-MM-DDThh:mm:ssTZ or YYYY-MM-DDZhh:mm:ss)
skype:	Focuses Skype (brings the Skype window to the foreground and gives it focus)

Not only can you enter the URLs in Table 4-1 into a browser's address bar to make them work, but you also can embed them in HTML/XHTML, as the following XHTML file, *skype.htm*, illustrates. If you load this file in a browser and click on the "Call echo123" link, Skype will open and call the Skype sound-test service (echo123). However, before you start including *skype:* links in all your web pages, you should be aware that they only work for browsers on machines that run Skype and that know how to handle *skype:* style URLs. If a user on a non-Skype machine clicks on a *skype:* link, it certainly won't work and will most likely be treated as an error, as shown in Figure 4-1.

Figure 4-1. Entering a skype: style URL or clicking on a skype: link in a web page on a machine that doesn't know how to handle skype: URLs will result in an error

```
<?xml version="1.0" encoding="UTF-8"?>
<!DOCTYPE html
    PUBLIC "-//W3C//DTD XHTML 1.0 Strict//EN"
    "http://www.w3.org/TR/xhtml1/DTD/xhtml1-strict.dtd">

<!-- File: skype.htm -->

<html xmlns="http://www.w3.org/1999/xhtml" xml:lang="en" lang="en">

    <head>
        <title>skype: URL</title>
    </head>

    <body>
        <p><a href="skype:echo123?call">
            Skype's sound test service (echo123)</a>
        </p>
    </body>

</html>
```

You can even enter *skype:* URLs from the run line (but not from the command prompt window), and from the Windows Explorer address bar! For example, select Start → Run…, enter "skype:echo123?chat", and press Enter or click OK. A chat window will open, enabling you to chat with Skype's sound-test service (echo123). Entering the same URL in the Windows Explorer address bar will achieve the same result.

callto://

When you enter a web address such as *http://www.oreilly.com* in your browser address bar, you are instructing the browser to use the HyperText Transfer Protocol (HTTP) to access the O'Reilly web site. Similarly, when you enter the web address *callto://echo123*, you are in effect telling the browser to do something with "callto," and what it does depends on how your browser is configured. This is because "callto" can be interpreted in many different ways.

When you install Skype on Windows, you are given the choice to associate *callto://* with Skype. However, if you failed to make that choice during installation, or if *callto://* simply isn't working properly, you can easily fix it using one of two methods.

First, select Skype → Tools → Options… → Advanced, and then under the Other category check the "Associate Skype with callto: links" checkbox. If that fails to work for you, you may want to try the second method (a third method uses the Windows registry, but I don't recommend it).

Second, from within Windows Explorer (the *file* browser that comes with Windows), select Tools → Folder Options… and in the dialog that opens click on the File Types tab. Scroll down the list of file types until you find URL: CallTo Protocol; highlight it, and then click on the Advanced button. In the Edit File Type dialog that opens, highlight the "open" action and click Edit…. That will open the dialog shown in Figure 4-2. Under "Application used to perform action," enter the command C:\Program Files\Skype\Phone\ Skype.exe "/callto:%1" (replacing the path to Skype.exe with your own, if required). Click OK, and now, any time Internet Explorer (or, indeed, Windows Explorer) encounters *callto://*, it will pass the request on to Skype.

After setting up *callto://* in this manner, you can use it to make calls in a number of different ways. The choice is yours.

Internet Explorer (or other browser)
Enter *callto://Skypename* in the address bar and press Enter or click Go.

Windows Explorer
Enter *callto://Skypename* in the address bar and press Enter or click Go.

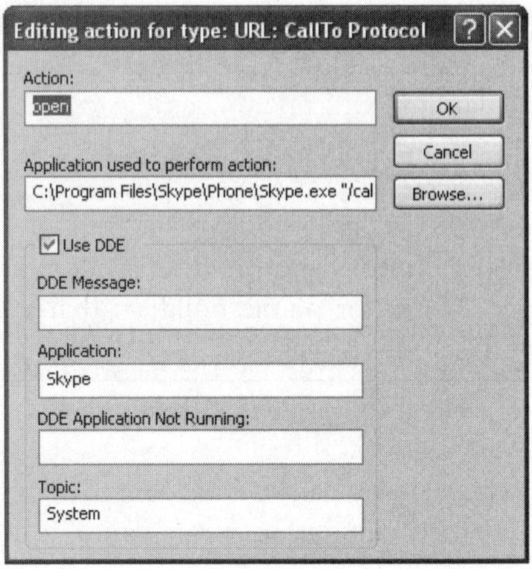

Make Calls from Your Web Browser

Figure 4-2. Configuring callto:// so that it uses Skype

Run...

Select Start → Run…, enter *callto://Skypename*, and press Enter or click OK.

Web-page link

Any web page with a *callto://Skypename* link embedded in it forms a hyperlink that you can click on to start a call using Skype. If you want to include such links in your own web pages, the following XHTML example will show you how:

```
<?xml version="1.0" encoding="UTF-8"?>
<!DOCTYPE html
    PUBLIC "-//W3C//DTD XHTML 1.0 Strict//EN"
    "http://www.w3.org/TR/xhtml1/DTD/xhtml1-strict.dtd">

<!-- File: callto.htm -->

<html xmlns="http://www.w3.org/1999/xhtml" xml:lang="en" lang="en">

    <head>
        <title>Skype Callto</title>
    </head>

    <body>
        <p><a href="callto://echo123">Call echo123</a></p>
    </body>

</html>
```

Skypename can be a Skype username or, if you are a SkypeOut subscriber, a regular telephone number.

Skype Toolbar

This neat add-on for Internet Explorer provides the following useful features, all of them available without leaving your browser:

- It recognizes phone numbers and provides a phone icon you can click on to make a call—even for phone numbers that aren't *callto://* links (see Figure 4-3).
- It lets you add phone numbers on web pages to your Contacts list.
- It lets you call and chat to existing contacts.
- It lets you change your online status.
- If you're a SkypeOut subscriber, it displays your remaining credit.

All this functionality is packed into a surprisingly small space on your Internet Explorer toolbar (see Figure 4-4). And best of all, the Skype Toolbar is free.

Figure 4-3. Fragment of a web page showing how the Skype Toolbar makes calling easy from web pages with phone numbers

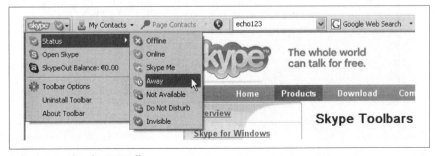

Figure 4-4. The Skype Toolbar

HACK Accelerate Skype Using Your Keyboard
#44
Make Skype fly, by speeding up common tasks with key sequences and hotkeys.

Works with: Windows version of Skype.

If you're proficient with the keyboard, sometimes driving Skype in this way can be easier, and faster, than if you use the mouse. Even if you're *not* one of these people, this hack will nevertheless help you speed up some Skype tasks.

> If you're visually impaired in some way, or if your motor skills with the mouse aren't quite what they used to be, or if you merely help such a person with their computer activities, you will find this hack very useful in terms of configuring Skype to make it easier to use.

Skype has the ability to control a very limited amount of its functionality using global hotkeys (see Figure 4-5). You can set these by selecting Skype → Tools → Options… → Hotkeys.

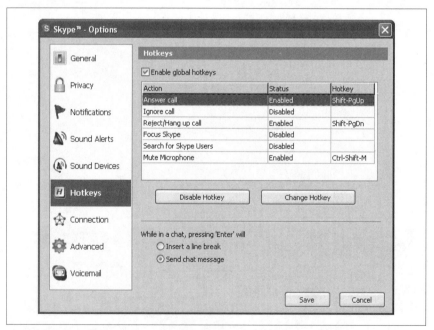

Figure 4-5. Skype's global hotkeys option dialog

Skype's global hotkey feature, though useful, is somewhat limited.

Another option is to drive Skype's GUI using key sequences. In this case, there's almost nothing you can do with the mouse that you cannot do with a key sequence entered at the keyboard. But if you want to use this approach, your efforts will be made a lot easier if you first set up a hotkey sequence to open Skype and give it focus. Once you do that, it will be a lot easier to drive Skype's GUI via the keyboard.

One method is to set a global hotkey sequence to Focus Skype (see Figure 4-5). However, this method has the annoying habit of minimizing Skype if it's already open! What we want is a foolproof way of always bringing Skype to the foreground and giving it focus wherever it may presently be lurking—behind another window, or in the system tray, or not running at all! Fortunately, such a method exists in the form of a hotkey sequence for a shortcut to *Skype.exe*. Create a shortcut that points to *Skype.exe* as its target, and then right-click on the shortcut and choose Properties. In the shortcut properties dialog that is displayed, select the Shortcut tab, click on the text entry field opposite "Shortcut key," press the key sequence you want as your hotkey (for example, Ctrl-Shift-S), and then click OK. Now you have a hotkey sequence that will bring Skype to the foreground of your desktop and give it focus—no matter where it might be hiding!

On my machine, I have the hotkey sequence Ctrl-Shift-S set up so that it always opens Skype and gives it focus. You may have to choose something different if this hotkey sequence conflicts with a hotkey sequence that already exists on your machine. However, for the remainder of this hack, we'll assume that Ctrl-Shift-S works as desired; but remember, it doesn't really matter what it is, just replace Ctrl-Shift-S in this hack with whatever you have set up instead.

Now we're ready to start driving Skype. Let's try some Skype keyboard acceleration:

Ctrl-Shift-S, Alt-F, Enter, A
    Will change your online status to Away.

Ctrl-Shift-S, Alt-T, R, Enter
    Will reopen your most recent chat session.

Ctrl-Shift-S, Alt-T, L
    Will clear your call list.

Ctrl-Shift-S, Ctrl-Tab (repeat)
    Will cycle through the tabs (Contacts, Dial, and Call List) in the Skype application window.

Ctrl-Shift-S, Alt-{down arrow}, Enter
    Will repeat the last call you made from the Skype address bar.

Don't be afraid to experiment, as it often takes a little trial and error (and sometimes a notepad and pencil) to find the right key sequence for what you want to do. This method works best, of course, when key sequences are short, as they're obviously easier to remember. However, even complex key sequences can be put to good use, and I'll show how next.

Hacking the Hack

Think of the following simple script, *drive_skype.vbs*, as a car you're meant to drive. You don't have to be a mechanic or look under the hood to drive a car, and so it is with this script. Just download the script from the book's web site (*http://www.oreilly.com/catalog/SkypeHacks/index.html*) and start using it to make Skype fly!

 This script uses the *Windows Scripting Host* (WSH), which comes with Windows XP but must be downloaded (from *http://www.microsoft.com/*) and installed separately for Windows 2000.

```
' File: drive_skype.vbs

' Invoke like this from the run-line:
'        drive_skype "^+S|%(TO)"
' where "^+S|%(TO)" is the key sequence to be sent to
' the Skype GUI (in this case ctrl+shift+S,
' followed by alt+T then alt+O)

Dim objShell, objArgs, keystrokes, keys, pause
Set objShell = WScript.CreateObject("WScript.Shell")
Set objArgs = WScript.Arguments
keystrokes = Split(objArgs(0), "|")
pause = 1500
For Each keys In keystrokes
    objShell.SendKeys keys
    WScript.Sleep pause
    If pause>100 Then pause=100 End If
next
```

To run this script, you will need to enter something like "C:\Scripts\drive_skype.vbs" "^+S|%(TO)" at the run line (Start → Run...), or use a similar command as the target of a shortcut (with or without a hotkey sequence assigned to it). Of course, if you put *drive_skype.vbs* in a folder on your path, you can dispense with *C:\Scripts*.

When I ran *drive_skype.vbs* from the command line in a command prompt window, it produced inconsistent results. It seems that sometimes, the command window grabs focus away from Skype before all the keystrokes have been sent to Skype. For this reason, I recommend that you run VBScripts that drive Skype's GUI (specifically, scripts that use the SendKeys command) using the run line, or as the target of a shortcut.

Let's look at some examples—and the power—of this simple script:

- drive_skype.vbs "^+S|%(TO)", if made into a shortcut and assigned a convenient hotkey sequence—say, Ctrl-Shift-O—will display the options dialog for Skype.

- drive_skype.vbs "^+S|%(TO)|{TAB}|{TAB}|{DOWN}|{DOWN}|{DOWN}|{DOWN}|{TAB}|{TAB}|L|{TAB}|L|{TAB}|L|{TAB}|{TAB}|{TAB}|{ENTER}" will, in my case, set the sound input and output device used by Skype to Logitech USB Headset (note the *L* in the script). An identical key sequence, but with *L* replaced with *C*, will, again in my case, set the sound input and output device used by Skype to C-Media USB Headphone Set. These two key sequences enable me to hot-switch between sound devices in a snap—even during the middle of a call! To use the key sequence yourself, simply experiment with replacing the *L*.

- drive_skype.vbs "^+S|%(TC)|Progress_Report|{TAB}|{DOWN}|{UP}|+({DOWN}{DOWN}{DOWN}{DOWN})|{TAB}|{TAB}|{ENTER}|{ENTER}" will start a conference call with the topic Progress_Report for the first four contacts in your Contacts list.

Clearly, some of the examples given here would stretch anyone's memory capacity, but when you use them in combination with the simple script presented in this hack, as well as with shortcuts, they can be extremely useful and great timesavers.

To help you explore the full power and possibilities of using *drive_skype.vbs* to drive Skype's GUI, here's a short crib sheet of the possible key sequences:

Letter keys
A–Z and numbers 0–9.

Special keys
+ for Shift, % for Alt, and ^ for Ctrl.

Function keys
{F1} through {F16}.

Tab and Enter keys
{TAB} and {ENTER}.

Arrow keys

{UP}, {DOWN}, {LEFT}, and {RIGHT}.

Miscellaneous keys

{BACKSPACE}, {BREAK}, {CAPSLOCK}, {DELETE}, {END}, {ESC} escape, {HELP}, {HOME}, {INSERT}, {NUMLOCK}, {PGDN} page down, {PGUP} page up, {PRTSC} print screen, and {SCROLLLOCK}. I've provided descriptions only for nonobvious keys.

Sequence of keys

To hold down one key—say, Alt (which is represented by %) and then press the keys T and O in sequence—all while holding down Alt, simply put the key presses in round brackets, like this: %(TO).

Now you are in a position to experiment for yourself. Using keyboard key sequences can really make Skype fly, and all it takes is a willingness to experiment, a systematic approach (having a notepad and pencil close by helps), and some imagination. Once a key sequence has been well thought out and tested, this way of using Skype can be both faster *and* less error prone than using the manual keyboard or the mouse!

HACK #45 Tweak Skype by Editing config.xml

config.xml is where Skype stores many of its configuration settings, and by editing it directly, you can have greater control over how Skype works.

Works with: all versions of Skype.

A word of caution. Hacking around with Skype's *config.xml* file can cause problems, especially if you tinker with settings not discussed in this hack. Skype, however, has the ability to rebuild a default—but valid—*config.xml* file when it encounters a problem with the existing *config.xml* file. This is the case even if you rename or delete *config.xml*—Skype simply builds a new one. Under such circumstances, Skype tries to restore as many of your personal settings and preferences in the new *config.xml* as possible, but it's always wise to make a backup of your current *config.xml* before you make any changes. That way, if things go wrong, you can restore the old version or copy across selected settings from the old to the new. You have been warned!

> Always stop Skype from running (by right-clicking on Skype in the system tray and choosing Quit) before making any changes to *config.xml* (or *shared.xml*), because even though your editor may tell you it has saved your updated version of *config.xml*, you may find that Skype ignores your changes and they are missing when you reopen *config.xml*. The procedure for editing any of Skype's configuration files should go like this: quit Skype (that is, stop it from running), edit (or delete) the configuration file, save the changes, and restart Skype.

You can find *config.xml* on all platforms, though the extent to which you can edit Skype on each varies. In terms of the opportunities for tweaking, the platform order, from the greatest to the least extent, goes like this: Windows, Linux, Mac OS X, and Pocket PC. Typically, you can find *config.xml* in these locations on each platform:

Windows
C:\Documents and Settings*Username*\Application Data\Skype*Skypename*\
    config.xml

Linux
/home/*Username*/.Skype/*Skypename*/config.xml

Mac OS X
/Users/*Username*/Library/Application Support/Skype/*Skypename*/config.xml

Pocket PC
\Application Data\Skype*Skypename*\config.xml

Username is your login name for the machine and *Skypename* is the name you use to log into Skype.

> If you cannot find *config.xml* (or *shared.xml*) it might not be because it is missing. Rather, on some platforms, files of this type are treated as "hidden" by the application you are using to search for them.
>
> You can fix this problem on Windows Explorer by selecting Tools → Folder Options... → View → Advanced Settings, and clicking on the "Show hidden files and folders" radio button. Alternatively, to find *config.xml* without having to enable "Show hidden files and folders," enter %AppData%\Skype*Skype logon name*\ in the Windows Explorer address bar and it will display all files, regardless of whether they're hidden.
>
> Mac OS X Finder displays all file types by default, but you may want to display the *.xml* file extension of *config.xml* (select Preferences → Advanced, and check "Show all file extensions").
>
> Most Linux file browsers have a similar option to show hidden files and folders. As such a wide choice of file browsers is available for Linux, look at the help file for your favorite file browser to find how to display hidden files and folders.

There is another file, *shared.xml*, from which Skype obtains configuration information that is common to all users of Skype on the same Windows machine, to all instances of Skype running in the same user session for Linux and Mac OS X, and to only one instance of Skype on Pocket PC, as Pocket PC supports neither multiple user sessions nor multiple running instances of Skype. You also can edit this file to tweak how Skype behaves, but the scope for tweaking is far more limited than for *config.xml*. You typically can find *shared.xml* in these locations on each platform:

Windows (version 1.3 and before)
C:\Documents and Settings\All Users\Application Data\Skype\shared.xml

Windows (version 1.4 and after)
C:\Documents and Settings*Username*\Application Data\Skype\shared.xml

Linux
/home/*Username*/.Skype/shared.xml

Mac OS X
/Users/*Username*/Library/Application Support/Skype/shared.xml

Pocket PC
\Application Data\Skype\shared.xml

config.xml Deconstructed

config.xml (and *shared.xml*) are what's known as Extensible Markup Language (XML) documents. XML files are human-readable text files that are made up of tags (named identifiers) that demark *elements* (items of data) that are organized in the structure of a tree (a collection of tags laid out in a root and branch fashion). Now that's a mouthful! However, it's all rather plain and easy if we look at an example—in this case, a fragment of *config.xml*:

```
<?xml version="1.0" ?>
<config version="1.0" serial="414" timestamp="1123702750.6">
    <Lib>
        <Call>
            <IncomingPolicy>everyone</IncomingPolicy>
            <MicVolume>255</MicVolume>
            <SkypeInPolicy>everyone</SkypeInPolicy>
        </Call>
        <CentralStorage>
            <LastBackoff>0</LastBackoff>
            <LastFailure>0</LastFailure>
                    .
                    .
                    .
                    .
</config>
```

The first line tells any application that uses this file that it is an XML file. From then onward, data is stored in a hierarchical fashion, with individual data elements and groups of elements always bracketed between two matching tags. Tags that have no data element are the exception and look like this: <NoDataTag attrib="value"/>. For tags with a data element, there's always an opening tag—for example, <Call>—and a corresponding closing tag—in this example, `</Call>`. Whatever you do, don't break this matched tag structure. Other than that, XML files are easy to edit. In fact, XML was specifically designed to be both easy to understand and easy to edit for a human, not just for a machine.

This hack deals with only a subset of the whole *config.xml* file, as it isolates only those tags that contain configuration data that does something useful from the perspective of a Skype user. Table 4-2 summarizes the tags we'll hack in this chapter. You can download a more complete table of *config.xml* tags and their meanings from the book's web site, *http://www.oreilly.com/ catalog/SkypeHacks/index.html*.

Table 4-2. Subset of config.xml tags used in this hack

Tag	Parent tag	Description	Platform	Default	Values
`<AGC>`	`<Call>` `<General>`	Automatic gain control	W	1	0, 1
`<AEC>`	`<General>`	Automatic echo correction	W	1	0,1
`<EC>`	`<Call>`	Echo correction	P	1	0,1
`<MicVolume>`	`<Call>`	Microphone volume control	WLMP		0–255
`<FriendsPopup>`	`<Calls>` and `<Messages>`	Pop-up notification from friends	W	1	0,1
`<OthersPopup>`	`<Calls>` and `<Messages>`	Pop-up notification from others	W	1	0,1

Key: W = Windows, L = Linux, M = Mac OS X, P = Pocket PC

Editing config.xml

XML files are text files. However, you can encode them in different character sets; specifically, wide character sets (ones with more than 256 characters in them). This may cause problems on different platforms and with different versions of Skype. One way to avoid this is to look at the encoding of your existing (working) *config.xml* file. If you always save your modified version of *config.xml* (or *shared.xml*) using the same encoding, encoding won't be a problem.

As a general rule, the default text editor on your platform should be up to the job of editing and saving *config.xml* (and *shared.xml*) in a format that Skype will recognize. Here are some suggestions, by platform (in all cases, make sure you save files in plain-text format without any formatting information of any sort).

Windows

> Notepad or WordPad. Perhaps the fastest way to edit *config.xml* on Windows is to right-click on it in Windows Explorer and choose Edit (or highlight *config.xml* and then choose File → Edit from the menu). That will immediately open *config.xml* in an editor window, from where you can make your changes directly or search for and, if necessary, replace text. Save your changes, close the window, and you're done!

Linux

> Emacs or Vim.

Mac OS X

> Vi and Emacs.

Tweaks

A number of tweaks are available to the Skype user who is willing to delve into *config.xml* and *shared.xml* and hack away. There are two motivations for doing so. First, some tweaks fix something that is broken with Skype. Second, some tweaks add functionality to Skype or otherwise enhance or improve it. Both are covered in the tweaks that follow, which are prefixed with "Fix" or "Enhancement" to help you distinguish between the two.

config.xml tweaks.

Fix (Windows): degraded sound and/or broken speech

> Find the automatic gain control tag, <AGC>, and set its value to 0. There should be two entries for <AGC>, one under the parent tag <Call> and the other under <General>; if either is missing, add it. When you're done, *both*<AGC> entries should be set to 0, and your *config.xml* file should look something like this:

```
<?xml version="1.0"?>
<config version="1.0" serial="327" timestamp="1125399449.34">
    <Lib>
        <Call>
            <AGC>0</AGC>
            <IncomingPolicy>everyone</IncomingPolicy>
            <MicVolume>173</MicVolume>
            <SkypeInPolicy>everyone</SkypeInPolicy>
        </Call>
        .
        .
        .
    </Lib>
    .
    .
    .
```

```
<General>
    <AEC>1</AEC>
    <AGC>0</AGC>
    <AdvancedFaF>0</AdvancedFaF>
    <AutoAudioSettingsAdjust>1</AutoAudioSettingsAdjust>
    .
    .
    .
</General>
    .
    .
    .
</config>
```

Fix (Windows): others cannot hear me

Select Skype → Tools → Options... → Sound Devices, uncheck the "Let Skype adjust my device settings" checkbox, and save. Find the microphone volume control tag, `<MicVolume>`. The valid range of values for this element is between 0 (off) and 255 (maximum). Try adjusting this value upward and downward, each time calling echo123 to test the result. After a little trial and error, hopefully you will find a microphone volume setting that enables others to hear you properly.

Fix (Windows and Pocket PC): echo

Find the automatic echo correction tag, `<AEC>`, on Windows (`<EC>` on Pocket PC), and try toggling its value between 0 and 1, each time testing the effect by calling the echo123 service. On Pocket PC, you can also toggle this setting using the user interface (select Skype → Tools → Options...).

Enhancement (Windows): disable pop ups

Pop-up notifications from Skype can be an irritation, particularly if you're in the throes of something important, like a video game! To disable pop ups, set both `<FriendsPopup>` and `<OthersPopup>` to 0; that is, set `<FriendsPopup>0</FriendsPopup>` and `<OthersPopup>0</OthersPopup>`. Now your *config.xml* file should look something like this:

```
<?xml version="1.0"?>
<config version="1.0" serial="327" timestamp="1125399449.34">
    .
    .
    .
    <UI>
        <Calls>
            <AllowMultiCalls>0</AllowMultiCalls>
            <FriendsAutoAnswer>0</FriendsAutoAnswer>
            <FriendsPopup>0</FriendsPopup>
            <OthersAutoAnswer>0</OthersAutoAnswer>
            <OthersPopup>0</OthersPopup>
```

```
            <PopupOnAll>0</PopupOnAll>
        </Calls>
      .

      .

      .

        <Messages>
            <AuthPopup>1</AuthPopup>
            <CafeMode>0</CafeMode>
            <DisplayCallInfo>0</DisplayCallInfo>
            <DisplayCallLogLimit>0</DisplayCallLogLimit>
            <FriendsFlash>1</FriendsFlash>
            <FriendsPopup>0</FriendsPopup>
            <ImChatStyle>0</ImChatStyle>
            <OthersFlash>1</OthersFlash>
            <OthersPopup>0</OthersPopup>
            <PopupOnAll>0</PopupOnAll>
            <ShowTime>1</ShowTime>
        </Messages>
      .

      .

      .

      </UI>
    </config>
```

shared.xml tweaks.

Enhancement (all platforms): refresh Skype super-node list

Refreshing your list of super nodes will change the way in which your Skype client interacts with the Skype network. It may change how calls are routed and have an impact on how many relays (hops from Skype client to Skype client) you have. Having a new and different super-node list sometimes improves how Skype runs. To refresh your super-node list, simply rename or delete *shared.xml*. The next time Skype starts it will build *shared.xml*, and your super-node list, anew.

See Also

- O'Reilly (*http://www.oreilly.com/*) has published a comprehensive range of books on XML, from beginner to expert level. Particularly noteworthy for someone new to XML is *Learning XML, Second Edition* (2003).

- "Eliminate Echo and Noise" **[Hack #39]** also uses some *config.xml* tweaks.

HACK #46   Run Skype from the Command Line

You can control how Skype is launched and behaves by running it from the command line with options.

Works with: Windows and Linux versions of Skype.

Skype runs in a graphical Windows environment. Nevertheless, for those diehards for whom anything but the command line is a strange and alien environment, there is good news. You can run Skype from the command line with options.

Even for those lesser mortals who are comfortable with the GUI in general, and with Skype in particular, running Skype from the command line offers some distinct benefits in terms of additional flexibility. Command-line options can be particularly useful when you combine them with shortcuts (see "Add Fast-Dial Shortcuts to Your Menu or Desktop" [Hack #49]).

> Running Skype from the command line with options is also a good way for the visually impaired to use Skype.

Windows

The Windows version of Skype currently supports the command-line options shown in Table 4-3.

Table 4-3. Command-line options for Skype on Windows

Command-line option	What it does
/callto: <Skype user or telephone number>	Places call to the specified user or number
/datapath:"<path>"	Specifies where user personal data is to be stored by Skype
/nosplash	Stops splash screen from displaying
/minimized	Runs Skype minimized in the system tray
/removable	Ensures that nonexistent paths aren't written to the Windows registry and does other housekeeping for running Skype from removable media
/shutdown	Stops Skype from running

Here are some things to try with command-line options entered in a command window (Start → All Programs → Accessories → Command Prompt) or from the run line (Start → Run, but if you choose this method, enter commands using quotes, like this: "Skype.exe" "/callto:echo123"). All of the following examples assume you have put the folder containing *Skype.exe* on your path:

- Skype /callto:echo123 will place a call to echo123, or to anyone else if you replace echo123 with their Skype name.
- Skype /callto:+442075551212 will place a call to a regular telephone number, provided you are a SkypeOut subscriber. Don't forget to use

the correct Skype dialing format ("+" and then country code, and then region/city code, and then phone number).

- `Skype /nosplash /minimized` will start Skype and put it in the system tray without anything appearing on the screen.

- `Skype /shutdown` will stop Skype from running (it's the equivalent of right-clicking on Skype in the system tray and choosing Quit).

Linux

The Linux version of Skype currently supports the command-line options shown in Table 4-4.

Table 4-4. Command-line options for Skype on Linux

Command-line option	What it does
`--callto: <Skype user / telephone number>`	Places call to the specified user or number
`--disable-api`	Disables Skype's Application Programming Interface (API)
`--use-session-bus`	Uses session bus rather than default bus

To make a call from the command line on Linux, enter this at the prompt in a terminal window, and press Enter:

```
/usr/local/bin/skype --callto:echo123 &
```

HACK Display the Technical Details of a Call
#47

Make a small change to your *config.xml* configuration file to have Skype display a wealth of detail about a call.

Works with: Windows and Linux versions of Skype.

This feature, on by default in earlier versions of Skype, is now off by default in the current version of Skype. Why Skype disabled this feature is a mystery, as it can provide a wealth of detail about what's happening during a call. Armed with this technical detail about a call, you will not only better understand what Skype is doing behind the scenes, but also perhaps get some clues as to why Skype is performing poorly. Even if Skype is performing well, the technical details provided by this hack might give you some ideas for further tweaking and tuning Skype's performance.

Fortunately, it's easy to switch call technical details back on. All you need to do is make a one-line change to your Skype configuration file, *config.xml*. Making this change is simple, especially if you follow the guidance provided in "Tweak Skype by Editing config.xml" **[Hack #45]**.

Note that you will have to quit Skype (right-click on Skype in the Windows system tray, and then choose Quit; select File → Close on Linux) and restart Skype for the changes to take effect. Editing *config.xml* while Skype is running will result in your changes being ignored by Skype. Quit Skype, and then in your *config.xml* file locate the appropriate tag and set its value to 1, like this:

Windows
```
<DisplayCallInfo>1</DisplayCallInfo>
```

Linux
```
<TechCallInf>1</TechCallInf>
```

> With version 1.4 of Skype for Windows, Skype reintroduced the option of setting `<DisplayCallInfo>` using its user interface (select Skype → Tools → Options… → Advanced, and then check or uncheck "Display technical call info"). On Linux, you can likewise change `<TechCallInf>` using the user interface (select Skype → Tools → Options… → Advanced, and then check or uncheck "Display technical call info").

Now, restart Skype and the ability to display call technical details will be enabled, so when you let your mouse hover over the picture in the middle of an active call window, it will display the technical details for that call (see Figure 4-6). This works for both outgoing and incoming calls, and for one-on-one and multiperson conference calls (though for the latter, CPU usage is displayed only in the case of the first, top-left, conference call participant on Windows, and not at all on Linux).

By activating call details, you get a lot of useful information about calls. However, the format of the information is somewhat terse and cryptic. So, I've provided the following explanations to help you interpret the displayed information:

Input and Output
Displayed are the sound-in and sound-out devices that Skype is using. If either of the devices listed against input and output doesn't match the hardware you are using, or intend to use, for making and receiving calls, that's a problem. You can change the sound devices Skype uses by selecting Tools → Options… → Sound Devices and selecting the devices you want from the Audio In and Audio Out pull-down lists. While there, you may also want to check the "Ring PC speaker" checkbox, as that will act as an additional notification of an incoming call.

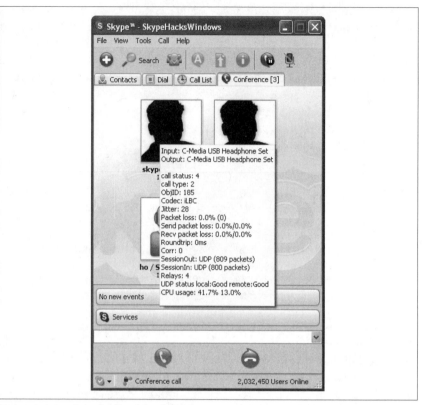

Figure 4-6. Display of call technical details

Call status

> The numeric code displayed has these meanings: 1 = connecting (you should hear a dial tone); 2 = failed call (the user is not on the line); 3 = ringing; 4 = connection established (the call is in progress); 5 = local hold; 6 = finished; 7 = missed; 8 = refused; 9 = busy; 14 = playing voice-mail greeting; and 15 = connected to voicemail (you can leave a voice-mail message, but only if the recipient is a Skype voicemail subscriber). A full list of call status codes and their meanings is available as a web extra from the book's web site, *http://www.oreilly.com/catalog/SkypeHacks/index.html*.

ObjID

> This is an internal reference used by the Skype programmers and has lit-tle meaning, or significance, from the user's point of view.

Codec

> *Codec* is an acronym that stands for code/decode. It is the software com-ponent of Skype that is responsible for converting speech into data

packets that are suitable for transmission across a network, and at the receiving end for converting those same data packets into sound that we can hear. There are many types of codecs. For Skype-to-Skype calls, one called ISAC from Global IP Sound (*http://www.globalipsound.com/*) is used, and for SkypeOut calls a G.279 codec is used (G.279 is a specification from the International Telecommunication Union, or ITU, *http://www.itu.int/*). This is part of the internal workings of Skype, so it is something over which the user has no control.

Jitter

Jitter is a measure of the variations between consecutive data packets arriving at the Skype client. The lower this number is, the better your voice connection will be. The jitter buffer in your network router holds incoming data packets until a bunch of them have been received and sequenced. Then it starts to release the packets as an even stream so that the sound you hear is continuous. Meanwhile, new data packets are being received. The idea behind the jitter buffer is that buffering increases the chances that, even if some subsequent packets arrive late, enough packets will be available in the buffer for the sound you hear to continue uninterrupted. Clever algorithms implemented in firmware within the router detect and try to compensate for the effects of jitter. In addition, Skype does its own jitter correction internally in software, so presumably, Skype's jitter number is some composite measure of the residual jitter arriving from the router and its own efforts at correcting jitter. High levels of jitter cause large numbers of data packets to be discarded by the jitter buffer. This may result in degraded call quality. Skype's jitter measurement is difficult to interpret in any precise way (outside of Skype); however, as already mentioned, the lower this number is, the better your voice connection will be. Many things cause jitter, and the time spacing between arriving data packets and other characteristics of the packets themselves can vary for a multitude of reasons, but common causes are network congestion and packet route changes. Skype's jitter number can peak in the thousands at the beginning of a call, but should then drop back to 300 or less. Since the jitter buffer and its corrective algorithms are built into your router, the level of jitter you experience is in part a function of your router's quality and sophistication. Upgrading to a new and improved router is one way to improve jitter. However, before doing this, it is worth checking your current router manufacturer's web site for firmware updates that will improve the router's performance. The "Roundtrip" section of this list provides some advice on router setup that may also help with jitter.

Packet loss and Send/Recv packet loss

"Send packet loss" shows the proportion of data packets lost at both ends of a call—that is, by you and the other party—for packets that are sent out. Likewise, "Recv packet loss" shows the proportion of data packets lost at both ends of a call, for packets that are received. "Packet loss" is a measure of the overall number of packets lost during the call. Loss of data packets is the bane of VoIP! High levels of packet loss mean poor voice quality and even dropouts, where the connection goes silent for seconds at a time. The ideal is to have zero packet loss, but this is rarely achieved in the real world unless you and the other caller have an outstanding network connection. As a rule of thumb, a packet loss of less than 5% (that is, 5% of data packets sent, or received, are "lost," and typically have to be re-sent) has very little noticeable effect on call quality. A packet loss of greater than 5% progressively degrades voice quality, to the point that when packet loss rises higher than 25%, call quality is significantly degraded and soon thereafter becomes unusable. You can address high packet loss by improving your network connection, specifically by giving Skype data packets higher priority than other data packets, which is a technique commonly referred to as Quality of Service (QoS). See "Improve Service Quality" [Hack #59] for ways in which you can improve your Skype QoS.

Roundtrip

This is a measure of your network connection's latency (see "Test Your Internet Connection Latency" [Hack #34]). Roundtrip times of 150 ms to 200 ms will mean excellent call quality and that there's very little need for you and the other caller to pause in your conversation just to know the other has stopped talking. When roundtrip times stretch to 350 ms and higher you will find yourself having to leave longer and longer pauses in your conversation just to know, without ambiguity, that the other party has stopped talking. Anything higher than 500 ms and conversations will become stuttered and very strained, as both calling parties will run the risk of talking over one another. If you use Skype, and you use a geostationary satellite link to connect to the Internet, you can expect this number to be quite high, but you can do little about it, as it is a consequence of the finite nature of the speed of light. Similar to jitter (discussed earlier), roundtrip data-packet transfer time is primarily a function of the speed and quality of your Internet connection. Also, *malware* and *adware*, which are common forms of *spyware* (unwanted software installed on your computer—often without your knowledge—that consumes processing power and Internet bandwidth; see *http:// arstechnica.com/articles/paedia/malware.ars/* for a good overview of the topic), can have a detrimental effect on roundtrip time. An excellent tool for removing spyware is Spybot—Search & Destroy, freely available from *http://www.safer-networking.org/en/spybotsd/index.html*. Also, upgrading your router firmware to the latest version can sometimes improve roundtrip time. Finally, if you're a real techie, you can tinker with the router port settings for the ports Skype uses (you can find Skype's port settings by selecting Tools → Options... → Connection); see "Fix Badly Behaving Routers" **[Hack #51]** for details on setting up port forwarding for Skype.

Corr
> The meaning of this term is unknown.

SessionOut and SessionIn
> These are counts of the number of UDP data packets both sent (out) and received (in).

Relays
> When a Skype call is a *relayed transfer*, it means that a direct connection between the caller and callee could not be established, so data packets must be routed via intermediate Skype nodes (peers, just like you, in the Skype network). The fewer the number of relay nodes, the smaller the number of "hops" data packets have to make from node to node, and the better your call quality will be. This is another call attribute for which the lower it is, the better it is for call quality. The ideal is to have zero relays, in which case the call is said to be in *direct transfer*. The most common cause for relayed transfer is because you, or the other party, are using a machine that lives behind a restrictive firewall or uses *Network Address Translation* (NAT). These are the areas to look at if you are suffering badly from relayed transfer. Note that relayed transfer not only affects voice-call quality, but it also severely impacts file transfers made through Skype, as file-transfer traffic is throttled back by Skype to a measly 1 kilobyte per second (so a 1MB file would take more than 15 minutes to transfer, and larger files would take correspondingly longer). You can improve file-transfer speed by not talking at the same time a transfer is taking place, because Skype gives voice packets priority over data packets. A high number of relays can also be a symptom of a malfunctioning or old router. Sometimes you can give an old router a new breath of life—including reduced relays—by upgrading its firmware.

UDP status
> The *User Datagram Protocol* (UDP) is a specification for a network protocol. UDP is one of the two methods by which Skype communicates with other Skype clients (nodes). The other is the *Transmission Control Protocol* (TCP). Together with the Internet Protocol (IP), UDP and

TCP/IP provide the network infrastructure on which Skype runs. Skype uses UDP when it can because it is the preferred protocol for small data packets, like the ones used by Skype. Skype indicates the quality of your (local) and the other party's (remote) UDP connection. If either end of a Skype call has poor UDP, call quality will suffer. The fix is for the offending end to make its network more UDP friendly.

CPU usage

This displays both your (local) and the other party's (remote) current CPU usage. High CPU usage numbers on either end of a call spell problems because Skype might not be able to get the processing power it needs to do its real-time job of encode → encrypt → send → receive → unencrypt → decode. Very high CPU usage (greater than 90%) may impact call quality. Oftentimes, high CPU usage is the result of other processes running on your or the other party's machine. In this case, you can improve things by shutting down the other non-Skype processes. Sometimes the problem is with Skype itself, in which case you should investigate and troubleshoot (see "Troubleshoot Skype" **[Hack #12]**).

HACK #48   Remove Unused Names from the Login List

Need to remove old, unused, or mistyped Skype usernames from the Skype login screen? A little work with files will get the job done.

Works with: Windows version of Skype.

Did you mistype your username when setting up a Skype account? Or were you bored with the old name, so now you use a new username? Regardless of why a Skype username becomes defunct, it is a rather surprisingly resilient fellow. It won't go away unless you take some direct action (see Figure 4-7).

Fortunately, removing the no-longer-welcome username is a breeze. Stop Skype from running (otherwise, you will find the directory locked), and then simply delete the account directory associated with it. For the example in Figure 4-7, delete this directory:

```
C:\Documents and Settings\Username\Application Data\Skype\thewrongname
```

Here, *Username* is your Windows login name.

Once the directory is gone, restart Skype, and your unwanted Skype username is banished from the Skype login screen, as shown in Figure 4-8.

A word of warning, however: Skype names persist "out there" on the Skype network. So, if at any time, you again log on to "thewrongname," it will again be added to the Skype login screen and you will have to repeat the preceding process to get rid of it!

Figure 4-7. Mistyped and old Skype usernames linger in the login screen, unless you delete them by hand

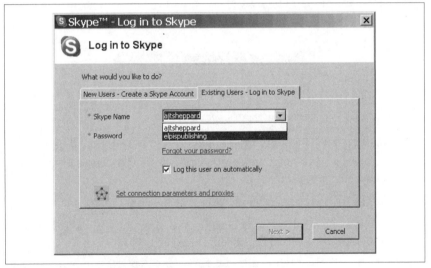

Figure 4-8. The unwanted Skype username is deleted from the login list

Add Fast-Dial Shortcuts to Your Menu or Desktop

#49   Add shortcuts to your menu or desktop for your most frequently called contacts.

Works with: Windows version of Skype.

When making a Skype call, the typical procedure goes something like this: double-click the Skype icon in the system tray or the Skype shortcut on the desktop, navigate to the Contacts tab, find the entry for the contact you want to call, and then double-click on it. Now, for some people of leisure, all this clicking is a great adventure. For the rest of us who must work for a living, wouldn't it be nice to make that call with as little as just one double-click? Fortunately, this is possible with the Windows version of Skype, as we can add shortcuts to the Windows desktop or menu for our most frequent calls.

Menu Shortcuts

Navigate to Skype on the Windows menu (select Start → All Programs → Skype), and right-click on the Skype icon. A pop-up menu should appear, from which you should choose Create Shortcut. This will create a shortcut under the Skype menu (see Figure 4-9).

Figure 4-9. A newly created menu shortcut for Skype

Next, right-click on the new shortcut (Skype (2)) and choose Properties. This will open a window in which you can edit the properties of the shortcut you have just created (see Figure 4-10).

With the Shortcut properties window open, you should follow these steps:

1. Go to the General tab and rename the shortcut. In the example in Figure 4-10, the shortcut has been named echo123.

2. Go to the Shortcut tab and in the Target box, enter a command such as this: `"C:\Program Files\Skype\Phone\Skype.exe" "/callto:echo123"`. Pay particular attention to the use of quotes, and if necessary, change the path to the *Skype.exe* executable.

3. If you want to associate a hotkey sequence with the shortcut, click on the Shortcut key text box and enter the key sequence you want to use for this shortcut—for example, `ctrl + shift + E`.

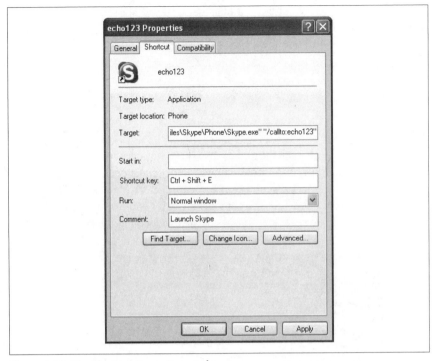

Figure 4-10. The Shortcut Properties window

Here's a nifty tip for when you associate hotkeys with short-cuts. If you have speed dial numbers set up for your Skype contacts, you can use them as part of your hotkey sequences. For example, suppose you gave echo123 the speed dial number 4 within your Skype Contacts list. You can assign the hotkeys ctrl + shift + 4 as its corresponding hotkey sequence. That way, your shortcut hotkeys match your speed dials. Unfortunately, as you can use only single digits within a hotkey sequence, this tip works only for speed dial numbers between 1 and 9. But if you assign 1 through 9 to your most important or most frequently called contacts, you'll always be only a short hotkey sequence away from making your most important calls.

Desktop Shortcuts

To create fast-dial shortcuts on your desktop, you have a couple of choices.

First, if you already have fast-dial shortcuts in your menu, you can simply right-click on any of them and choose Send To → Desktop. That will create an identical shortcut, but one that lives on your desktop instead (see

Figure 4-11). Double-clicking on a fast-dial desktop shortcut will start a call to whomever you have entered as the /callto: name (or to the regular phone number, if you're a SkypeOut subscriber).

Skype   echo123

Figure 4-11. Desktop fast-dial shortcuts for Skype and for echo123

Second, you can simply right-click anywhere on an unoccupied area of your desktop. From the pop-up menu that appears, select New → Shortcut. This will create an empty shortcut on your desktop, as well as open the Shortcut Wizard. Use the Browse... key to find *Skype.exe* (see Figure 4-12).

Figure 4-12. The newly created desktop shortcut and the Shortcut Wizard

In effect, the shortcut we're creating will run Skype from the command line, and as such we can add command-line options. The command-line option we will add is /callto:*Skypeuser*, where *Skypeuser* is the name of the Skype user we want to contact when we double-click on the shortcut. Under "Type the location of the item" in the wizard, add the /callto: command-line option after *Skype.exe*, like this: "C:\Program Files\Skype\Phone\Skype.exe" "/callto:echo123". Pay particular attention to the use of quotes, and if necessary, change the path to the *Skype.exe* executable. Click Next, then name the shortcut, and then click Finish. Now you should have a freshly minted fast-dial shortcut on your desktop, like that shown in Figure 4-11.

Note that a careful naming convention for your Skype desktop shortcuts will pay dividends when it comes to organizing your desktop. This is particularly true if you have more than a few shortcuts. Using a short prefix, such as Skype–, for shortcut names will mean that when you organize your desktop icons by name or file type, all your fast-dial shortcuts will group together nicely as a block. This should make finding and calling your most frequent Skype contacts quicker and easier still.

With this hack, calls are now just a double-click away!

Fix Windows Wireless

H A C K
#50

Windows Wireless is largely self-configuring and mostly problem free. But Windows can sometimes shoot itself in the foot, and so it is sometimes with its Wireless Zero Configuration Service.

Works with: Windows version of Skype.

The Windows *Wireless Zero Configuration Service* (WZCS) is meant to help you, by doing all of the wireless configuration on your behalf. But it can become as much of a hindrance as a help as far as Skype is concerned.

During operation, the WZCS constantly hunts around for a better WiFi connection, and if it finds one, it switches you to that connection and away from your current connection. However, this switch is not instantaneous. This is not a problem if you are, say, browsing the Internet, as the momentary disruption to your Internet connection is not noticeable. However, Skype is sensitive to both latency and packet loss, both of which are adversely affected during the switch. If you are in a WiFi "noisy" location, the WZCS might constantly try to switch your machine from one access point to another, and possibly back again. Even the WZCS's habit of continuously hunting around for a better wireless connection by hopping from access point to access point can degrade call quality, as latency is injected into your connection and packets are lost.

Fortunately, the WZCS, which is switched on by default in Windows, can be disabled, but only after Windows startup; otherwise, your wireless services will fail to start. After Windows startup, you can stop the WZCS by selecting Start → Control Panel → Administrative Tools → Services, right-clicking on Wireless Zero Configuration, and choosing Stop.

Alternatively, if you don't want to have to remember this sequence of actions every time you start Windows, you can add the following entry to the Windows registry using RegEdit (select Start → Run…, enter "RegEdit," and click OK) to do the job for you:

```
HKEY_CURRENT_USER
   Software
```

```
Microsoft
    Windows
        Current Version
            Run
                WZCS-Killer REG_SZ "c:\windows\system32\net.exe" stop WZCSVC
```

See Also

- If you have a wireless or nonwireless router that is causing problems, you might want to look at "Fix Badly Behaving Routers" **[Hack #51]**.

Fix Badly Behaving Routers

Skype works without a problem with most routers, both wireless and nonwireless. This hack is for those of you who have a router that behaves badly with Skype, or vice versa!

Works with: all versions of Skype.

If Skype habitually drops calls, suffers from poor call quality, or simply doesn't work at all, after testing all else you should turn your attention to your network router. By working your way through this list of things to try, you stand a good chance of either fixing the problem or resigning yourself to buying a new router!

Reset your router
  If problems have started to occur only recently and prior to that, your Skype calls were largely trouble free try resetting your router. You can do this by either pressing the Reset button (most routers have one, though it's oftentimes tucked away so that the router is not easily reset by accident), or powering the router off and then on again.

US Robotics router
  Go to the configuration settings, and under Access/Special App, look for a setting named PC-to-Phone. Enable it.

Other routers
  Look for a setting similar to that for the US Robotics router and enable it.

Avoid being a super node
  Skype uses a lot of simultaneous port connections. When you become a super node, the number of connections can increase substantially. This might overwhelm your router, especially if it has very limited built-in processing power. If you stop Skype from using ports 80 and 443 for incoming connections (select Skype → Tools → Options... → Connection on Windows or Skype → Tools → Options... → Advanced on

Linux; this option is not available on Mac OS X or Pocket PC), you will very likely not become a super node. However, I must say that Skype is continuously being developed, and the rules by which a regular Skype node (client) becomes a super node are not public, so you can never be sure your node is not operating as a super node.

Enable ports 80 and 443

Letting Skype use ports 80 and 443 for incoming connections can improve things, as it gives Skype more options and flexibility in terms of routing traffic. However, doing so does increase the probability that you may become a super node, which can create problems of its own (as discussed earlier). At first glance, this suggestion may seem to contradict the advice I gave earlier under the "Avoid being a super node" heading, which argues in favor of closing off ports 80 and 443. The point is that both enabling and disabling ports 80 and 443 has advantages and disadvantages, in both cases. I suggest you try both approaches to see which brings the greatest net benefit.

Port scanning

Routers sometimes block Skype because it uses a large number of ports (TCP and UDP). Some malware programs go from port to port, in a process call port scanning, probing each to find a vulnerability to exploit. Because Skype tries to use so many ports, it can be mistaken for port-scanning malware and therefore be blocked. If your router blocks this type of behavior, disable its port-scanning blocking feature. However, bear in mind that doing so might make you more vulnerable to port-scanning malware.

Port forwarding

You can find out the port number, let's call it N, that Skype prefers to use for incoming connections, under connection options (select Skype → Tools → Options... → Connection on Windows, Tools → Options... → Advanced on Linux, or Skype → Preferences... → Advanced on Mac OS X; this option is not available for Pocket PC). If your machine lives behind a restrictive NAT or firewall, it might not be accessible to other machines outside on the Internet, so Skype won't work. However, by using port forwarding, incoming connection requests to port N (and/or ports 80 and 443) can be forwarded directly to your machine, allowing machines on the Internet to connect with your machine and, in so doing, enabling Skype to work. You can find an excellent resource for support documents specifically on port forwarding for individual router models at *http://www.portforward.com/routers.htm*. You can find a more general tutorial on port forwarding at *http://www.dlink.com.au/tech/drivers/files/modems/DSL-302G_Open.ports_DMZ.zip*. Although this tutorial is specific to a D-Link router, it nevertheless has information useful to anyone considering opening ports for forwarding.

Erratic or strange router behavior

For unknown reasons, some routers (wireless and nonwireless) behave erratically with Skype. Common router models reported to have this problem are the D-Link 604 (nonwireless), D-Link 614 (wireless), Linksys BEFSR41 (nonwireless), and Linksys BEFSX41 (nonwireless). There are others. If upgrading your router firmware doesn't fix the problem, there's very little you can do, other than buy a new router!

Upgrade firmware

This is always worth a try and it costs you nothing. By upgrading to the latest firmware for your router (visit the manufacturer's web site), you might not only cure all sorts of problems, but also boost your router's performance.

Buy a new router

This is always a last resort, but it's worth considering if all else has failed and you're fairly sure that the problem is with your router.

See Also

- It might also be worth testing your Internet connection for Skype friendliness (see "Test Your Connection for Skype Friendliness" [Hack #38]).

- You can get a handle on jitter, packet loss, and other things influenced by your router's behavior by looking at the technical details of the calls you make (see "Display the Technical Details of a Call" [Hack #47]).

Skype at Work
Hacks 52–59

It might be some time before large organizations adopt Skype, partly because Skype lacks the features and reliability demanded by such organizations, and partly because of simple inertia—the bigger the organization, the slower it moves, or so it seems. Skype is known to be working on "enterprise" features and even a specific version of Skype targeted at business users. Even so, Skype as it is now has a lot to offer businesses, local government agencies, and charities that are willing to give it a try. Perhaps, as happened for instant messaging, Skype is a technology that will come in through the back door!

One advantage of Skype is that it's not an all-or-nothing proposition, as you can run it in parallel with existing phone systems, often with very little initial outlay in terms of both cost and effort. In addition to the possible cost savings of using Skype, you also should not overlook the technological wonders Skype can perform, as its capabilities are utterly different from, and in my opinion superior to, those of any regular phone system you have seen before. So, if you're thinking of giving Skype a try in a small business, department, agency, or whatever, these hacks should help get you started and give you some ideas of how Skype can improve your organization's phone services.

HACK #52

Automate Skype Installation

These tips will simplify installation if you need to install Skype on anything more than a handful of machines.

Works with: Windows version of Skype.

Walking from machine to machine and installing Skype can be a thankless task. Automating the installation process makes the job a lot more palatable, and enables you to customize the installation easily.

To help customize the installation of Skype on Windows, Skype has thoughtfully provided its installer, typically a file named *SkypeSetup.exe*, with several command-line options (see Table 5-1).

Table 5-1. Skype's install program command-line options on Windows

Command-line option	What it does
/NoStart	Do not start Skype when Windows starts.
/NoWpFinished	Skip the "finish page" during installation.
/Silent	Show installation progress only.
/VerySilent	Show nothing during installation.
/NoCancel	Install cannot be cancelled.
/Lang=<language>	Specifies the language for installation.
/Dir="X:\Directory"	Specifies the installation directory.
/NoIcons	No shortcut icon on the desktop.

Using these command-line options, you can very easily create a Windows batch file that will simplify the whole installation process. Here's a step-by-step how-to guide:

1. Put *SkypeSetup.exe* in a folder on a shared network drive, which maps to, say, S:\Shared\Install\ on all your target machines.

2. Create a batch file, *install_skype.bat*, and save it in S:\Shared\Install\:

   ```
   REM File: install_skype.bat

   MKDIR C:\Apps\Skype
   S:\Shared\Install\SkypeSetup.exe /VerySilent /Lang=en /Dir="C:\Apps\Skype" /
   NoIcons
   ```

3. Send an email to all the users whom you want to install and run Skype. At a minimum, this email should specify how to run *install_skype.bat* and how to set up a Skype name. If you are rolling out Skype, not as a trial, but in a rather more systematic fashion, this same email should also perhaps include additional information, such as the Skype name to be used by each user, and advice on how best to configure their sound hardware to use Skype, among other things.

This procedure might look like something that Rube Goldberg (*http://www.rube-goldberg.com/*) might dream up, but it beats wandering from machine to machine, especially if those machines are in different offices, or even different buildings!

Hacking the Hack

If you want to roll out Skype, but with restricted functionality—such as with file transfer and Skype's API disabled—you can instruct the batch file installer to do this at the time of installation.

First, create a registry file, *skype_disable.reg*, and save it in *S:\Shared\Install*:

```
; File: skype_disable.reg

Windows Registry Editor Version 5.00

[HKEY_LOCAL_MACHINE\SOFTWARE\Policies\Skype\Phone]
"DisableFileTransfer"=dword:00000001
"DisableApi"=dword:00000001
```

Next, add a line to the existing batch file to create a new installation file—say, *install_skype_reg.bat*—so that the appropriate registry keys to disable Skype file transfer and its API are created during the installation process:

```
REM File: install_skype_reg.bat

MKDIR C:\Apps\Skype
S:\Shared\Install\SkypeSetup.exe /VerySilent /Lang=en /Dir="C:\Apps\Skype" /
NoIcons

RegEdit.exe /s S:\Shared\Install\skype_disable.reg
```

For Skype file transfer and the Skype API to be disabled, the users who run *install_skype_reg.bat* must have the necessary privilege to edit the registry under [HKEY_LOCAL_MACHINE\SOFTWARE\Policies. Incidentally, this also means that they can switch these features back on if they're willing to hack around in the registry! Clearly, this method of installing Skype is not the most foolproof if your users are relatively sophisticated and experienced with Windows.

See Also

- Skype has a briefing document directed specifically at network administrators responsible for installing and running Skype; see *http://www.skype.com/security/guide-for-network-admins.pdf*.

- For details on how to disable Skype file transfer, see "Disable Skype File Transfer" [Hack #58].

- For details on how to disable the Skype API, see "Disable the Skype API" [Hack #100].

Set Up a Toll-Free Number for SkypeIn

Set up a toll-free number for your customers and have calls automatically redirected to your SkypeIn number.

Works with: all versions of Skype.

Even in these days of ubiquitous email, many customers expect a business to provide a toll-free number for ordering or support. Sure, you can also put a Skype name—SalesAtMegaXYZCorp, or whatever—on your web site for people to call, but you cannot expect non-Skype users to download and install Skype just to talk with you, can you?

Toll-free numbers are free to the caller, but are not free to you, the recipient. Even so, consider the advantages of providing your U.S. customers with a toll-free number:

Consumers like toll-free numbers
Because toll-free numbers are free to call, customers are more likely to call you if you provide a toll-free number.

Toll-free numbers are portable
Changing your SkypeIn number doesn't mean you have to give up your toll-free number.

You can create the right image for your company
A toll-free number makes your company look professional and, if you're a non-U.S. company, extends your reach globally.

You can widen your markets
A toll-free number lets you serve customers by having a national presence in the U.S.

You can pay as you go
Many toll-free plans charge only for what you use, so your bills grow only in proportion to your business!

You can do the vanity thing
A *vanity toll-free number* is a number that spells something meaningful in relation to your company or business. 1-800-GO-FEDEX is an example of a well-known vanity number.

Well, thankfully, you can provide your customers with a toll-free number that you can link with your SkypeIn number so that calls made to the toll-free number are redirected automatically to your SkypeIn number. In fact, you can have any number of toll-free numbers redirected to the same SkypeIn number.

This also means that if you're a non-U.S. company, you can have a toll-free number in the U.S. (that is, a number with the prefix 800, 888, 877, or 866 which is linked to a U.S. SkypeIn number), but have those calls redirected to wherever you are located around the globe. Now, how's that for convenience for your U.S. customers! Plus, it says volumes for the global reach of your company!

First, you must get a U.S. SkypeIn number. This number will look like any regular Public Switched Telephone Network (PSTN) number to a toll-free service provider. If asked whether you have a Plain Old Telephone System

(POTS) or PSTN number (see Chapter 1), you can simply answer yes and give your SkypeIn number.

Next, you need to find a toll-free service provider to give you a toll-free number and have calls to that number redirected to your SkypeIn number. Google on "" and you'll find yourself spoiled with choices. However, beware that some toll-free plans require a contract, perhaps also an up-front fee, and a recurring monthly maintenance fee; other plans are such that you pay only for what you use (or rather, what your customers use, to be precise). So shop around to get the best deal based on your needs; you should find, without effort, a plan that costs less than 5 cents per minute. To get you started, here are a handful of toll-free plans to look at:

- *http://www.officedepot.telecomsvc.com/tollfree/index.asp?nav=home*
- *http://www.smart800now.com/*
- *http://www.kall8.com/*
- *http://www.teliax.com/*
- *http://www.get1800.com/*

None of these companies comes with any recommendation or endorsement from the author or publisher; they're just to be used as a rough guide to the sorts of toll-free plans available.

All of this should take a few days, at most, to set up and begin working. Extending your global reach to your customers has never been so easy.

H A C K #54 Set Up a Call Center

A single Skype username—say, XYZCorpCustomerService—can support many simultaneous callers, therefore supporting call center functionality at a fraction of the normal cost.

Works with: Windows version of Skype.

If you have an existing call center, or are thinking of setting one up on the cheap, you might be surprised at how simple Skype makes this. Presumably, you already have the computers and network infrastructure in place, as no modern-day call center can do without those, so it's just a question of configuring Skype to connect your call center with your customers.

One particularly useful feature of Skype is its ability to run on multiple computers under the *same* Skype username—say, XYZCorpCustomerService. Then, when someone calls XYZCorpCustomerService, all running instances of Skype logged on under the username XYZCorpCustomerService will ring (see Figure 5-1). Whoever picks up first will take the call (see Figure 5-2).

Now, while that first call is in progress, suppose someone else calls XYZCorpCustomerService. All instances of Skype not already engaged in a call will ring (see Figure 5-3). Whoever picks up this second call first will take that call (see Figure 5-4), and so it goes, until no available instances of Skype under the username XYZCorpCustomerService are left. As calls are completed and parties hang up, running instances of Skype are returned to the pool of available phone lines for XYZCorpCustomerService. Skype's behavior in this regard is just what a call center needs.

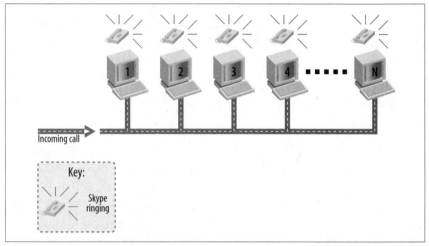

Figure 5-1. An incoming call rings all instances of Skype logged on under the same Skype name

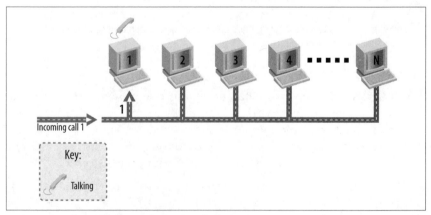

Figure 5-2. Whoever picks up first, takes the call

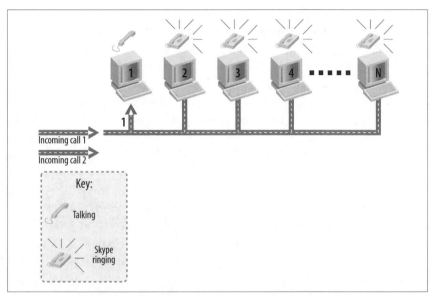

Figure 5-3. A second incoming call rings all instances of Skype not already engaged in a call

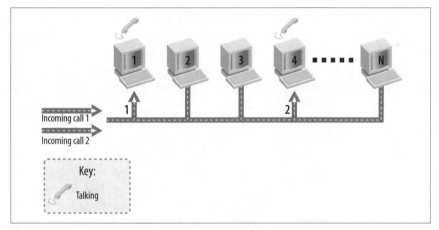

Figure 5-4. Whoever picks up first, takes the second call

Even though setting up a call center using Skype is simplicity itself, you may find it useful to work through this checklist, in the order shown:

1. Check your bandwidth and latency. All the computers that participate in your call center will most likely share the same connection to the Internet. As the Internet is a shared resource, you must make sure that your connection has sufficient bandwidth, and low enough latency, to make call quality acceptable. You should budget 128 Kbps, both

upstream and downstream, per concurrent phone call. Thus, for N machines (instances of Skype), you should have a minimum bandwidth of $N \times 128$ Kbps. Latency should be less than 0.2 of a second. You can measure both the bandwidth and the latency of your Internet connection using "Test Your Internet Connection Bandwidth" **[Hack #33]** and "Test Your Internet Connection Latency" **[Hack #34]**.

2. Install Skype on your computers and set them up so that the same Skype username is used on each one. If you have to roll out Skype across more than a handful of computers, you may find "Automate Skype Installation" **[Hack #52]** useful.

3. Fit each machine with headsets or handsets. If users are expecting to spend prolonged periods in calls with customers, headsets are probably best, as they're both comfortable (if well chosen) and hands free.

4. Publicize your call center Skype name to let your customers know how to contact you. And if they're not already Skype users, suggest they download and install Skype.

5. Using Skype-to-Skype is clearly the most cost-effective method of Skype-enabling your call center. However, if you think it's unreasonable to expect all your customers to use Skype just to talk with you, you can set up one or more SkypeIn numbers for XYZCorpCustomerService.

What I've described so far is merely the most obvious way of configuring Skype to achieve the functionality commonly associated with a call center. But don't be afraid to experiment, because if you do, you will surely find new and innovative ways to use Skype's technology to raise to a new level the services offered by your call center.

Hacking the Hack

If your call center is your first point of contact for your customers, you might want to back it up with a second rank, such as technical support. Again, Skype makes this very easy to do. By giving your technical support staff Skype names—say, XYZCorpTech1, XYZCorpTech2, and so forth—you can use Skype's conference call feature to add technical support staff to a call on an ad hoc basis.

Using our existing example, suppose that whoever is talking with the customer on call 2 decides that technical support is needed. In this case, here are the steps required to bring technical support into the call:

1. Put the customer, whose Skype name is, say, XYZCustomer, on hold (select Skype → Call → Hold).

2. Create a conference call with XYZCustomer and, say, XYZCorpTech1, as the participants (select Skype → Tools → Create a Conference Call...;

in the conference call dialog that appears, add XYZCustomer and XYZCorpTech1 and start the conference call).

3. Wait for XYZCorpTech1 to pick up. On pickup, all three of the call participants will appear in the call window.

4. If necessary, talk briefly with XYZCorpTech1, and then take XYZCustomer off hold (select Skype → Call → Resume → Conference with XYZCustomer).

5. Now, all three conference call participants—XYZCorpCustomerService, XYZCustomer, and XYZCorpTech1—are able to speak (see Figure 5-5).

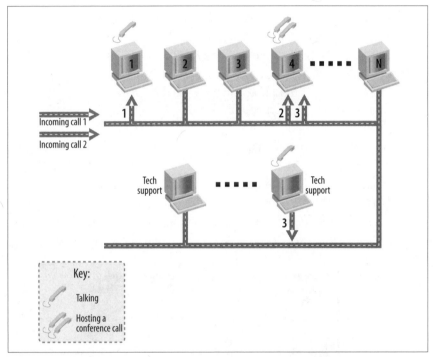

Figure 5-5. Adding someone from technical support to a conference with a customer

Integrate Skype with Microsoft Office

Here are some productivity-enhancing tips for using Skype with Microsoft Office.

Works with: Windows version of Skype.

Presented in this hack are a handful of ways in which you can more closely integrate Skype with Microsoft Office.

This hack uses the URL prefix *callto://* extensively. However, with version 1.4 of Skype on Windows, a new prefix
was introduced: *skype:* (note that there's no *//*, as *skype:*
won't work if you use them). The *skype:* prefix can be used
in place of *callto://* and can do a lot more; for example, it can
start a Skype chat session rather than place a call. See "Make
Calls from Your Web Browser" **[Hack #43]** for more details.

Skype Toolbar for Outlook

Skype's free toolbar add-on for Outlook adds these features to Outlook by
means of a couple of pull-down menus and buttons (see Figure 5-6):

- All your contacts, for both Skype and Outlook, are together in one
  place.
- Make SkypeOut calls (if you're a SkypeOut subscriber) to contacts that
  are not yet using Skype.
- Call Skype names and phone numbers that appear in email you receive
  (select Outlook → Skype pull down → Call <Skypename> or Call
  <Number>); see Figure 5-7.
- Chat with Skype names that appear in email you receive (select Out-
  look → Skype pull down → Chat with <Skypename>); see Figure 5-7.
- Change your Skype online status from within Outlook (select Outlook
  → Skype pull down → Status); see Figure 5-6.
- Create journal entries for incoming and outgoing calls; see Figure 5-8.
- ...and more (select Outlook → Skype pull down → Configure)!

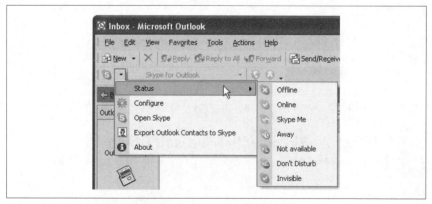

Figure 5-6. Skype toolbar for Outlook

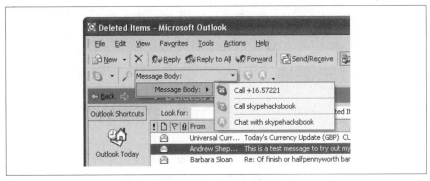

Figure 5-7. Call or chat directly with contacts embedded within email

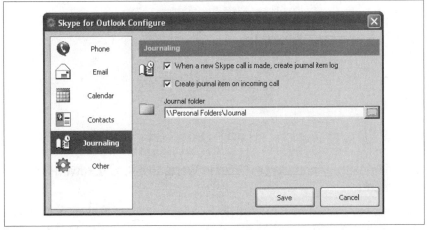

Figure 5-8. Setting up the Skype toolbar to create journal entries for outgoing and incoming calls

You can download the Skype toolbar for Outlook at *http://www.skype.com/ products/skypetoolbars/*.

> The Skype toolbar for Outlook is an add-on that uses the Skype Application Programming Interface (API). Consequently, when you first run Outlook after installing the toolbar, Skype will display a window asking you for permission for the toolbar (specifically, the file *SkypeOBE.exe*) to access Skype. You must click the radio button labeled "Allow this program to use Skype" for the toolbar to work.

Importing Outlook Contacts

You can import your Outlook contacts directly into Skype. Simply use Skype's own contact import facility by going to Skype → Tools → Import

Contacts…, and following the instructions provided by the Import Contacts Wizard. This is a great way to start using Skype, as you'll have a ready-made contact list to begin with.

Skype's import facility for contacts also works with contact lists stored in MSN Messenger, Opera, and Outlook Express.

If you are using the Skype toolbar for Outlook (discussed earlier), an alternative way to get your Outlook contacts into Skype is to use the toolbar's Export Outlook Contacts to Skype function (see Figure 5-9).

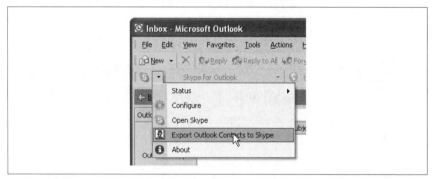

Figure 5-9. Export your Outlook contacts to Skype using the Skype toolbar for Outlook

Inserting callto:// and skype: Links in Word, Excel, and PowerPoint Documents

Inserting hypertext links into office documents that, if clicked, will start a Skype call to the specified Skype name requires nothing more than a few clicks and keystrokes. Of course, for the links to work, Skype must be installed and properly configured to use *callto://* (select Skype → Tools → Options… → Advanced, and check the "Associate Skype with callto: links" checkbox) on the machine on which the document is opened.

Word. Place your cursor at the point where you want to insert the Skype link, and then go to Insert → Hyperlink…, which will open an Insert Hyperlink dialog into which you can enter the text for the link and its address (URL). Later, if necessary, you can edit the link by right-clicking on it and choosing Edit Hyperlink… (see Figure 5-10).

Excel. Select the cell into which you want to insert the Skype link, and then go to Insert → Hyperlink…, which will open an Insert Hyperlink dialog into which you can enter the text for the link and its address (URL). Later, if necessary, you can edit the link by right-clicking on the cell and choosing Edit Hyperlink… (see Figure 5-11).

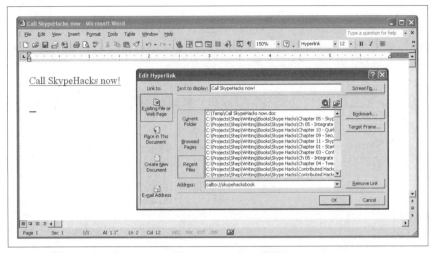

Figure 5-10. Inserting/editing a callto:// link in a Word document

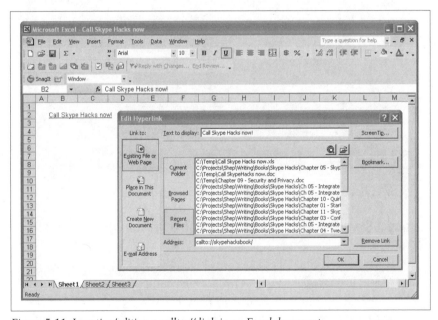

Figure 5-11. Inserting/editing a callto:// link in an Excel document

PowerPoint. To insert a Skype hyperlink into a PowerPoint presentation, you must first insert an object that can then be associated with the link. The simplest object is a text box with the link text you want to display (select Insert → Text Box, click on a slide, and enter text). Next, click on that object to select it (and select the text in the box, if you're using a text box). Then from the PowerPoint menu, choose Insert → Hyperlink…, which will open an Insert Hyperlink dialog into which you can enter the text for the link and its address (URL). Later, if necessary, you can edit the link by right-clicking on the text and choosing Edit Hyperlink… (see Figure 5-12).

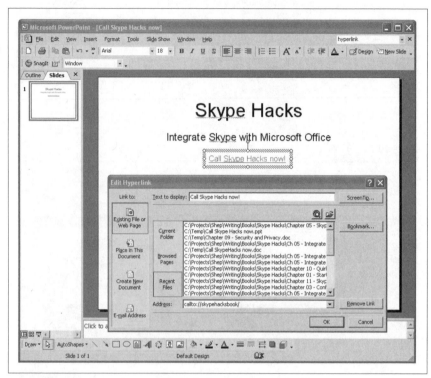

Figure 5-12. Inserting/editing a callto:// link in a PowerPoint slide

Adding a Skype Me Button to a Web Page or to Your Outlook Email Signature

You can add a Skype Me button to any web page. Simply go to the Skype Me buttons web page, pick a button style, and then cut and paste the HTML for that button into your web page HTML. Anyone who clicks on your Skype Me button in a web page they are viewing in a browser, and has Skype installed and properly configured to use *callto://* (select Skype → Tools → Options… → Advanced, and check the "Associate Skype with callto: links" checkbox), will start a Skype call to you. You can find the Skype Me buttons web page at *http://share.skype.com/tools_for_sharing/tools_for_ sharing/skype_me_buttons*.

Here's an example of the HTML needed for a very simple web page, shown in Figure 5-13, that displays only your Skype name and Skype Me button:

```html
<!DOCTYPE HTML PUBLIC "-//W3C//DTD HTML 4.0 Transitional//EN">

<!-- File: skype_hacks_button.htm -->

<HTML>
    <HEAD>
        <TITLE>Skype Hacks Button</TITLE>
    </HEAD>
    <BODY>
        <P>Skype Hacks
           <A href="callto://skypehacksbook">
           <img src="http://goodies.skype.com/graphics/skypeme_btn_yellow.gif"
               border="0">
           </A>
        </P>
    </BODY>
</HTML>
```

Simply replace *skypehacksbook* in the preceding HTML with your own Skype name to create your own Skype Me button in a web page. Remember that you can insert your Skype Me button HTML (everything between and including the <A> ... </A> tags) into any HTML web page where inserting an anchor (hypertext link) is valid.

Figure 5-13. A Skype Me button embedded in a web page

To include a Skype Me button in your email signature for Outlook, go to Outlook → Tools → Options…, and in the Options dialog that appears, navigate to the Mail Format tab and click on the Signatures… button. That will

open a Create Signature dialog, in which you should click on the New...
button. That, in turn, will display a Create New Signature dialog. Give the
signature a name, and click on the radio button labeled "Use this file as a
template." Click the Browse... button and use the file navigation dialog that
appears to locate and use this template HTML file (which you can create in
Notepad, or download from the book's web site):

```
<!DOCTYPE HTML PUBLIC "-//W3C//DTD HTML 4.0 Transitional//EN">

<!-- File: skype_hacks_outlook.htm -->

<HTML>
    <HEAD>
        <TITLE>Skype Hacks Outlook Signature</TITLE>
    </HEAD>
    <BODY>
        <P>Skype Hacks
            <A href="callto://skypehacksbook">
            <img src="http://goodies.skype.com/graphics/skypeme_btn_yellow.gif"
                border="0">
            </A>
        </P>
    </BODY>
</HTML>
```

Simply replace *skypehacksbook* in the preceding HTML with your own Skype
name to create your own Skype Me button in the HTML signature template.

In the Create New Signature dialog, click Next. That will display an Edit
Signature dialog that will allow you to edit the signature further, using fonts
and other elements of your choice. Once you're done editing your signature, click Finish and then click OK in the Create Signature dialog. In the
Options dialog, choose the name of your newly minted signature in the "Signature for new messages" pull-down menu and click OK. Now, any email
you send will have a signature that includes a Skype Me button on which the
recipient can click to place a Skype call to you. You can check out what your
signature will look like by sending yourself a test email (see Figure 5-14).
The recipient of an email from you can click on the Skype Me button to
place a Skype call to you.

If you are using the Skype toolbar for Outlook (as discussed earlier), there's
an even easier way to insert a Skype Me button as part of your email signature. Select Outlook → Skype pull down → Configure → Email, and then use
the settings under Signatures (see Figure 5-15).

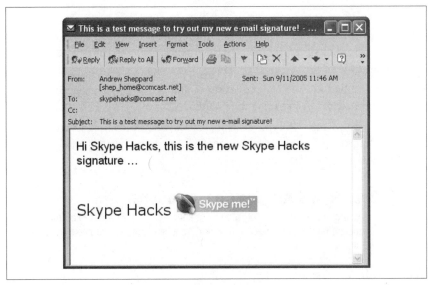

Figure 5-14. Outlook signature with a Skype Me button

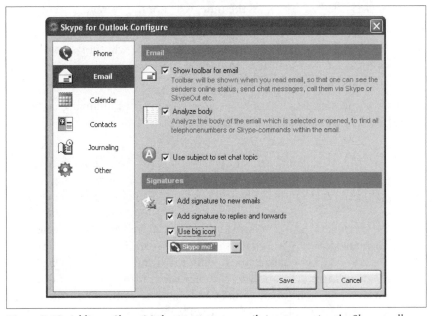

Figure 5-15. Adding a Skype Me button to your email signature using the Skype toolbar for Outlook

See Also

- To learn how to add your Skype online status to a web page or to your Outlook email signature, see "Show Your Online Status in a Web Page" [Hack #88].

- For a detailed how-to on importing contacts into Skype, see *http://share. skype.com/blog/insight/importing_contacts/*.

- Several third-party Skype add-ons are available that help integrate it with Microsoft Office applications. See the Skype Extras Gallery at *http:/ /share.skype.com/directory/* for details.

HACK #56   Record and Archive Conversations

There are many reasons for recording and archiving Skype calls, from conducting online interviews to regulatory requirements. All you need are a few simple tools.

Works with: all versions of Skype.

There are many reasons why you might want to record phone conversations. Heck, if the FBI does it all the time, why not the average citizen!

However, recording conversations is (unfortunately) not a feature currently built into Skype. Nor is there one simple tool that will work on all platforms. So to do it, you will need to hack around with some additional software and, possibly, some hardware.

Here are some suggestions for ways of recording and archiving conversations, by Skype platform:

Windows

> By far, the easiest method is to use the Pamela Professional Skype add-on (€17.50—about $22—*http://www.pamela-systems.com/*). Recording Skype conversations is just one feature of this veritable Swiss army knife of Skype add-ons. To start recording and archiving your Skype calls, go to Pamela → Tools → Options → Call recording, and select the recording options you want (see Figure 5-16). Then, every time you make and receive a call, Pamela will record the conversation based on the setting you chose, and you can play those recordings back using the Pamela application (open Pamela and navigate to the "Recorded calls" tab, then select a call and click on the Play button).

Linux

> The method I use to record Skype conversations on Linux uses four software components:

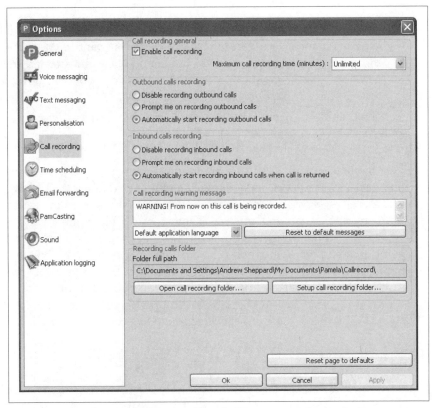

Figure 5-16. Configuring the Pamela add-on for Skype to record conversations

Framework for User-Space Devices (FUSD)

Pronounced "fused," this component enables a user-space (rather than a kernel-space) device to be created for audio streams that can be a JACKed client (discussed next). You can download FUSD at *http://www.circlemud.org/%7Ejelson/software/fusd/*.

JACK

JACK allows multiple applications to connect to a sound device and share audio with each other. You can download it at *http://jackit. sourceforge.net/*.

Secret Rabbit Code (a.k.a. libsamplerate)

This is a sample rate converter for audio, which you can use to determine the sound quality of Skype voice recordings. You can download it at *http://www.mega-nerd.com/SRC/download.html*.

oss2jack

This application allows several applications to use the same sound card simultaneously. To record Skype calls, you want to configure things so that the same sound-in and sound-out audio streams are used by both Skype and a recording application. You can download oss2jack at *http://fort.xdas.com/~kor/oss2jack/*.

You also can download all of these software components at *http://fort.xdas.com/~kor/oss2jack/*.

Mac OS X

This method uses two software applications: WireTap Pro ($19, from *http://www.ambrosiasw.com/utilities/wiretap/*) and Detour ($12, from *http://www.rogueamoeba.com/detour/*). WireTap takes an audio stream from any application and converts it into a sound file in any one of a variety of common formats, and Detour—as its name suggests—allows you to redirect the destination of audio from any application. For this hack, Detour redirects sound from Skype to WireTap so that you can save it as a sound file. Set up Detour to redirect sound in the manner shown in Figure 5-17, and set up WireTap to capture that redirected sound and save it as a file in a specified sound format (see Figure 5-18).

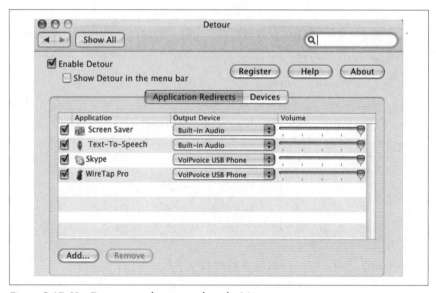

Figure 5-17. Use Detour to redirect sound on the Mac

Pocket PC

See the next section, "Hacking the Hack."

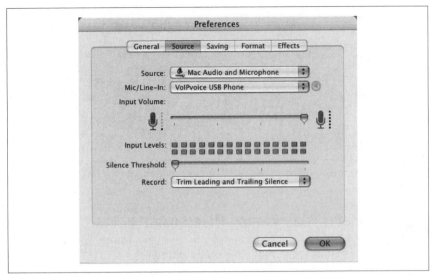

Figure 5-18. Use WireTap to save a redirected sound to a file in an audio format of your choice

Hacking the Hack

This is a low-tech, but utterly reliable, way to record your voice-call conversations. A lot of software solutions for recording Skype conversations can be a pain to configure and a pain to use, and may let you down when you need them most.

This method is very low tech, as it uses a simple $1.50 pickup microphone (available from *http://www.alltronics.com/*) that has a suction cup on it. Just stick the cup to the handset, plug the 3.5mm jack into your sound card (or an iMic if you have a Mac, *http://www.griffintechnology.com/products/imic/index.php*), fire up your favorite (or default) sound recorder application for your platform (select Start → All Programs → Accessories → Entertainment → Sound Recorder, for example, on Windows), and record your conversation. The advantages of this method are that it's simple, cheap, and trouble free; and it works for Windows, Linux, Mac OS X, and Pocket PC (using a PC to do the recording).

This method works with any USB handset used by Skype; and as an added bonus, it works with regular phones too! You can even stick the pickup microphone onto the back of your PDA or mobile phone to record conversations (see Figure 5-19). This might bring back memories of 1960s-era spy-type B-movies, but it does work, and very reliably at that!

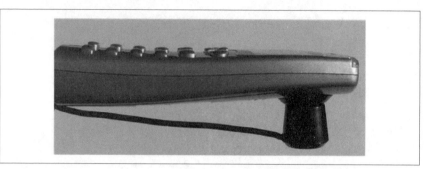

Figure 5-19. The low-tech way to record phone conversations: a stick-on pickup microphone

 Transfer Files Among Diverse Machines

#57 Use the Skype file-transfer feature on a home or office network to transfer files among machines running different operating systems.

Works with: Windows, Linux, and Mac OS X versions of Skype.

If your home or office has a diversity of machines, transferring files among them is a snap if you use Skype. With Skype installed on each machine, Windows, Linux, and Mac OS X can finally "play nice" together in terms of seamless file transfer.

To transfer files among machines in, say, a household where Dad runs Windows, Mom runs Mac OS X, and Junior runs Linux, just go to the machine that will be the source of the file, open Skype, and initiate a file transfer (there are several ways of doing this; see "Transfer a File Using Skype" [Hack #8]). Then, walk over to the destination machine, where a confirmation window will be displayed (see Figure 5-20). Click on Save As... and save the file to the location of your choice. Figure 5-21 shows an example of a home having a mix of different machines running different operating systems; however, the same principles apply whether you're transferring files among machines in a home, a small business, or a department in a large organization.

File transfer is that easy with Skype! No more FTP'ing up to a server and then down from the server (or from machine to machine, in which case the receiving machine must be running an FTP client/server program). No more playing around with Samba or NFS, to mount shared network folders. No more burning to CD-ROM, DVD, or zip disks and swapping from drive to drive—in short, no more hassle.

Moreover, the machines among which you want to transfer files do not have to be in the same physical location; they can be spread around the globe. In

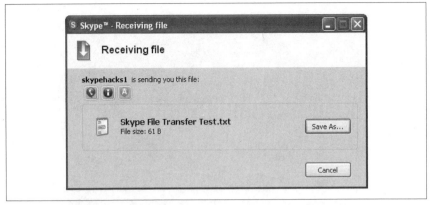

Figure 5-20. All Skype file transfers must be confirmed on the receiving machine

that case, it's worth remembering that Skype file transfer is encrypted end to end and therefore is secure.

> You cannot transfer a file to yourself. That is, Skype will transfer files only among different Skype names. So, for example, if you want to transfer a file between a Windows machine and a machine running Mac OS X, both machines must have Skype running, but under a *different* Skype logon name.

Incidentally, Skype file transfer is superior to sending files as email attachments, for several reasons. But the two main reasons are as follows:

- Skype file transfers are not limited in size. Email attachments, on the other hand, are limited to the size of the inbox on your mail server (typically only 10 to 20 megabytes).

- Skype file transfer is encrypted end to end, so it is more secure than email (unless you first encrypt the attachment, in which case the receiving machine must have compatible decryption software installed, which introduces additional steps into the transfer process).

If any of the machines to which you want to transfer files is located behind a restrictive Peer to Peer (P2P)-unfriendly firewall or router, Skype will use what it calls "relayed transfer" and your file transfer will slow to a crawl. Relayed transfer is signaled by "Your transfer is being relayed" appearing in the "Sending file" window (see Figure 5-22).

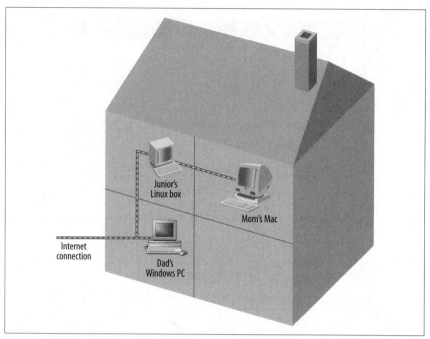

Figure 5-21. Use Skype to transfer files among diverse machines

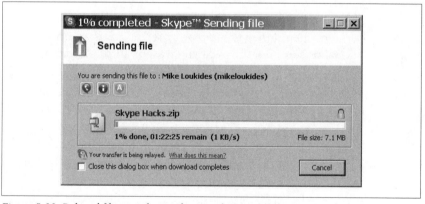

Figure 5-22. Relayed file-transfer notification (bottom left)

See Also

- "Transfer Folders, Not Just Individual Files" [Hack #84]
- "Scan Files Received via Skype for Viruses" [Hack #75]

HACK #58 Disable Skype File Transfer

Perhaps corporate policy dictates it, or perhaps you just think it's a good idea. In any event, disabling Skype's file-transfer function requires only a single registry setting.

Works with: Windows version of Skype.

With the release of version 1.4 for Windows, Skype included the ability to disable file transfer selectively. In many businesses, disabling this function may be dictated by corporate policy, or it might be at the request of your network administrator. Provided you're willing to hack the Windows registry, selectively disabling file transfer is a snap.

Open RegEdit (select Start → Run..., enter "RegEdit," and press Return or click OK) and add this key: HKEY_LOCAL_MACHINE\Software\Policies\Skype\ Phone. Under this key, add a new DWORD value having the name DisableFileTransfer. Setting DisableFileTransfer to 1 will disable Skype file transfer (see Figure 5-23), and setting it to 0 (or omitting or deleting the key altogether) will leave file transfer enabled. Note that you don't have to stop and restart Skype for this change to take effect.

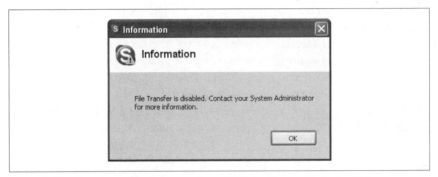

Figure 5-23. The pop-up window you will see if Skype file transfer is disabled

Of course, this hack works sensibly only when regular user accounts are set up so that they can't edit the registry under HKEY_LOCAL_MACHINE themselves; that is, specifically, they should not be able to change DisableFileTransfer.

Hacking the Hack

If you don't want to hack this registry setting yourself, or if you have to roll Skype out across a large number of machines, you might find the following VBScript (*disable_file_transfer.vbs*) helpful:

```
' File: disable_file_transfer.vbs

Dim objShell
Set objShell = WScript.CreateObject("WScript.Shell")
```

```
objShell.RegWrite "HKLM\Software\Policies\Skype\Phone\DisableFileTransfer", _
                1, "REG_DWORD"
```

Here is the opposite (*enable_file_transfer.vbs*), just in case the policy that prohibits file transfer changes:

```
' File: enable_file_transfer.vbs

Dim objShell
Set objShell = WScript.CreateObject("WScript.Shell")
objShell.RegWrite "HKLM\Software\Policies\Skype\Phone\DisableFileTransfer", _
                0, "REG_DWORD"
```

Note that both scripts will, if necessary, create the registry entry if it does not exist already.

HACK #59 Improve Service Quality

Supporting several Skype users on the same outgoing Internet connection may require implementation of bandwidth rationing (per user) using Quality of Service (QoS) to maintain good call quality.

Works with: all versions of Skype.

The Internet is a shared resource, even for a single user. Web browsing, file downloads, streaming audio, and Skype calls are all vying for use of the data pipe. When several machines share the same Internet connection, this conflict over how bandwidth is shared among the competing users can be exacerbated. Certain activities, such as file downloads, are not bandwidth or latency critical in the sense that a slow file download is still a file download! In contrast, for VoIP applications such as Skype, being squeezed for bandwidth and latency by other applications might result in poor call quality.

Clearly, some way to prioritize Internet traffic is needed so that VoIP data packets get precedence over all other types of data packet. This is the goal of *Quality of Service* (QoS), which seeks—in advance—to guarantee a certain level of service in terms of bandwidth and latency, plus other secondary characteristics, such as error rates. In this hack, I'll focus only on QoS for bandwidth and latency. Improving bandwidth and latency for Skype VoIP traffic will always improve voice-call quality.

What makes QoS difficult in the case of Skype is that it doesn't use any fixed port numbers for outgoing traffic. QoS normally works by binding the port numbers used by an application to a QoS feature built into the router, which then takes care of prioritizing traffic for those fixed ports. However, for the outgoing part of a call, Skype uses available ports above and including 1024; that is, it randomly selects the User Datagram Protocol (UDP) and/or Transmission Control Protocol (TCP) ports it needs between and including port numbers 1024 and 65535. QoS typically needs fixed ports to operate, so traditional QoS doesn't work for Skype.

However, it is possible to set up a "QoS-like" service for Skype by selectively rationing bandwidth.

For a single user, one way of setting up a QoS-like service is to use a bandwidth-shaping tool such as NetLimiter (*http://www.NetLimiter.com/*). Using such a tool, you can divvy up your available bandwidth among the applications running on your computer that require Internet bandwidth. Specifically, you can make sure there's always enough bandwidth left over for Skype to work, and work well in terms of call quality.

Let's look at a concrete example. Figure 5-24 shows the available Internet bandwidth for a machine. Let's play it safe, and say that there's 1,400 Kbps of available bandwidth, both uplink and downlink. If we reserve, say, 250 Kbps for Skype, that means we can allocate the remaining 1,150 Kbps of bandwidth among the remaining applications running on the machine that require Internet access. Using a tool such as NetLimiter, you can do this very easily. With the limits shown in Figure 5-25, no matter what else is being done on the machine, there should always be enough bandwidth left over for Skype to work well.

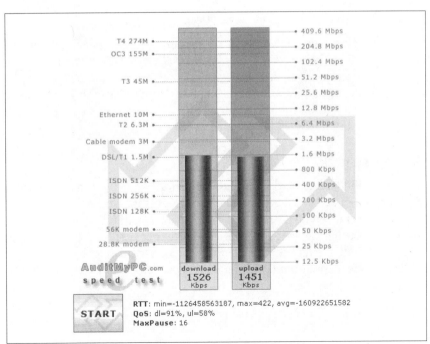

Figure 5-24. Available bandwidth (as measured by http://www.auditmypc.com/)

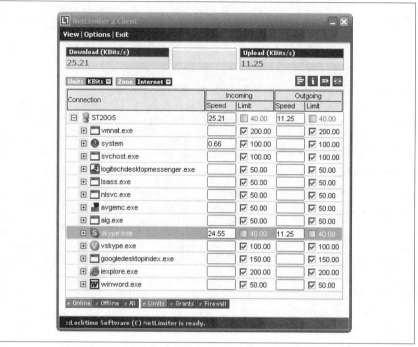

Figure 5-25. Using NetLimiter to ration bandwidth

For multiple machines and users that share an Internet connection, you can put a similar method of budgeting and bandwidth rationing in place by using nothing more than simple arithmetic and by running NetLimiter on each machine. That way, no matter what any machine is doing in terms of accessing the Internet, no Skype call will be squeezed out, so to speak, and good call quality can be maintained for all users.

Hacking the Hack

Measuring, budgeting, and enforcing bandwidth limits with a tool such as NetLimiter can become tedious and can be a less-than-optimal way to manage your overall bandwidth when more than a handful of machines are involved. Fortunately, network devices are coming onto the market (see Figure 5-26) that effectively implement QoS in hardware by prioritizing Internet traffic based on monitoring data packet characteristics, rather than using fixed port numbers.

Figure 5-26. Broadband Booster from Hawking Technology (http://www.hawkingtech.com/)

Such devices sit between your router and your broadband Internet connection and divide Internet traffic into streams of packets having different characteristics. Then, they give priority to those packets whose delivery is time sensitive, such as the VoIP packets Skype uses. Best of all, these devices are Plug and Play (PnP), requiring little or no user configuration.

Hawking Technology claims its HBB1 Broadband Booster provides improvements of up to 400%, in terms of uplink throughput, for certain types of applications that use the Internet. The HBB1 improves upstream traffic only, and does not differentiate between different machines or applications, so you can't fine-tune Internet traffic prioritization as you can with tools such as NetLimiter. It is worth reminding the reader that most asymmetric broadband Internet connections have substantially less uplink bandwidth than downlink bandwidth, so the HBB1's focus on upstream traffic improvement makes sense. These units do work (see *http://www.tomsnetworking.com/Reviews-210-ProdID-HBB1.php* for a real-world review) and are an inexpensive method for implementing QoS for a group of Skype users that share a Digital Subscriber Line (DSL) or cable broadband connection.

Mobile Skype
Hacks 60–64

The hacks in this chapter might prove useful to mobile users, travelers, and people otherwise on the move that use Skype. They might also prove useful to live-away-from-home students and their families.

HACK #60 Make Cheap Long-Distance or International Calls from Your Mobile Phone

Route calls using Skype, and take advantage of Skype's low long-distance and international call rates.

Works with: Windows version of Skype.

Many mobile phone plans offer low-cost, or even free, limited calling within their "home" geographic area. Not so with long-distance and international calls, for which you normally have to pay a bundle. Using this hack, you can effectively substitute Skype's very low long-distance and international call rates for the more expensive call rates of your mobile plan.

This hack takes advantage of three Skype services: SkypeIn, SkypeOut, and Skype call forwarding. SkypeIn is a prepaid subscription service (see "Try SkypeIn, Risk Free" [Hack #5]), but is a comparatively low-cost way of getting a regular dial-in phone number. SkypeOut is likewise a prepaid subscription service that allows you to call regular phones anywhere in the world at very low rates (see "Try SkypeOut, Risk Free" [Hack #4]). Skype call forwarding is a function that is built into Skype and costs you nothing. In fact, if the international "number" you want to call is actually another Skype user, you don't need SkypeOut at all!

To make cheap long-distance and international calls you need to set up Skype on a machine at home that basically routes your long-distance and international calls by forwarding them to a specified destination (in fact, up to three destinations at once). The three destinations you forward to can be any mix of Skype users, regular phones, and mobile phones. In the case of regular and mobile phones, you'll need to be a SkypeOut subscriber and you will pay the appropriate SkypeOut call rate for the destination.

Now, Figure 6-1 makes the routing process look rather more intimidating than it really is, because configuring Skype to do this is easy:

1. Create a Skype account for the desired destination; for example, *aunt_ peg_in_paris*.

2. Sign up the Skype account *aunt_peg_in_paris* for SkypeIn and, if Aunt Peg isn't a Skype user, SkypeOut also. Let's assume that Aunt Peg is a Skype user and has the Skype name *aunt_peg* and that your new SkypeIn number—chosen to minimize the cost of your mobile phone calls to this number—is +12035551212.

3. Set up *aunt_peg_in_paris* to forward calls to *aunt_peg* whenever you call the SkypeIn number you have set up for *aunt_peg_in_paris* (select Skype → Tools → Options → Call Forwarding & Voicemail), as shown in Figure 6-2.

4. Have *aunt_peg* authorize *aunt_peg_in_paris* as a new contact.

5. After you've set up *aunt_peg_in_paris* as described, the easiest way to make this hack work is to leave the account you have set up for this purpose logged off at all times except for intermittently checking your SkypeOut balance, if required. That way, your calls are forwarded immediately.

6. Now, whenever you call +12035551212 on your mobile phone, the call will automatically be routed to *aunt_peg* and your overall call cost will be that between your mobile phone and +12035551212, plus *nothing* to forward the call to *aunt_peg*!

Now, to make all this effort worthwhile, long-distance or international calls from your mobile phone to the desired destination must currently cost you more than a SkypeIn subscription, plus mobile-to-SkypeIn call costs, plus (perhaps) SkypeOut call costs to the final call destination. Fortunately, working out your savings requires just simple arithmetic, as the example in Table 6-1 shows.

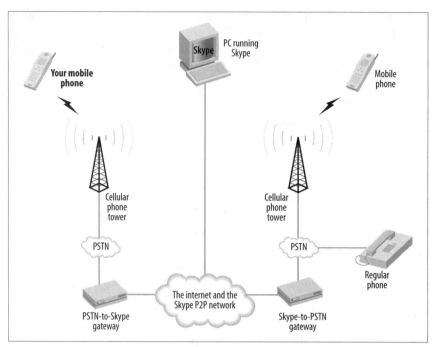

Figure 6-1. Routing calls from your mobile phone through Skype, to make cheap international calls

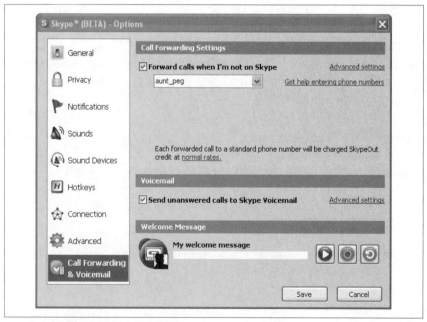

Figure 6-2. Setting up call forwarding

Table 6-1. *Figuring your savings for forwarding mobile calls to a long-distance or international destination using Skype, rather than dialing direct (an example)*

Cost component	Cost
Number of minutes of talk time per year	1,200
Mobile only	
Per-minute call rate to destination	$0.20
Total annual cost	$240
Mobile plus Skype	
Mobile-to-SkypeIn call rate	$0.05
SkypeOut-to-destination call rate	$0.03
Call costs per year	$96
SkypeIn annual subscription (€30 per year)	$37.50
Total annual cost	$133.50
Cost comparison	
Total annual savings using this hack	$106.50
Percentage savings	44%

SkypeOut rounds calls up to the whole minute, but your mobile phone plan might have the same, or a shorter, rounding time increment. Shorter time increments are to your advantage, and longer time increments are to the advantage of your phone service provider (including Skype). If your mobile plan rounds calls using a time increment of substantially less than 1 minute, you might want to factor in the effects of call rounding (see "Round Call Time to Your Advantage" [Hack #23]).

Another way of looking at the money-saving potential of this hack is to consider a business scenario. Suppose that a European company has 50 sales representatives that travel throughout the U.S. and check in each day with the European head office by mobile phone. On average, these calls are, say, 20 minutes in length per sales representative. Using representative costs, the estimated savings might look something like Table 6-2.

Table 6-2. *Cost savings from using Skype to forward mobile phone calls from traveling sales representatives in the U.S. to a European head office*

Cost component	Cost
Number of minutes of talk time per day	1,000
Mobile only	
Per-minute call rate to destination	$0.10
Total daily cost	$100

Table 6-2. Cost savings from using Skype to forward mobile phone calls from traveling sales representatives in the U.S. to a European head office (continued)

Cost component	Cost
Mobile plus Skype	
Mobile-to-SkypeIn call rate	$0.05
Call-forwarding cost (Skype-to-Skype)	Free
Total daily cost	$50
Cost comparison	
Total daily savings	$50
Percentage savings	50%

Hacking the Hack

You can extend this hack to any number of long-distance or international call destinations by setting up a new Skype account for each. This might sound cumbersome, until you realize that this hack works best when *none* of the accounts set up for this purpose is logged in. That is, apart from checking your SkypeIn subscription status and SkypeOut credit balance from time to time, you can just forget about them.

See Also

- "Give Your Mobile Phone an International Dial-In Number" [Hack #62]

Communicate Using Skype, Even When Bandwidth Is Low

Even when bandwidth is too low for voice communication, that doesn't mean you can't communicate with other Skype users.

Works with: Pocket PC version of Skype.

Many devices that can run Windows Mobile 2003, but don't meet Skype's minimum requirements (see Table P-1 in the Preface) or don't have a Wireless Fidelity (WiFi) connection, can still use Skype.

General Packet Radio Service (GPRS) and *Enhanced Data rates for Global Evolution* (EDGE) are two mobile phone technologies that allow mobile phones to connect to the Internet, but at data rates insufficient to support Skype's voice-call features. Even so, when your device lacks the processing power and/or Internet connection bandwidth for voice, you can still use Skype chat.

Hacking the Hack

It is even possible to make Skype voice calls from a GPRS-3G phone, such as the Nokia 6630, Nokia 6680, Nokia 6681, or Nokia 6682. How, you ask? Well, if you strip out all the encryption/decryption and other overhead from a regular Skype call, even GPRS has just enough bandwidth to support a voice call, though the quality of that call may depend a lot on the quality and speed of your GPRS Internet connection.

To make this work you will need to use a Skype add-on (for instance, the Useful GPRS-3G Skype add-on software, which you can get for $22 from *http://www.useful-apps.com/new_page_21.htm*) that runs on both your mobile phone and your home PC. The add-on client that runs on your mobile phone will relay your voice from your mobile phone to your home PC, where a second component of the Skype add-on is running and feeds your voice into Skype, which then relays the call to its destination in the usual Skype way.

To make Skype voice calls, even over GPRS, follow these steps using the Useful GPRS-3G Skype add-on software:

1. Before you leave home, make sure Skype and the PC-based component of the add-on are running.

2. From your mobile phone, connect to the Internet using GPRS.

3. Start the mobile phone component of the add-on.

4. Input a number to call (SkypeOut) or the name of a Skype contact into the mobile phone add-on, and then click Call (see Figure 6-3).

Your call should be routed to its destination, with the first leg of the call being relayed between your mobile phone and your home PC by the add-on over GPRS, and thence from your home PC to its final destination by Skype.

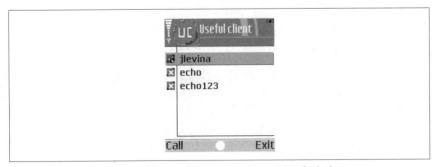

Figure 6-3. By using Skype add-on software, even devices that lack the Internet connection bandwidth for a regular Skype call can still make voice calls using Skype

HACK #62 Give Your Mobile Phone an International Dial-In Number

Use SkypeIn and call forwarding to give your mobile phone one or more international dial-in telephone numbers.

Works with: Windows version of Skype.

Giving your mobile phone one or more international dial-in numbers has a number of advantages, not the least of which is a reduced call rate for callers who are in the same country as your dial-in number, and the fact that you can have an international presence at a distance.

This hack uses three Skype services: SkypeIn, SkypeOut, and call forwarding. By giving a Skype account one or more SkypeIn numbers, you can use Skype call forwarding and SkypeOut to automatically forward to your mobile phone all calls that come in to these dial-in numbers (see Figure 6-4).

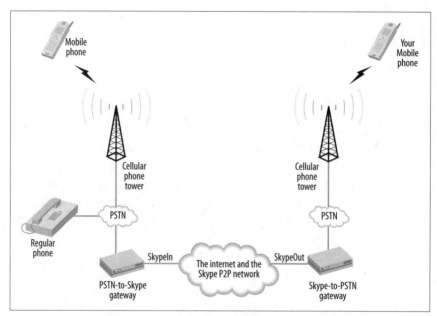

Figure 6-4. Routing calls to your mobile phone through Skype effectively gives your mobile phone multiple dial-in phone numbers

To give your mobile phone one or more international dial-in numbers, follow these steps:

1. Set up a Skype account just for this purpose—say, *my_mobile*.

2. Sign up *my_mobile* for SkypeIn and SkypeOut. Choose your SkypeIn number for the country of your choice; for example, +442075551212 would be a phone number for London. SkypeIn is available for many countries, and even regions of those countries; see *http://www.skype. com/* for a complete list.

3. Set up *my_mobile* so that incoming calls to your international SkypeIn number are automatically forwarded to your mobile phone (select Skype → Tools → Options… → Call Forwarding & Voicemail). For this exercise, we'll assume your mobile phone number is +12035551212 (see Figure 6-5).

4. Log off of *my_mobile*. Call forwarding for this hack works best when the *my_mobile* Skype account is logged off.

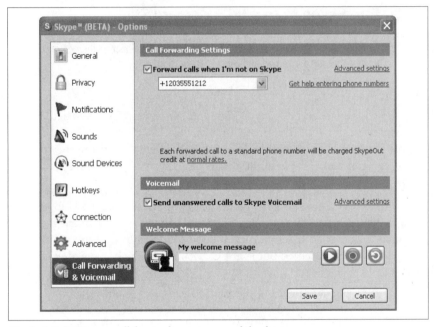

Figure 6-5. Setting up call forwarding to your mobile phone

Now, any calls to your international SkypeIn number will be forwarded to your mobile file automatically.

Unfortunately, all of this is not free, and you must decide for yourself whether the benefits of having an international dial-in number for your mobile phone outweigh the costs (see Table 6-3).

Table 6-3. Cost of adding an international dial-in number to your mobile phone (an example)

Cost component	Cost
Number of minutes of talk time per year	1,200
Per-minute SkypeOut-to-mobile call rate	$0.03
Cost of SkypeOut calls to mobile	$36
SkypeIn annual subscription (€30 per year)	$37.50
Total annual cost	$73.50

See Also

- "Make Cheap Long-Distance or International Calls from Your Mobile Phone" [Hack #60]

HACK #63 Run Skype from a USB Memory Stick

You can take Skype with you wherever you go, by putting it on a USB memory stick that hangs on your key ring, and then connecting through any machine having a USB port and Internet connection.

Works with: Windows version of Skype.

Wouldn't it be nice to take Skype with you, wherever you go? Whether from a business center PC at a hotel, or from an Internet cafe—indeed, from almost any PC to which you have access and which has an Internet connection—you can make a Skype call by carrying Skype in your pocket.

USB memory sticks are a popular way of carrying your essential data with you wherever you go. But you can also carry applications on a USB memory stick. This hack will show you how to put Skype on a memory stick, run Skype on a borrowed machine, and most importantly, clean up afterward so that your data is preserved but is not left behind on the borrowed machine.

 Simply running Skype on a machine that is not your own and then logging on to your Skype account is dangerous, because if you fail to remove your Skype datafiles properly, someone else might be able to use your Skype account later. You must therefore be careful to clean up and delete your Skype personal data from the borrowed machine.

For this hack, you will need a USB memory stick with enough spare memory to install Skype and some extra files, and to store your downloaded files—say, a minimum of 32 MB. And, unless you are certain the machine you will be plugging your USB stick into has a microphone and sound output, you will also need a USB handset or headset too.

For the file manipulations that follow, actions you perform at the command line you also can perform just as easily in the Windows Explorer file browser, if you find that environment more comfortable. To find out where the %appdata% environment variable points to just type "echo %appdata%" at the command line.

Loading Skype onto a USB Stick

Load Skype and your Skype data onto the memory stick by following these steps:

1. Stop Skype from running on your desktop machine (right-click on Skype in the system tray, and then choose Quit).

2. Plug your memory stick into a free USB port. In Windows Explorer, it should appear as a new drive letter—say, F:\.

3. Copy *SkypeSetup.exe* (which you can download from *http://www.skype.com/download/*, if you don't have it on your hard drive) to your memory stick's root directory.

4. Create a new directory on your memory stick using this command: MKDIR F:*Skypename*, where *Skypename* is the Skype name under which you log onto Skype.

5. Copy your Skype data from your desktop machine to the memory stick by running this command: XCOPY /E /H /Y "%appdata%\Skype*Skypename*" F:*Skypename*.

Installing, Configuring, and Running Skype

If Skype isn't installed on the borrowed machine, install it by running the command U:\SkypeSetup.exe, and following the instructions of the Skype setup program.

With Skype installed on the borrowed machine, here's all you need to do now to get up and running with Skype:

1. Stop Skype from running on the borrowed machine.

2. Plug your memory stick into a free USB port. We'll assume it maps to drive U:\ this time.

3. Create a new directory on the borrowed machine by running this command: MKDIR "%appdata%\Skype*Skypename*".

4. Copy your Skype data to the borrowed machine by running this command: XCOPY /E /H /Y U:*Skypename* "%appdata%\Skype*Skypename*".

5. Restart Skype and log on as *Skypename*.

6. Check that the sound device settings are compatible with the borrowed machine (select Skype → Tools → Options... → Sound Devices).

7. Check that the Internet connection settings are compatible with the borrowed machine (select Skype → Tools → Options... → Connection).

8. Call the Skype sound test service (echo123) and test that everything is working.

Cleaning Up

Leaving your personal Skype data on a borrowed machine runs several risks, from compromising your privacy, to allowing others to use your Skype account and SkypeOut credits. Follow these steps after you're done with Skype on the borrowed machine so that your Skype personal data goes with you on your USB memory stick and, at the same time, is not left behind on the borrowed machine:

1. Stop Skype from running on the borrowed machine.

2. Copy your Skype personal data from the borrowed machine back to your USB memory stick using this command: XCOPY /E /H /Y "%appdata%\ Skype*Skypename*" U:*Skypename*.

3. Erase your Skype personal datafiles from the borrowed machine with this command: RMDIR /S /Q "%appdata%\Skype*Skypename*".

4. Unplug your USB memory stick.

> Version 1.4 of Skype for Windows introduced a command-line option that enables you to specify the location where Skype will store your personal data. By running Skype like this: skype.exe /datapath:"U:\Skypename" /removable; you can have Skype save your personal data directly to your USB memory stick and so avoid having to clean up on the borrowed machine. The /removable command-line option ensures that nonexistent paths aren't written to the Windows registry and does other housekeeping for running Skype from removable media.

If you had to install Skype on the borrowed machine before you could use it, you should uninstall Skype before stepping away from the borrowed machine (select Start → Control Panel → Add or Remove Programs, select Skype from the list of currently installed programs, and click the Remove button).

See Also

- There is a method of running Skype from a USB memory stick that maps most of your Skype data onto your memory stick. It uses a third-party utility to create Windows "junction points." However, the method works only for NTFS filesystems and requires a fairly highly privileged user account to get working. See *http://forum.skype.com/viewtopic.php?t=25052*.

- If you like the idea of carrying Skype on your key ring wherever you go, but you are not confident of your ability to follow the necessary configuration steps in this hack, commercial products are available. See *http://www.mplat.com/* and *http://www.echostore.com/*.

Make Free Calls While on the Move

HACK #64

Skype Zones provides Skype connectivity around the globe, but at a price. Save money by using free alternatives.

Works with: all versions of Skype.

Skype provides a subscription-based service for Skype users who want to make calls and chat while on the move; in fact, Skype has partnered with Boingo to provide wireless access points that span the globe (see "Roam the World with Skype Zones" **[Hack #7]**). But free alternatives are available.

Skype WiFi Program

Seemingly in competition with its paid subscription service, Skype Zones, Skype has a free WiFi program. Through this program, Skype asks that independent providers of wireless Internet access give free Skype-only access to Skype users, and advertise the fact in addition to making their wireless access points Skype friendly. Sadly, a list of participating partners and their locations is not available, so you'll have to keep a sharp eye out for the Skype logo on your travels. To find out more, visit *http://www.skype.com/partners/wifi.html*.

Hotspots

Hotspots are publicly available wireless access points. Sometimes hotspots are well publicized and other times you have to hunt them down, an activity commonly known as *wardriving*. Once you've found a free Internet access hotspot, you may be able to use Skype to make and receive calls. Many public libraries offer free wireless Internet access, as do some hotels, cafes, and even metro-area communities. Googling on "free wifi ("access point" OR hotspot)" will return a list of directories for free, open-access hotspots; here are a couple of web sites to get you started:

- *http://metrofreefi.com/*
- *http://www.wififreespot.com/*

The usual rules about bandwidth and latency (see "Test Your Internet Connection Bandwidth" [Hack #33] and "Test Your Internet Connection Latency" [Hack #34]) as well as Skype friendliness apply, but this is a great way to make and receive free calls while on the move.

Use Someone Else's Machine

You can use a machine with Skype already installed by simply logging off the current Skype user, and then logging in yourself. Of course, first you should ask the machine owner's permission, and you should be aware of the dangers of leaving personal information behind after you're done (see "Erase a Skype User Account" [Hack #98]). But, this is one of the less painful ways to use Skype on the move, as you're starting from the baseline from which Skype already works on that machine!

Carry Skype with You

You can install Skype on a borrowed machine, or run Skype from a USB memory stick on a borrowed machine (see "Run Skype from a USB Memory Stick" [Hack #63]). Both methods might require that you do some extra machine configuration (sound, network, etc.) before Skype is up and running properly, and there's the danger that you might leave some personal Skype information behind on the hard disk; but with a little patience, most machines with the right specification (see Table P-1 in the Preface) and a decent, Skype-friendly Internet connection can be coaxed into running Skype.

## CHAPTER SEVEN

Skype Fun and Play
Hacks 65–69

"Have fun and play with your landline phone!" That sentence doesn't quite ring true, does it? Perhaps the reason why is that your regular landline phone has been in stasis for decades, as it's based on a boring technology that appears to be dead and unmoving. That's most definitely *not* the case with Skype.

Skype is based on new technologies and a new mindset. It is a telephony tool that is evolving rapidly and encourages—indeed, almost begs—you to experiment and hack with it. So have fun and play around with these hacks. I hope they are a stimulus to the creative and fun side of your imagination. Don't be afraid to experiment and have fun on your own!

HACK #65 Fun with Ringtones

Are you tired of that boring, old "ring-ring" sound Skype makes? Change it to something new and funky!

Works with: Windows version of Skype.

Now you can buy ringtones directly through Skype as part of its Personalise Skype service: *http://personal.skype.com/wnf/t74us/0/m*. But at $1.20 for each ringtone you purchase, it's a form of customization that can get expensive quickly.

The good news is that you can very easily make your own ringtones, and this hack shows you how.

> Skype uses *.wav* files (that is, files with a *.wav* extension, which denotes a Windows audio file format) for ringtones. But there are a couple of restrictions: they must be mono and not stereo, they must be of short duration (seconds, not minutes), and the recordings must be made at relatively low sample rates, and therefore have a small file size.

Ringtones are distinctive sounds that signal certain events in Skype. By going to Skype → Tools → Options... → Sounds (see Figure 7-1) you can change the ringtones that are associated with those events.

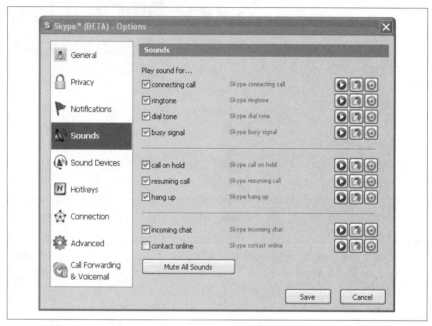

Figure 7-1. Setting up ringtones for specific Skype events

Few people realize that by default, Windows comes with a whole bunch of "ringtones" that you can use with Skype. In fact, these "ringtones" are the default sounds you hear for certain Windows events and other sounds, but you can use them as ringtones within Skype. To use these ringtones with Skype, go to Skype → Tools → Options... → Sounds, and click on one of the middle buttons opposite the Skype event. So, for example, to change the sound for "ringtone" to something different, click on the middle button opposite the word *ringtone*. This will display the My Sounds window (see Figure 7-2). Click on Browse..., and a file navigation and select dialog will appear. Navigate to *C:\Windows\Media* and pick one of the *.wav* files—say, *tada.wav*. The word *tada* will be added to the list in the My Sounds window. Select it and click OK. Now, whenever you receive an incoming call, Skype will repeatedly play the "ta-da" sound until you pick up or cancel the call. Windows comes with a small but adequate number of *.wav* sound files that you can use as ringtones within Skype. And they're all free!

In terms of creating your own ringtones for Skype, you have several options. I cover three of them in the following three sections.

Figure 7-2. Choosing a ringtone sound for a Skype event (in this case, Ringtone, which is the sound you hear when an incoming call rings)

Note that ringtones don't travel. That is, if you log onto Skype on a different machine under your usual Skype name—and for which you've set up custom ringtones—you will have only the default Skype ringtones available to you.

Use Windows Recorder

Windows Recorder is a utility that comes with Windows (select Start → All Programs → Accessories → Entertainment → Sound Recorder). This simple sound recorder takes sound input from, and outputs sound to, whatever sound devices you have configured in Windows (select Start → Control Panel → Sounds and Audio Devices). By feeding music, other sounds, or your voice into Windows Recorder, you can create a *.wav* file suitable for use as a ringtone for Skype. You even have the option of applying some very basic sound effects to your recording (select Windows Recorder → Effects).

To hear a simple ringtone I made using Windows Recorder, download *woop-woop-woop.wav* from the book's web site, *http://www.oreilly.com/catalog/SkypeHacks/index.html* (see Figure 7-3).

Figure 7-3. Use Windows Recorder to create your own Skype ringtones

To use with Skype the ringtones you create using Windows Recorder, simply put your *.wav* files in a convenient location and follow the procedure outlined earlier for Windows' own *.wav* files.

Find Free .wav Files to Use as Skype Ringtones

Googling on "free .wav (ringtones OR "sound effects")" will produce a lot of hits. However, one web site I particularly like for its free Skype-compatible ringtones is at *http://www.partnersinrhyme.com/*. Partners In Rhyme is a web site that has lots of royalty-free music and sound effects. Clicking on the Free Sound Effects link on the home page will display a page of sound effects, by category (see Figure 7-4). Partners In Rhyme is a source of literally hundreds of sounds that you can use either directly as Skype ringtones, or as ringtones after you've converted them to the proper audio file format (discussed shortly).

To use with Skype the ringtones that are freely available on the Internet, simply download *.wav*-format files (remember, they must be mono, not stereo) to your hard disk at a convenient location and follow the procedure outlined earlier for Windows' own *.wav* files.

Convert Ringtones from Other Formats to .wav

Many commercial, free, and open source audio file conversion utilities are available—just try Googling on "sound file conversion software" and you'll be overwhelmed with choices. However, one audio file conversion utility I can recommend is SoX. This open source utility, which you can download at *http://sourceforge.net/projects/sox/*, boasts of being the Swiss army knife of sound-file conversion utilities. And frankly, this is no idle boast!

SoX is a command-line utility that has a multitude of command-line options for twiddling with and fine-tuning audio file-format conversions. From echo to reverb effects, and from stretching sounds to changing their sample rate, SoX can do it all. Even so, for simple, no-frills conversions from one audio file format to another, SoX makes the task easy.

Figure 7-4. The Partners In Rhyme web site has lots of royalty-free sound effects that you can download and use as Skype ringtones

Here's an example of how easy it is:

1. Download a sound from *http://www.partnersinrhyme.com/* that isn't in *.wav* format—say, *gunshots.aiff* (an Apple audio format file), from the Fight Sounds category.

2. Open a command prompt window (select Start → All Programs → Accessories → Command Prompt).

3. In the command prompt window, navigate to the directory where you put *gunshots.aiff*.

4. Run this command at the prompt: sox gunshots.aiff gunshots.wav

5. To use your newly created ringtone, *gunshots.wav*, follow the procedure outlined earlier for Windows' own *.wav* files.

Of course, this example assumes you have already downloaded *SoX-win* from *http://sourceforge.net/projects/sox/* and placed *sox.exe* somewhere on your execution path.

Band Together with Skype

Are your band members spread all over the world? No problem, you can practice and jam together online with Skype.

Works with: Windows version of Skype.

Jamming over the Internet by using Skype might not be your first choice for band practice, but if it's your only choice, it's worth a try. Here's how to do it.

Before even thinking about jamming using Skype, there are three things to consider:

Bandwidth

> You can jam with up to four other band members by means of a conference call. But whoever hosts the conference call should have enough available bandwidth to support the conference call, which roughly scales with the number of participants. So, figure out who in your band has the best bandwidth and nominate that person as the host for the jam session. Use "Test Your Internet Connection Bandwidth" [Hack #33] to test your Internet connection bandwidth. Whoever is hosting the jam session should budget a minimum of 128 Kbps of bandwidth per session participant, uplink and downlink, and ideally have substantially more than this minimum—say, 256 Kbps per participant.

Latency

> This is the real killer for online jamming. If the Skype Internet connection of one of your band members has a latency that's greater than 250 ms, tempo and synchronization will be difficult to maintain. Use "Test Your Internet Connection Latency" [Hack #34] to test your Internet connection latency.

Interfacing your musical instrument

> At a minimum, you will probably need a Musical Instrument Digital Interface (MIDI)-capable sound card, and more likely, you will need a full-featured music-mixing device (something like an M-Audio FireWire 410; see *http://www.m-audio.com/products/en_us/FireWire410-main. html*) for your PC to make your Skype jam sessions really rock! Of course, for nonelectronic instruments, you'll also need a microphone.

This last item is important because without it, you face two problems. You'll probably need a preamp to get the raw signal output from your electronic instrument into a form that is suitable to feed into your sound card, and you will need to mix multiple audio streams—at a minimum, your instrument and headset—and feed them into and out of Skype (select Skype → Tools → Options... → Sound Devices). Both of these problems are neatly side-stepped by many music-mixing devices that typically interface to your computer through USB or FireWire and come with a whole host of musical instrument interfaces, audio mixing, and sound driver (software) features (see Figure 7-5).

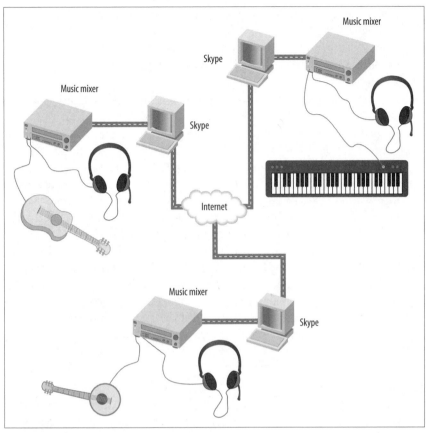

Figure 7-5. Jamming together with Skype

 ### HACK #67 Stop Incoming Calls from Interrupting Game Play

Skype will switch to the desktop during game play unless you configure it not to interrupt your fun.

Works with: Windows version of Skype.

Many games run in full-screen mode and don't like it when Skype notifications, calls, or chat interfere with game play—for example, by minimizing a game at some critical moment. This problem is exacerbated if you want to use Skype as part of your online gaming activities for communication with other players.

To minimize interference by Skype with your game play, try these suggestions:

Change your online status

Changing your online status for Skype will affect how Skype behaves; specifically, whether the Skype window will open and grab focus away from your game (see Table 7-1). Clearly, setting your online status to Offline or Do Not Disturb will stop Skype from opening and grabbing focus away from your game; but these modes also mean that you cannot use Skype to accept incoming calls while you play.

Stop pop ups

You can stop Skype from popping up windows for incoming calls and chat messages, which can interfere with game play. To do this, stop Skype from running (right-click on Skype in the system tray and choose Quit). Find your *config.xml* file, which is normally located at *C:\Documents and Settings\Username\Application Data\Skype\Skypename\config. xml*, where *Username* is the name under which you log onto your machine and *Skypename* is the name that you use to log onto Skype. Open *config.xml* in Notepad or some other text editor. Locate the `<FriendsPopup>` and `<OthersPopup>` XML tags under *both* the `<Calls>` and `<Messages>` parent tags. Set their values to 0; that is, set them like this: `<FriendsPopup>0</FriendsPopup>` and `<OthersPopup>0</OthersPopup>` under both `<Calls>` and `<Messages>`. Save your changes, and then restart Skype. Now your game play won't be interrupted by pop ups. These settings override the behavior described in Table 7-1. You may also want to combine these settings with the setting you'd use to have Skype automatically answer calls (select Skype → Tools → Options… → Advanced, and then check the "Automatically answer incoming calls" checkbox).

Switch off notifications

Notifications are small pop ups that appear briefly, at the lower right of your screen just above the system tray. These too can interfere with game play, depending on the game you're playing. You can selectively switch off these notifications by selecting Skype → Tools → Options… → Notifications (see Figure 7-6).

Multiple monitors

If your machine has multiple monitors attached, some games will play in full-screen mode on only one monitor, leaving your other monitors to display the remainder of your desktop. Moreover, if you last opened Skype so that it was displayed on one of the monitors that isn't used by your game when in full-screen mode, and if you set up Skype to automatically answer calls (by selecting Skype → Tools → Options… → Advanced, and checking the "Automatically answer incoming calls" checkbox), an incoming call will open Skype on one of the free screens and answer the call, but it might not minimize your game in the process, and therefore, it might not spoil your fun. I say it *might* not minimize your game because different games behave differently to other on-screen activity, even if on a separate monitor.

Run Skype under a separate user on your machine
This is the only method guaranteed not to interrupt game play. If you run Skype in a different user session, it can't affect your game play. You still can use Skype to receive calls—and even play a role in your game-play activities—but without any possibility of interference. See "Set Up Multiple Phone Lines" [Hack #37] for details on how to run Skype concurrently in a separate user session.

Table 7-1. How your Skype online status affects Skype's open and focus behavior

Online status	Incoming call will...
Skype not running	Not open Skype window
Online	Automatically open and focus Skype window
Offline	Not open Skype window
Skype Me	Automatically open and focus Skype window
Away	Automatically open and focus Skype window
Not Available	Automatically open and focus Skype window
Do Not Disturb	Not open Skype window
Invisible	Automatically open and focus Skype window

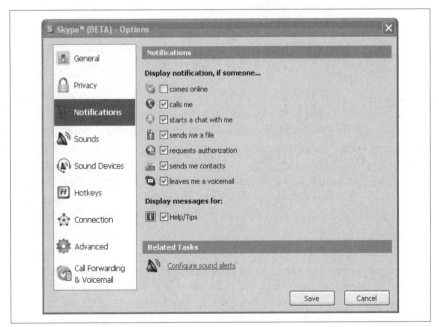

Figure 7-6. Control what notifications appear, and don't appear, by selectively enabling and disabling them

See Also

- For advice on how best to edit *config.xml* and for other Skype tweaks, see "Tweak Skype by Editing config.xml" **[Hack #45]**.

Learn to Speak a Foreign Language

HACK #68

Improve your spoken foreign-language skills by joining a practice group that includes native speakers, or by finding individual Skype users willing to talk with you in any language of your choice.

Works with: all versions of Skype.

You can think of Skype as an international community that spans the globe. So if you are learning a language and you want to practice speaking it with native speakers of that language, this hack will help you.

To use this hack sensibly, you must properly understand what Skype Me as an online status actually means. Skype Me is rather like hanging out a notice that says, "I'm here and I want to be contacted by the wider Skype community." This mode of being online disables all of your privacy settings, but only for the period when you are in Skype Me mode. Also, this is the only online status mode that you can use as part of a search for Skype users (select Skype → Tools → Search for Skype Users…, and then check the "Search for people who are in 'Skype Me' mode" checkbox).

If you're merely interested in speaking one on one with a native speaker of a language, by far the fastest method of finding someone willing to talk with you is to use the Skype-Me! forum. Open a web browser, enter the URL *http://forum.skype.com/search.php* in the address bar, and in the web page that is displayed type the language you're interested in. Then select the Skype-Me! forum to search, and click on the Search button (see Figure 7-7). This will display a new web page (or, more typically, several web pages) of Skype users—and Skype user groups—who are interested in the language you specified and, most importantly, are willing to accept calls from people they don't know (see Figure 7-8).

An alternative way of finding native-language-speaking partners and groups of people interested in practicing speaking in a specific language is to join a Skype community of language learners. One such community is the Jyve language-learning group: *http://community.jyve.com/lang_learning/language_learning.php*. Jyve integrates well with Skype in that it's very easy to talk and chat with other Skype users. Jyve requires that you register to use its Skype-centric communities, but using these communities is free. Jyve allows you to

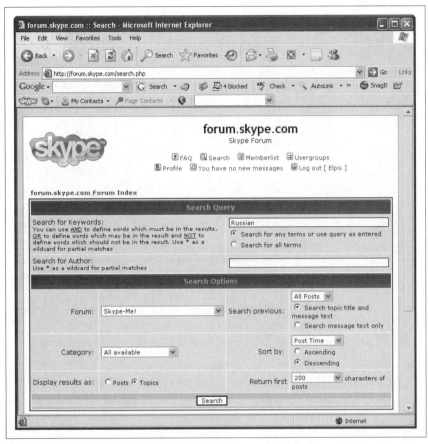

Figure 7-7. Search the Skype-Me! forum for native speakers of a language (in this case, Russian)

focus your efforts when searching for Skype foreign-language-speaking partners, because Jyve captures a good deal of information on your language proficiency level and learning interests. By using Jyve's search tools, you can easily and quickly find fluent speakers of your chosen language, or find others like yourself who are at the same proficiency level and are willing to talk online using Skype to practice speaking (see Figure 7-9).

HACK #69 Build Skype Communities

Create a directory of Skype users who share similar interests, therefore building a community.

Works with: all versions of Skype.

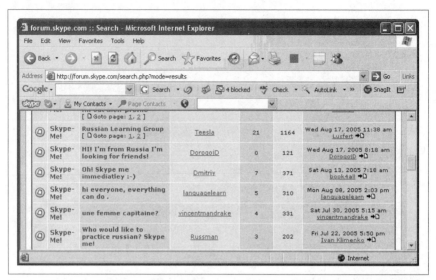

Figure 7-8. Native Russian speakers willing to talk with other Skype users

Are you passionate about a particular area or subject? Then why not build your own Skype community around that interest to share information, talk and chat, and generally form a community of like-minded Skype users!

You first encountered Skype communities in "Learn to Speak a Foreign Language" [Hack #68], where Jyve (*http://www.jyve.com/*) was introduced. However, Jyve is far more than just a community for language learners, as you can use it to create your own interest groups. Here's a step-by-step guide to creating your very own Skype-centric community:

1. First, you must register with Jyve. To register with Jyve you must either be a Skype user, or commit to installing Skype and becoming a user in the near future. Jyve, after all, is an online community that uses Skype as the "glue" that binds the community together. During the registration process, you must give up some personal information (see Figure 7-10); but no one checks the accuracy of this information, so you don't need to divulge anything you don't feel comfortable with.

2. Next, go to the Group area in Jyve and select from one of the top-level categories listed. For example, click on Computers & Technology.

3. Below the top-level categories, you will usually find a number of subcategories that further subdivide the interest area. Continuing our example, click on Software.

4. The Software category is further subdivided into additional categories. Let's click on the Mobile Computing category.

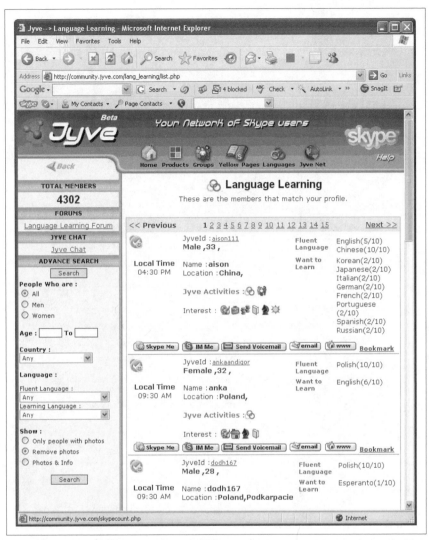

Figure 7-9. Jyve has built communities of Skype users around specific interests, including learning a foreign language

5. Under Mobile Computing, there are no more subcategories. For our example, let's now create a new group called Hacking Mobile Devices. On the web page at Home → Computers & Technology → Software → Mobile Computing, which is where we've navigated to so far in our example, there's a Start New Group for Mobile Computing button. Click on it and you'll be presented with a web page in which to set up the new group (see Figure 7-11).

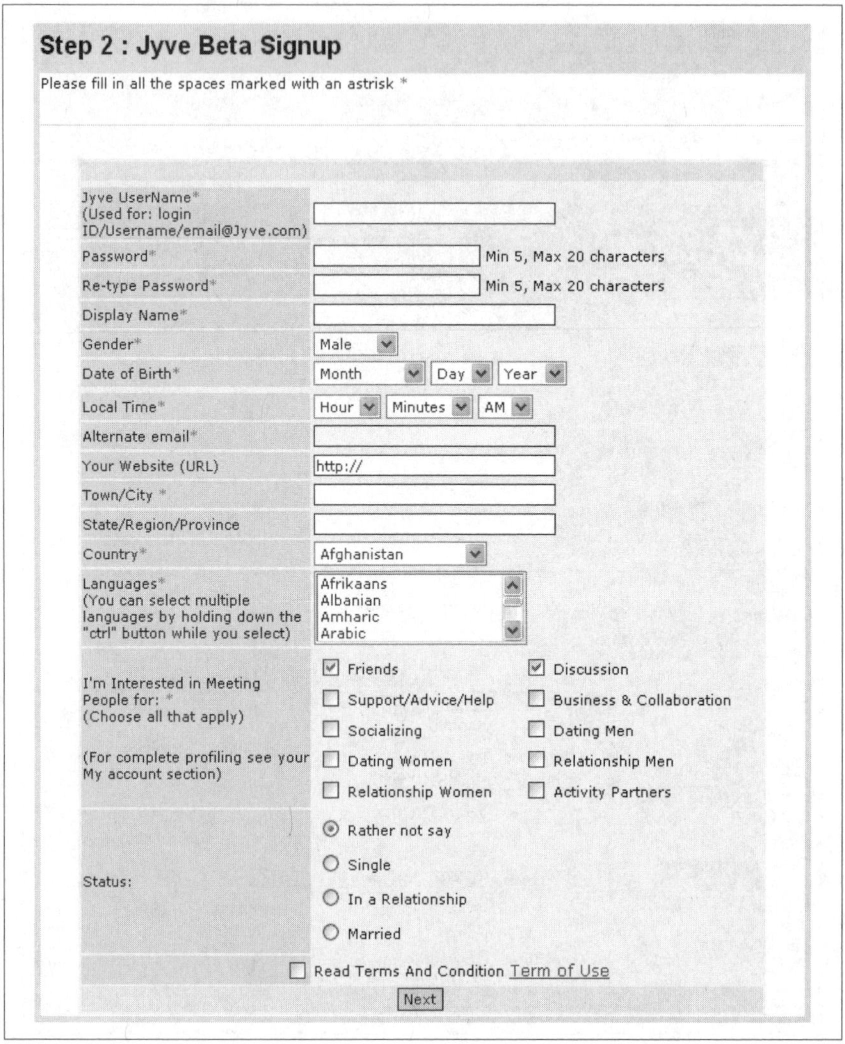

Step 2 : Jyve Beta Signup

Please fill in all the spaces marked with an astrisk *

Jyve UserName* (Used for: login ID/Username/email@Jyve.com)	[_____]
Password*	[_____] Min 5, Max 20 characters
Re-type Password*	[_____] Min 5, Max 20 characters
Display Name*	[_____]
Gender*	Male ▼
Date of Birth*	Month ▼ Day ▼ Year ▼
Local Time*	Hour ▼ Minutes ▼ AM ▼
Alternate email*	[_____]
Your Website (URL)	http://
Town/City *	[_____]
State/Region/Province	[_____]
Country*	Afghanistan ▼
Languages* (You can select multiple languages by holding down the "ctrl" button while you select)	Afrikaans / Albanian / Amharic / Arabic

I'm Interested in Meeting People for: *
(Choose all that apply)

(For complete profiling see your My account section)

☑ Friends ☑ Discussion
☐ Support/Advice/Help ☐ Business & Collaboration
☐ Socializing ☐ Dating Men
☐ Dating Women ☐ Relationship Men
☐ Relationship Women ☐ Activity Partners

Status:

◉ Rather not say
○ Single
○ In a Relationship
○ Married

☐ Read Terms And Condition Term of Use

[Next]

Figure 7-10. Information captured by Jyve during the registration process

6. Once you've created your new group, you can customize it with such things as your own logo, invite others to join the group, and otherwise manage the group's activities (see Figure 7-12).

Now you have a new Skype community whose members are free to call and chat with each other using Skype, as well as use other Jyve online features such as community forums, a shared calendar of events, and much more.

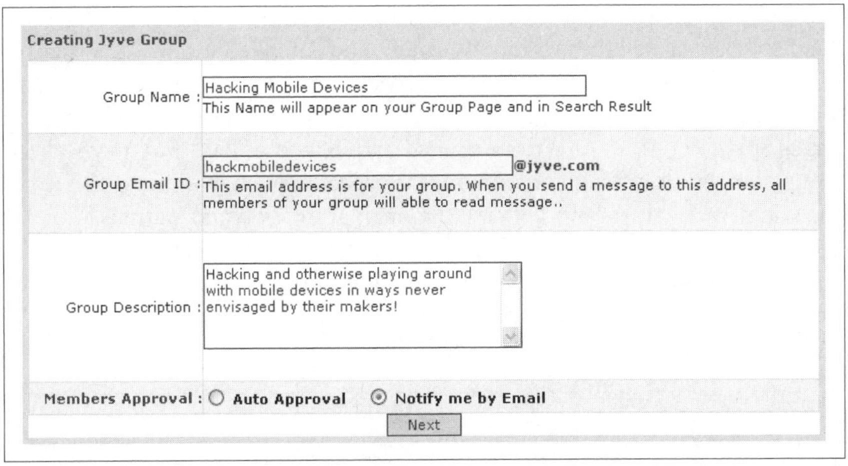

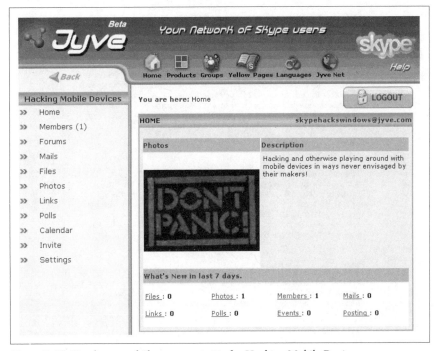

Figure 7-11. Creating a new Jyve interest group

Figure 7-12. Newly created Skype community for Hacking Mobile Devices

Hacking the Hack

Jyve is currently the most Skype-centric community available for Skype users. But other such communities are sure to follow. In addition, you should perhaps not overlook alternative ways of forming Skype communities.

Yahoo! (*http://www.yahoo.com/*) and Google (*http://www.google.com/*) have their own group features: Yahoo! Groups and Google Groups. A search of either using the search term "Skype" shows groups and activities that are centered on Skype users (see Figure 7-13). Yahoo! Groups and Google Groups are not as Skype-centric,or as well integrated with Skype as Jyve. But they've been around longer, have a larger user base, are probably more familiar to most people, and in many ways have better and more mature tools and features for managing online communities and groups. If being Skype-centric is not that important to building your online Skype community—remember, anyone can make their Skype name available by including it with their ordinary name in message postings—Yahoo! Groups or Google Groups is worth considering.

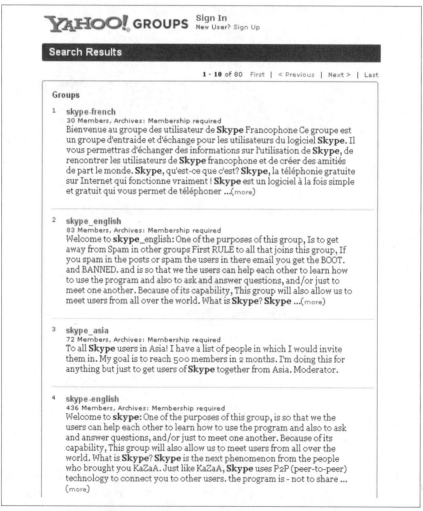

Figure 7-13. Yahoo! Groups already has several active Skype communities

Skype Chat and Voicemail
Hacks 70–73

Sometimes it is easy to forget that Skype is about more than just voice calls. Skype chat and voicemail are key features of Skype in their own right—and both are well worth hacking!

The VBScripts in this chapter use a neat COM component called ActiveS, which you can download free of charge from the KhaosLabs web site, *http://www.khaoslabs.com/actives. php*. It is available in both source code and binary form under a BSD-style license.

VBScripts run using *Windows Scripting Host* (WSH), which is available by default on Windows XP, but which you must install separately on Windows 2000. You can download WSH at *http://www.microsoft.com/downloads/*. Use the keyword "WSH" to find the appropriate download page.

HACK #70 Log Chat Sessions Outside of Skype

Skype can keep a history of your chat sessions, but there are many reasons why you might want to log chat sessions outside of Skype: to publish to a blog, or as an RSS feed, or just as a permanent record, for instance. This hack shows you how to build your own simple chat logger.

Works with: Windows version of Skype.

There are a multitude of reasons why you might want to keep a permanent record of your chat sessions outside of Skype in the form of a simple text file. Having such a file might be useful if you want to publish your chats to a blog, or as an RSS feed, or just for your records. Whatever the reason, switching chat logging on and off is a snap using this hack.

You can set up Skype to keep a history of your chat sessions (select Skype → Tools → Options → Privacy → Keep chat history), but each session is kept separately. So if you want the text for a particular chat session, or all chat sessions, you'd better brace yourself for a lot of cut and paste! This hack provides a means of creating a single logfile outside of Skype for all of your chat sessions.

This hack uses two scripts, *start_chat_log.vbs* and *stop_chat_log.vbs*, to start and stop logging of chat sessions, respectively.

Use this script, *start_chat_log.vbs*, to start logging a Skype chat session:

```
' File: start_chat_log.vbs

' To use this script yourself, you will need to change
' the path and filename of the chat log file stored
' in the variable strLogFile.

Dim objFSO, objLogFile, objSkype, objSemaphore
Dim strTempFolder, strSemaphoreName, strLogFile
Set objFSO = WScript.CreateObject("Scripting.FileSystemObject")
Set objSkype = WScript.CreateObject("SkypeAPI.Access", _
                                    "SkypeAPI_")
strLogFile = "C:\Temp\Skype\ChatLog.txt"
Set objLogFile = objFSO.OpenTextFile(strLogFile, 8, True)

' Skype event handlers
Sub SkypeAPI_ChatMessageSent(ChatMessage)
Dim msg_from
Set msg_from = ChatMessage.MessageFrom
    objLogFile.WriteLine("Chat sent by " & msg_from.Handle & _
                         " at " & Now & ":")
    objLogFile.WriteLine(ChatMessage.Body)
    objLogFile.WriteLine("")
End Sub
Sub SkypeAPI_ChatMessageReceived(ChatMessage)
Dim msg_from
Set msg_from = ChatMessage.MessageFrom
    objLogFile.WriteLine("Chat received from " & msg_from.Handle & _
                         " at " & Now & ":")
    objLogFile.WriteLine(ChatMessage.Body)
    objLogFile.WriteLine("")
End Sub

' Main script begins here
strTempFolder = objFSO.GetSpecialFolder(2)
strSemaphoreName = objFSO.BuildPath(strTempFolder, _
                                    "chat_logging.tmp")
Set objSemaphore = objFSO.CreateTextFile(strSemaphoreName, true)
objSemaphore.Close
objSkype.ConnectAndWait 15000
Do While objFSO.FileExists(strSemaphoreName)
    WScript.Sleep 500
Loop
objLogFile.Close
```

Use this script, *stop_chat_log.vbs*, to stop logging a Skype chat session:

```
' File: stop_chat_log.vbs

' Main script begins here
Dim objFSO, strTempFolder
Set objFSO = WScript.CreateObject("Scripting.FileSystemObject")
strTempFolder = objFSO.GetSpecialFolder(2)
objFSO.DeleteFile objFSO.BuildPath(strTempFolder, _
                            "chat_logging.tmp")
```

The easiest way to use these scripts is to turn them into shortcuts and assign them hotkeys. Create a shortcut named Start Chat Log that points to *start_chat_log.vbs* as its target, then right-click on the shortcut and choose Properties. In the shortcut properties dialog that is displayed, select the tab named Shortcut, click on the text entry field opposite "Shortcut key," press the key sequence you want as your hotkey (for example, Shift-Alt-L for "Log"), and then click OK. Do the same for *stop_chat_log.vbs*, giving its shortcut the name Stop Chat Log and a different hotkey sequence (for example, Shift-Alt-O for "Off"). Now, before—or even during—a chat session, you can switch logging on and off using only a couple of hotkey sequences!

Automatically Forward Voicemail

Have all incoming voicemail forwarded to an email address of your choice as soon as it arrives.

Works with: Windows version of Skype.

This is one of those features you feel sure should be built into Skype, but isn't. Until it is, you'll need a Skype add-on to do the job, and for automatically forwarding all your voicemail to an email address, there is no better tool than Pamela Professional (€17.50, about $22, from *http://www.pamela-systems.com/*).

Skype uses a proprietary and undocumented (outside of Skype, at least) format for its voicemail audio files, which have a *.dat* file extension and can normally be found in this folder: C:\Documents and Settings*Username**Application Data**Skype**Skypename**voicemail*, where *Username* is the name used to log on to the machine and *Skypename* is the name used to log on to Skype. This is unfortunate, as it means you cannot easily listen to, archive, or exchange Skype voicemail outside of Skype.

Setting up voicemail forwarding in Pamela is simplicity itself. Select Pamela → Tools → Options → Email forwarding, and set up how, and to what email address, you want your voicemail forwarded (see Figure 8-1).

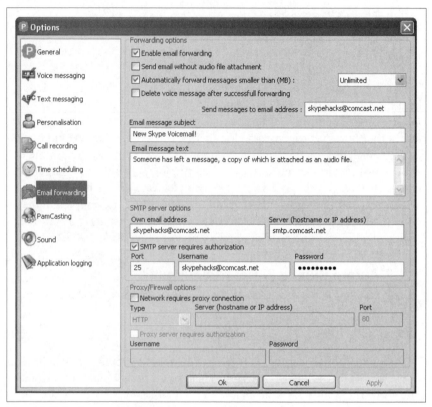

Figure 8-1. Setting up voicemail forwarding using Pamela

Pamela forwards your voicemail as *.wav* files, which you can play easily by opening them (in your default playback application for *.wav* files) from directly within the received email (see Figure 8-2), or by saving them to disk for later. Just right-click on the *.wav* file attachment and choose Open or Save As....

Pamela uses a format for the name of the attached voicemail audio file that tells you a good deal about who left you voicemail, and when. Its format is *msg_skypename_dd_mmm_yyyy_hh_mm_ss.wav*, where *skypename* is the name of the Skype user who left the voicemail, *dd_mm_yyyy* is the date on which the voicemail was left, and *hh_mm_ss* is the time at which the voicemail was left.

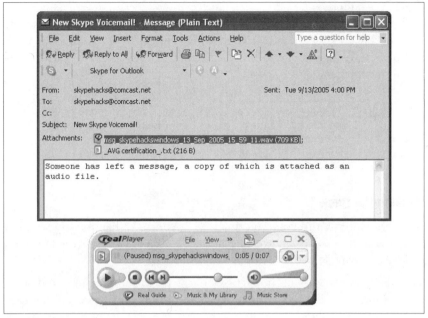

Figure 8-2. Playing voicemail (in this case, using RealPlayer) forwarded by Pamela, directly from the email message

Listen to Voicemail Using a USB Handset

HACK #72

Are you tired of switching from your USB handset to your PC sound system just to hear your voicemail? With this hack, you don't have to switch from your USB handset to listen to voicemail.

Works with: Windows version of Skype.

Until I came up with this hack, I had to switch my playback audio device within Skype (by selecting Skype → Tools → Options... → Sound Devices) just to hear my voicemail messages. And if I forgot to switch back to my USB handset for audio-out, no sound would come out of the handset during my next call. All very irritating.

The good news is that you can listen to your voicemail messages using a USB handset that has a keypad, if you do the following. First, switch to the Dial tab. Otherwise, when you press the # key on your handset, Skype will most likely start a call if you are in either the Contacts or the Call List tab. Pressing the # key on your handset while in the Dial tab will effectively put the handset into listen and speak mode, but as there's no number or contact to dial from within the Dial tab, no call will be started. Now switch to the Call List tab and select the voicemail message to listen to, and then click the

Play button. Once you're done listening to your voicemail message, hang up in the usual way and everything will be back to the way it was. No longer will you have to scramble to switch audio devices in the middle of a call because you're able to speak into your handset, but you can't hear the person at the other end of the call.

> On many USB handsets, the # key tells Skype to start a call and effectively puts the handset into listen and speak mode. However, if your handset doesn't use the # key for this function, you may have to experiment to find the correct key to do the same thing.

Hacking the Hack

Now you can listen to your voicemail using your USB handset. So why not also record your voicemail greeting using a USB handset that has a keypad, instead of having to use a microphone or headset?

This hack is a variation of the first part of the hack, and the same comments and warnings for that hack apply here. Recording your voicemail message using your USB handset, without all the fuss and without needing to switch the audio-in device back and forth from within Skype, is simple, if you follow these steps.

First, switch to the Dial tab. Press the # key on your USB handset to put it into listen and speak mode. Now, go to Skype → Tools → Options... → Call Forwarding & Voicemail and click on the Record button (see Figure 8-3). Speak your greeting into your handset to record it. Stop recording by clicking the Stop button. Click the Playback button to replay your message using your handset speaker. If you're satisfied, save your voicemail recording and hang up as you would normally. You've recorded your voicemail greeting, without the fuss of switching audio devices.

Run Commands Remotely Using Chat

#73   Have you ever wanted to run a shell command on a remote machine? This hack shows a simple way you can do this using Skype chat as the communications mechanism.

Works with: Windows version of Skype.

Have you ever wanted to run a command on a remote machine? If so, this hack is for you.

By leaving Skype and this script, *run_command.vbs*, running on a remote machine, you can use Skype chat to send commands—in fact, any command

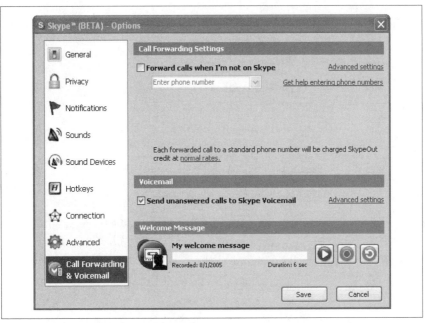

Figure 8-3. Record and play back your voicemail greeting

you could run from the command line were you sitting at that computer—to be executed on the remote machine. Moreover, as commands will be executed *only* for a named Skype user, and because Skype chat is encrypted end to end, you can run the commands in a relatively secure fashion.

```
' File: run_command.vbs

' To use this script yourself, you will need to change:
' 1) The name of the Skype user, held in strSkypeHostName,
'    on the host machine that will run commands.
' 2) The name of the remote Skype user, held in
'    strSkypeRemoteName, who is allowed to run commands
'    on the host machine.

Dim objShell, objSkype, objExec, strChatID
Dim strSkypeHostName, strSkypeRemoteName
Set objShell = WScript.CreateObject ("WScript.shell")
Set objSkype = WScript.CreateObject("SkypeAPI.Access", _
                                    "SkypeAPI_")

' Only process commands on this host for this remote user
strSkypeHostName = "ajtsheppard"
strSkypeRemoteName = "skypehackswindows"

' Initialize
strChatID = ""
Set objExec = Nothing
```

```
' Skype event handler
Sub SkypeAPI_ChatMessageReceived(ChatMessage)

    On Error Resume Next
    Dim objMsgFrom, objChat

    Set objChat = ChatMessage.Chat
    strChatID = objChat.Name

    Set objMsgFrom = ChatMessage.MessageFrom

    If objMsgFrom.Handle = strSkypeRemoteName Then
        Set objExec = objShell.Exec(ChatMessage.Body)
        If Err <> 0 Then
            objSkype.SendBlockingCommand("CHATMESSAGE " & _
                                        strChatID & _
                                        " Unable to run: " & _
                                        ChatMessage.Body)
            strChatID = ""
            Set objExec = Nothing
        End If
    Else
        objSkype.SendBlockingCommand("CHATMESSAGE " & _
                                     strChatID & _
                                     " You are not authorized" & _
                                     " to run: " & ChatMessage.Body)
        strChatID = ""
        Set objExec = Nothing
    End If
End Sub

' Main script begins here
objSkype.ConnectAndWait 15000
Do While True
    WScript.Sleep 500
    ' Send a chat message back when the command has completed
    If Not (objExec Is Nothing) Then
        If objExec.status <> 0 Then
            objSkype.SendBlockingCommand("CHATMESSAGE " & _
                                         strChatID & _
                                         " StdOut: " & _
                                         objExec.StdOut.ReadAll)
            objSkype.SendBlockingCommand("CHATMESSAGE " & _
                                         strChatID & _
                                         " StdErr: " & _
                                         objExec.StdErr.ReadAll)
            strChatID = ""
            Set objExec = Nothing
        End If
    End If
Loop
```

The script *run_command.vbs* will continue running until it is either killed explicitly, you log off, or you shut down your machine.

Running commands remotely has never been so easy. For example, by running Skype and *run_command.vbs* on the target (or host) machine with "ajtsheppard" logged onto Skype, "skypehackswindows" on a different machine can send a command as a chat message to "ajtsheppard"—say, calc (which is what you would enter at the command line on the remote target machine to run Calculator, were you sitting there)—and it will run and pop up "Calculator" on the remote target machine (see Figure 8-4). Running Calculator on a remote machine is just an example, because *any* command you could enter and run at the command line while sitting at the remote target machine, you can now run remotely using this hack.

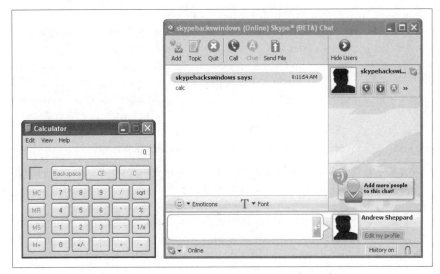

Figure 8-4. Running Calculator on a remote machine using Skype chat

It's also important to realize that while the target machine must be running Windows to take advantage of this hack, *any* other version of Skype running anywhere can be used to send commands to that target machine using chat.

## CHAPTER NINE

Security and Privacy
Hacks 74–78

Skype, like any social community, has its pluses and minuses, its pros and cons. It is also a community with a truly global reach. There probably isn't a country in the world that doesn't have some sort of representation within the Skype community, and for some countries those numbers are now very large. However, like all social communities and networks, Skype represents all sorts of people, both good and bad. For that reason, you must take responsibility for, and control over, how you interact with the Skype community at large. The hacks in this chapter will help you do exactly that, as they address security and privacy issues arising from using Skype.

Having said that, I should make you aware of two additional security issues that I discuss elsewhere in this book. File transfer has the potential to infect your computer with a virus, an issue I discuss in this chapter. However, it is possible to disable Skype's file-transfer function altogether (see "Disable Skype File Transfer" [Hack #58]). Similarly, the Skype Application Programming Interface (API) has the potential to be misused by malicious Skype add-ons, and can similarly be disabled (see "Disable the Skype API" [Hack #100]).

Manage Your Skype Privacy Settings
Manage your privacy settings to avoid being contacted by people with whom you don't want to speak or chat.

Works with: all versions of Skype.

You can think of Skype as a large online community of people that spans the globe. This can be a wonderful resource and an almost inexhaustible source of social contacts. However, if you value your privacy, or are simply less interested in the social aspects of Skype, use the advice in this hack to tailor your privacy settings so that you have the visibility within the Skype community that you desire.

Before I discuss the specifics of Skype's privacy settings, you need to understand how your online status, which is available to other Skype users, affects how you interact with others in the Skype online community:

Online (default)
You can make and receive calls, chat, and voicemail. You can also send and receive files. Who can contact you depends on your privacy settings.

Offline
This shuts down Skype's connection to the Internet, so no traffic flows between Skype running on your machine and the Skype network. This means you can't make and receive calls, chat, and voicemail. Nor can you send and receive files.

Skype Me
This is like hanging out a notice that says, "I'm here and I want to be contacted by the wider Skype community." This mode of being online disables all your privacy settings, but only for the period in which you are in Skype Me mode. Also, this is the only online status mode that you can use as part of a search for Skype users (select Skype → Tools → Search for Skype Users..., and in the search window check the "Search for people who are in 'Skype Me' mode" checkbox).

Away
This mode lets people know you are online, but that you're away from your computer. You can set this online status to activate automatically after a period of inactivity (select Skype → Tools → Options... → General, and enter the number of minutes of inactivity after which you want to automatically switch to Away status; the default is 5 minutes, but entering a value of 0 will mean that you'll never automatically switch to Away).

Not Available
This is similar to Away, but indicates that you are away from your computer for a prolonged period. You can set this online status to activate automatically after a period of inactivity (select Skype → Tools → Options... → General, and then enter the number of minutes of inactivity after which you want to automatically switch to Not Available status; the default is 20 minutes, but entering a value of 0 will mean that you'll never automatically switch to Not Available).

Do Not Disturb
To others you are "Online," but you will not be disturbed by ringing or pop-up notifications for incoming calls or chat. All that you will see is a different Skype icon in the system tray indicating that an event has occurred.

Invisible

> To others you are Offline, but you can continue to use Skype freely. However, you only *look* Offline, and in reality, your privacy settings for being Online are in effect.

You can change your online status using the following methods:

Windows

> Use the pull-down menu in the lower-lefthand corner of the Skype window (see Figure 9-1). Or, from the menu bar, select Skype → File → Change Status and pick one of the settings.

Linux

> Use the pull-down menu in the lower-lefthand corner of the Skype window. Or, from the menu bar, select Skype → File → Change Status and pick one of the settings.

Mac OS X

> Use the pull-down menu in the lower-lefthand corner of the Skype window. Or, from the menu bar, select Skype → Account → Change Status and pick one of the settings.

Pocket PC

> Click on the online status button at the bottom of the screen, and then pick one of the settings.

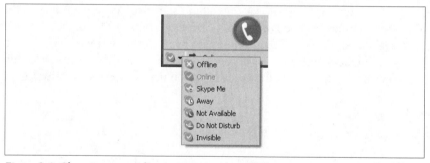

Figure 9-1. Changing your online status using the pull-down menu

Skype has several privacy-related settings that are under your control. Unfortunately, you can't set them en masse, so to speak. So you can't, for example, simply click on a single button or menu item and have your privacy settings be set to "high." You have to set privacy settings one by one. However, to help you construct a privacy policy of your own that is consistent with "very high," "high," "medium," and "low" privacy, you may find Table 9-1 helpful. Likewise, these descriptions of the terms used in the table may also be helpful:

Anyone

As its name suggests, this privacy setting means anyone can call you or send chat to you.

Contacts only

No one outside your Contacts list can call or chat with you. In this case, people who try to call you will be refused, but with an informative message (see Figure 9-2).

Authorized people only

This means that only people you have explicitly authorized can call or chat with you. When someone requests authorization, you have three choices: allow the person to see and contact you (in which case, you also have the choice of whether to add them to your Contacts list); allow the person to contact you, but don't notify them when you're online; and block the person from contacting you.

Known numbers

Known numbers are numbers that you have set up in your SkypeOut list. Skype will accept only incoming calls from these numbers.

History

Your chat history may contain some private exchanges with others, so it is something you might want purged from your computer from time to time.

Show my picture

You can choose for which contacts your profile picture should appear during a call or chat.

Enable Bonjour

Bonjour is a zero-configuration wireless connection technology from Apple. You can auto-authorize Bonjour contacts for use within Skype.

Figure 9-2. When you tell Skype to restrict the calls you receive, any nonauthorized caller normally gets an informative message as to why their call failed

You always have the option of accepting or rejecting file-transfer requests. Clearly, don't accept any file transfer from anyone you don't know. In fact, think twice about accepting file transfers from people you do know! Accepting files from anyone, known or unknown, runs the risk of infecting your computer with a virus. That is why you should scan every file you download for viruses. I discuss this topic in another hack in this chapter (see "Scan Files Received via Skype for Viruses" [Hack #75]).

Table 9-1. Suggested privacy settings for "low," "medium," "high," and "very high" privacy

Privacy setting	Default	Low	Medium	High	Very high
Online status: Online	✔		✔		
Online status: Skype Me		✔			
Online status: Do Not Disturb				✔	
Online status: Invisible					✔
Calls: Anyone	✔	✔			
Calls: Contacts only			✔		
Calls: Authorized people only				✔	✔
SkypeIn: Anyone	✔	✔			
SkypeIn: Known numbers			✔		
SkypeIn: My contacts				✔	✔
Chat: Anyone	✔	✔			
Chat: Contacts only			✔		
Chat: Authorized people only				✔	✔
Chat: History	✔	Forever	One month	Two weeks	None
Show my picture (Mac only)	Authorized	Anyone	Contacts	Contacts	Authorized
Enable Bonjour (Mac only)		✔			

You can set privacy options for SkypeIn only if you are a SkypeIn subscriber. And even if you are a SkypeIn subscriber, you can't set SkypeIn privacy options using the Pocket PC version of Skype.

You can change your online status using one of the methods described earlier in this hack. You can set the other options in Table 9-1 as follows.

Windows and Linux
> Select Skype → Tools → Options... → Privacy (see Figure 9-3).

Mac OS X
> Select Skype → Preferences... → Privacy, and Skype → Preferences... → Chat for chat history.

Pocket PC
> Select Skype → Tools → Options....

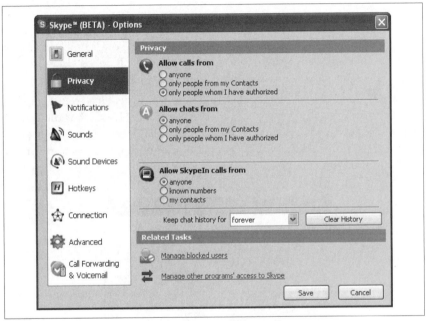

Figure 9-3. Privacy options (if you are not a SkypeIn subscriber, the category "Allow SkypeIn calls from" does not appear)

Relationships change. Partnerships change. For this reason, Skype allows you to change the authorization status of existing contacts and, if necessary, block them. Note that deleting a contact does not necessarily block the contact, as that depends on your privacy settings. For example, if you allow calls from "Anyone," a deleted contact can still call. In contrast, blocked users cannot see your online status, nor can they contact you in any way.

To block unwanted calls, chats, and SkypeIn calls, you must either raise the level of your privacy settings, or block specific Skype users. To do the latter, you have the following methods available to you.

Windows and Linux

In the Contacts or Call List tab, right-click on a contact or call and choose "Block this User." This will display a dialog that will enable you to block and, if desired, remove the selected user from your Contacts list (see Figure 9-4). Alternatively, or to manage your complete list of blocked users, select Skype → Tools → Managed Blocked Users... or (Windows only) Skype → Tools → Options... → Privacy and click on "Manage blocked users."

Mac OS X

In the Contacts or Call List tab, click on a contact or call, and then select Skype → Contacts → Block. To manage your complete list of blocked users, select Skype → Contacts → Manage Blocked Users....

Pocket PC

In the Contacts or Log tab, click and hold the stylus on a contact or call, and then from the pop-up list, choose "Block this User." For the Pocket PC version of Skype, there is no option available to manage your complete list of blocked users. You must block and unblock each user from within the Contacts or Log tab.

Figure 9-4. Blocking a user

If necessary, you can unblock blocked users. The procedure is more or less identical to that for blocking a user, except you will need to choose "Unblock this User" at the same points at which you were previously given the choice to "Block this User."

HACK #75 Scan Files Received via Skype for Viruses

Check files you receive via Skype file transfer immediately for viruses.

Works with: Windows, Linux, and Mac OS X versions of Skype.

File transfer using Skype is both simple and secure. Secure in the sense that files are transferred using end-to-end encryption, *not* in the sense that they are free from viruses.

You should never accept file transfers from strangers. But even receiving files from friends and contacts is not without some risk. Whoever is sending you a file might be doing so from a machine—unknown to them—that is infected with viruses. By sending you a file, they may unwittingly infect your machine too. Skype is well aware of this potential *vector* (means of infection) for viruses, and that is why the recipient of a file transfer always has the option of accepting or rejecting the file transfer. Moreover, Skype is quite explicit about the need to scan received files for viruses (see Figure 9-5).

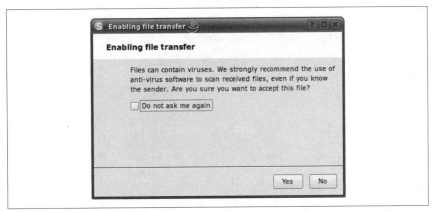

Figure 9-5. Skype warns of the potential for infecting your machine with a virus by accepting a file transfer (Linux)

Fortunately, scanning files for viruses and, in some cases, fixing them is easy with most of today's antivirus software. Most antivirus software has a nice GUI that allows you to scan your whole machine, or a specific file or folder. So, immediately after receiving any file, you should—before opening it—scan it for viruses. By default, Skype deposits transferred file into these folders:

Windows
    C:\Documents and Settings\UserName\My Documents\My Skype Received Files

Linux
    /home/UserName

Mac OS X
    /home/UserName/Library/Application Support/Skype/SkypeName

UserName is the username you use to log on to your machine, and SkypeName is the name under which you signed into Skype.

If you are the type of person who shuns the GUI, you always have the option of scanning received files at the command line. Here are some examples of scanning from the command prompt:

Windows (AVG Free Edition, http://free.grisoft.com/)

```
cd C:\Documents and Settings\Andrew Sheppard\My Documents\My Skype
Received Files

AVG /clean /arc /report scan.log /scan *.*
```

Linux (Clam AntiVirus, http://www.clamav.net/)

```
cd /home/shep

clamscan --recursive -remove --stdout . > scan.log
```

Mac OS X (Clam AntiVirus, http://www.clamav.net/)

```
cd /home/shep/Library/Application Support/Skype/skypehacksmac

clamscan --recursive --remove -stdout . > scan.log
```

In these examples, I used the free antivirus software listed. However, if you use something different, check your product's documentation, as you will most likely find that you can run it from the command line.

Hacking the Hack

Scanning transferred files can soon become a chore you could do without. Fortunately, automating the process is easy, as these scripts demonstrate. Each time a new file appears in your default file-transfer folder, it will be scanned and, if possible, cleaned of any viruses. Or, if necessary, the file will be removed (deleted).

> All the scripts presented in this hack will start scanning files in your default Skype file-transfer folder only *after* they start running. In the case of Windows and Linux, you can have the scripts do an initial scan on startup as well by changing the initial file count *outside* the do-while loop, like this: num_files = 0 (Windows), numfiles = 0 (Linux).

Windows (VBScript, AVG Free Edition).

```
' File: virus_scan.vbs

' To use this script yourself, you will need to
' change skype_file_transfer_folder and
' run_anti_virus to be compatible with folder
' locations and the anti-virus software you
' have installed on your computer. Files infected
' with a virus are cleaned automatically.
```

```
Dim objShell, objFSO, objFolder, objFiles, objExec
Dim skype_file_transfer_folder, num_files, run_anti_virus
Set objShell = WScript.CreateObject("WScript.Shell")
Set objFSO = WScript.CreateObject("Scripting.FileSystemObject")
skype_file_transfer_folder = "C:\Documents and Settings\" & _
                             "Andrew Sheppard\My Documents\" & _
                             "My Skype Received Files"
run_anti_virus = "C:\Program Files\Grisoft\AVG Free\AVG.exe " & _
                 "/clean /arc /report scan.log /scan *.*"

Set objFolder = objFSO.GetFolder(skype_file_transfer_folder)
Set objFiles = objFolder.Files
num_files = objFiles.Count

Do
    If objFiles.count > num_files Then

        objShell.CurrentDirectory = skype_file_transfer_folder

        Set objExec = objShell.Exec(run_anti_virus)

        Do While objExec.Status = 0
            WScript.Sleep 100
        Loop

    End If

    num_files = objFiles.count

    WScript.Sleep 5000 ' Go to sleep for 5 seconds

Loop While True
```

Linux (Python, Clam AntiVirus).

```
#!/usr/bin/env python
# -*- coding: iso-8859-15 -*-

# File: virus_scan.py

# To use this script yourself, you will need to
# change the paths to be compatible with folder
# locations and the anti-virus software you
# have installed on your computer. Files infected
# with a virus are removed automatically.

import os, time, sys

def num_files():
    file_count = 0
    for root, dirs, files in os.walk('/home/shep/skype_file_transfer'):
        file_count += len(files)
    return file_count
```

```
def main( ):
    numfiles = num_files( )
    while 1:
        if num_files( ) > numfiles:
            output = os.popen('clamscan --recursive ' \
            + '--remove --stdout ' \
            + '/home/shep/skype_file_transfer').read( )
            file = open(r'/home/shep/' + \
            'skype_file_transfer/scan.log', 'a')
            file.write('---- START SCAN ----\n\n')
            file.write(output)
            file.write('\n---- END SCAN ----\n\n')
            file.close( )
            print output
        numfiles = num_files( )
        time.sleep(5)
    return 0

if __name__ == "__main__":
    main( )
```

Mac OS X (AppleScript, Clam AntiVirus). This AppleScript, *virus_scan.scpt*, can be attached to a folder-action—in this case, the "new item alert" action—that will run the script every time a new file is added to your default folder for file transfers. This means that every time you accept a file transfer to this folder, the script will run and check it for viruses.

To set up a folder-action, in the Finder application locate the default Skype file-transfer folder, Ctrl-Click on it, choose Attach a Folder Action..., and then attach the *virus_scan.scpt* script. Now, every time you accept a file transfer, you know it will be scanned for viruses immediately. This script will run on action until you disable or delete the folder-action with which it is associated. Even after rebooting, it'll still be there doing its job!

To have *virus_scan.scpt* available as a folder-action script, you must put it in the folder-action scripts folder, */Library/Scripts/Folder Action Scripts/*:

```
-- File: virus_scan.scpt

-- To use this script yourself, you will need to
-- change the path to be compatible with folder
-- locations and the anti-virus software you
-- have installed on your computer. Files infected
-- with a virus are removed automatically.

do shell script "cd /home/shep/Library/Application Support/Skype/ ¬
skypehacksmac ; clamscan --recursive --remove --stdout . >> scan.log"
```

Manage (or Delete) Your Skype Public Profile

Having a comprehensive online public profile for Skype can be a great way
for people to find you, but you should be careful in terms of what you make
public and what you keep private.

Works with: Windows, Linux, and Mac OS X versions of Skype.

Your public profile is how you advertise whom and what you are to the
Skype community. As such, it can be a great resource. But like any resource,
it should be managed.

Before discussing how to manage (or delete) your Skype profile, it's worth
pausing a moment or two to understand how Skype maintains your profile.
Without such an understanding, you cannot manage your profile intelligently.

Your profile is stored on the Skype network. This is good in the sense that
your profile follows you wherever you go: fly halfway around the world and
log onto Skype, and there it will be; the same profile you last saw at home.

But because of how Skype's peer-to-peer technology works, your profile typically persists for only around 72 hours following your last use of Skype.
That is, after 72 hours of being offline, someone who is searching for you by
means of the profile you stored on the Skype network might not find you.

Another thing to bear in mind is that Skype names persist forever; that is,
names are never recycled or reused. So, in some sense, you never can delete
a Skype name. Later in this hack, I will show you how to get as close as possible to eradicating a Skype account from the face of the Earth!

Manage Your Profile

You manage your profile through the My Profile dialog (select Skype → File
→ My Profile... on Windows, Skype → File → Your Personal Profile... on
Linux, or Skype → Account → My Profile... on Mac OS X; managing your
profile is not available on Pocket PC); see Figure 9-6.

When creating and later managing your Skype profile, you should think
carefully about the following:

- All profile information is optional.
- Your profile is what you make public to the Skype community. Be careful not to give too much away. Everything in your profile, except your
  email address, is available for any Skype user to see. However, even your
  email address can be used in a Skype user search (in which case, the person searching must clearly already know it).

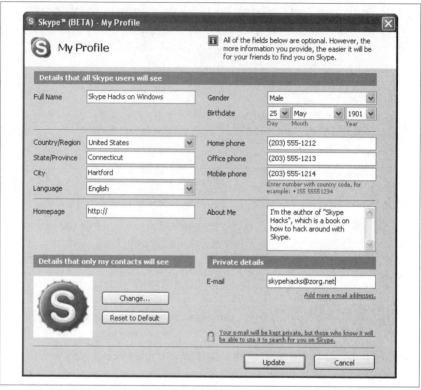

Figure 9-6. Updating your Skype profile

- Your profile follows you wherever you go, but your avatar picture will not.

- Some people don't accept calls or chat from anyone who doesn't have a fairly complete profile. The rationale is that if you're willing to share details about yourself, you're less likely to be a mischief-maker and people can find you more easily.

- The information you put in your profile doesn't have to be true (which negates the preceding point to some degree), as it's not checked or validated by Skype, or by anyone else.

- All profile data is signed digitally, to make it impossible to tamper with it.

Delete Your Profile

Because your profile as stored on the Skype network typically expires after 72 hours of being offline, one option to "delete" your Skype profile is simply to let it expire and die a natural death. However, as Skype is a closed source application and its policy of how profile data is stored is subject to change, how can you really know when, and if, all your profile data was deleted? For this reason, and for peace of mind, I recommend overwriting your entire profile with junk data and updating your online profile.

Hacking the Hack (Windows Only)

To help you to delete (overwrite) your Skype profile with a simple click of the mouse, you can use the following keystroke sequence. Note that this keystroke sequence uses the VBScript *drive_skype.vbs*, which you'll need to have on your machine and on your path (see "Accelerate Skype Using Your Keyboard" [Hack #44] for details). Simply make the following command the target of a shortcut, or run it from the run line (select Start → Run...), and your profile will be history in a few heartbeats! This command might be particularly useful if you have, or as part of your job are responsible for, several Skype names, and all of them need to have their profiles zapped. If you don't want to enter this command by hand and would prefer to use cut and paste, you can download the command as a text file, *delete_profile.txt*, from the book's web site, *http://www.oreilly.com/catalog/SkypeHacks/index.html*.

```
drive_skype.vbs "^+S|%(FM)|{DEL}|{TAB}|{DEL}|{TAB}|{DEL}|{TAB}|{DEL}|
{TAB}|{DEL}|{TAB}|{DEL}|{TAB}|{DEL}|{TAB}|{DEL}|{TAB}|{DEL}|{TAB}|
{DEL}|{TAB}|{DEL}|{TAB}|{DEL}|{TAB}|{DEL}|{TAB}|^A{DEL}|{TAB}{TAB}|
{ENTER}|{TAB}|{DEL}|{TAB}|{ENTER}"
```

HACK #77   Avoid Skype "Spammers"

Skype, like any other online service, has its dark side. Here are some tips on how to avoid spammers.

Works with: all versions of Skype.

Unless you have incredibly restrictive Skype privacy settings, you will at some time or another experience some form of unwanted attention from spammers. The term *spammer*, as used in this hack, is a person who contacts you (or attempts to contact you, possibly repeatedly) by voice (phone calls or voicemail messages), chat, or file transfer and who wants something from you. Characteristically, this attempt to communicate with you is unsolicited on your part.

Fortunately, Skype provides several tools to thwart spammers. These, in combination with some common sense, can do a lot to make spammers only an occasional nuisance, rather than a continuous annoyance. Here's a checklist of things to do to thwart spammers:

- Choose a sensible Skype name. Avoid anything provocative or that might attract unnecessary attention.
- Configure your Skype privacy settings as described earlier in this chapter.

- Control when you are online, by using your online status or by controlling when Skype runs. Never make your status "Skype Me," as that temporarily ignores your privacy settings.

- If you have a SkypeIn number (which allows people with regular telephones to contact you), be careful whom you give it to. Also, add your number to a registry that lists your number as not wanting unsolicited calls from telemarketers. Such registries include *https://www.donotcall. gov/* in the U.S., and *http://www.tpsonline.org.uk/tps/* in the UK. You can lodge complaints through these web sites too.

- Some SkypeIn calls list the number that is calling in the call window. This number also is recorded in your call list. If the spammer is particularly offensive or persistent, or both, you can always pass this number on to the police and see what they can do. In this case, you might want to record some of the calls as evidence.

- Don't let children use Skype without close parental supervision.

Unfortunately, there is no meaningful mechanism for reporting spammers to Skype so that it can take action on your behalf. As a last resort, you always have the option of setting up a new Skype name and a new SkypeIn number, as there's no restriction on how many you can have of either of these. This may be inconvenient for contacts you want to call, as you need to inform them of your new Skype name (and SkypeIn number, if you are a subscriber), but hopefully, it will solve your old spammer problem. Of course, you still run the risk that new spammers will find you!

Hacking the Hack (Windows Only)

Spammers might be more reluctant to target you repeatedly if you can fight back. Perhaps they might be more reluctant to call again if you can tell them that you have their IP address, which in some cases, can be used to trace where they are calling from.

Here's how you can find a spammer's IP address (voice call or chat):

1. Enable "Display technical call info" (select Skype → Tools → Options... → Advanced, and check the "Display technical call info" checkbox), as this will allow you to determine during a phone call whether the other party is connected directly with you or whether the call is being relayed. Unfortunately, this doesn't work for chat, so you'll have to *assume* a direct connection. This method of finding a spammer's IP address works only if your connection is direct and is *not* being relayed.

2. Keep the other person talking or exchanging chat messages while you follow steps 3 through 6, as this procedure works only while there is a communications link between you and the other person.

3. Check whether the person you are talking to has a direct connection with you. With "Display technical call info" enabled, let your mouse hover over their avatar picture in the call window and the technical details of the call will be displayed in a pop-up window. Look at the number of "Relays" you have; for direct communication, you will see a value of 0.

4. Open a command prompt window (select Start → Accessories → Command Prompt), enter the command netstat –b, and press Return. You should see something similar to that shown in Figure 9-7 (incidentally, the figure shows a fake IP address).

5. Armed with the output of netstat, you can enter the IP address you found in an "IP locator" web page (Googling on "IP locator" will provide a list), which may then be able to tell you the caller's physical location (see Figure 9-8, which shows the output you get from the IP locator at *http://www.geobytes.com/IpLocator.htm*). You should be aware that this is not an exact science, and finding someone's location from their IP address is by no means certain; indeed, some IP locators give an estimate of the certainty with which they have located the remote IP address (see the Certainty box in Figure 9-8).

6. Send this chat message if chatting, or say this if in a call: "I know where you are, you're calling from *X*" (substitute the location you obtained from the IP locator for *X*). This might be a sufficient deterrent for scaring away some spammers.

Sadly, like many weapons, netstat and IP locator are like a two-edged sword, in that another person can use them to find out where you are! This is one occasion in which sitting behind a restrictive and Peer-to-Peer (P2P)-unfriendly firewall works to your advantage, as it is more likely that your calls will be relayed rather than directed.

Figure 9-7. Running netstat during a call or chat session can sometimes reveal the other party's IP address

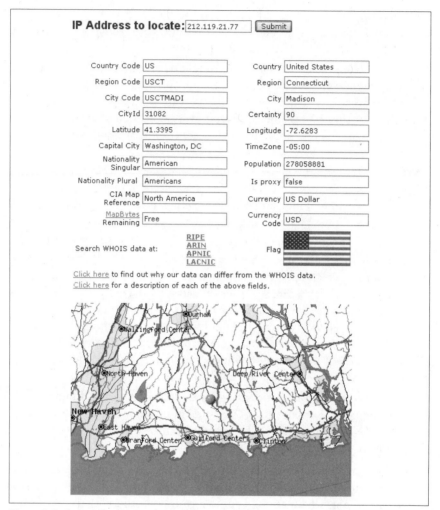

Figure 9-8. Output from an IP locator that indicates the physical location of an IP address

See Also

- "Manage Your Skype Privacy Settings" **[Hack #74]**
- "Choose the Right Username to Avoid Being Harassed" **[Hack #78]**
- "Run Skype Based on Time of Day" **[Hack #41]** or "Schedule When Skype Runs the Mac Way" **[Hack #42]**

Choose the Right Username to Avoid Being Harassed

Choosing the wrong Skype username can cause you a lot of aggravation, particularly if you are a woman. Follow these simple rules to make yourself a less likely target for harassment.

Works with: all versions of Skype.

This hack begins with a true story. After I'd been using Skype for about a year, I decided to set up a Skype account and username for my wife. For her Skype name, I chose the nickname by which she is known at work, which happens to include the word girl in it. Within four hours of setting up the name, she had received five authorization requests, all clearly from men, all clearly requesting some form of intimate communication (or worse), and from all over the world. I don't speak Finnish, Italian, or Dutch, but the two messages in English that accompanied the authorization requests were explicit. All of this occurred in the space of four hours, presumably because my wife's username included the word girl! In stark contrast, the previous year I had received only one unwanted request for authorization, and that request very obviously came from someone who clearly knew someone else with the same name.

In my mind, this quickly drove home the message that there are large numbers of men out there—in the Skype community—who do little else than search for Skype users having seductive female names. I'm not saying that these men are over-represented in the Skype community, only that they're there, just as they are in society.

Before working through a checklist of what makes for a good Skype username, let's first review the rules of constructing a valid Skype name. Such a name:

- Must be at least 6 characters in length and, at most, 32 characters
- Must start with a letter (digits [0 through 9] can be used anywhere, except as the first character)
- Cannot have any spaces or tabs
- Can include underscores (_), hyphens (-), periods (.), and commas (,)
- Cannot include the following characters: ! @ # $ % ^ & * ( ) [ ] { } + = | \ ~ ` : ; " ' < > ? /

If you want to avoid being harassed just because of the words used in your Skype name, you can follow this "recipe" of things to *leave out* of your Skype name:

What sex you are
  Avoid *jane_single_female*.

What faith you are
  Avoid *muslim_jane*.

Where you live
  Avoid *jane_branford_ct_usa*.

How old you are
  Avoid *fourteen_year_old_jane*.

What ethnicity you are
  Avoid *chinese_jane*.

Where you work
  Avoid *jane_small_xyz_corp*.

What you do
  Avoid *jane_the_physician*.

How wealthy you are
  Avoid *loads_of_money_jane*.

It's strange that something as simple as your Skype name can make you a target for harassment and ne'er-do-wells, but as my wife's experience proved, it most certainly can. Clearly, *anyone* can be a target if he's not careful about how he chooses his Skype name. As for me, I seem to be doing rather well using the Skype name *grumpy_old_man_naff_off*!

See Also

- To set up your privacy settings within Skype, see "Manage Your Skype Privacy Settings" [Hack #74].

Quirks, Gotchas, and Workarounds
Hacks 79–85

Skype is a sophisticated piece of software and bundle of services. But it ain't perfect, as the saying goes.

This chapter deals with Skype's shortcomings—the ugly underbelly of Skype, so to speak. The good news is that Skype is continuously improving, so many of the quirks and gotchas that are with us today will be fixed over time. But in the meantime, the following workarounds may be of help.

HACK #79 Avoid Problems with Interactive Telephone Services

Skype is known to have real problems when interacting with telephone systems that instruct callers to enter key codes by pressing numbers on the phone's keypad. At best, it is unreliable, and at worst, it doesn't work at all. But a neat Skype add-on called KhaosDial might do the trick.

Works with: Windows version of Skype.

Dual Tone Multi-Frequency (DTMF) is the term used to describe the tones you hear when you press the keys on your phone's keypad. Each key generates a different tone that can be used to represent the numbers 1 through 9, the letters A through Z, and the characters * and # to an *Interactive Voice Response* (IVR) telephone system. IVR telephone systems provide services without another human being at the other end of the line. When they work, they are a very convenient and efficient way of delivering services. When they don't work, they suck!

Skype is known to have real problems working with IVR systems—just visit the Skype community forums (*http://forum.skype.com/*) to get a glimpse of the pain and suffering the misbehavior of this feature has caused.

When using Skype from your computer, the normal way of entering DTMF codes is to use the buttons on the Dial tab (see Figure 10-1, right). Alternatively, if you use a phone handset to make and receive calls using Skype, you can try the keypad on the handset to enter your DTMF codes (see Figure 10-1, left).

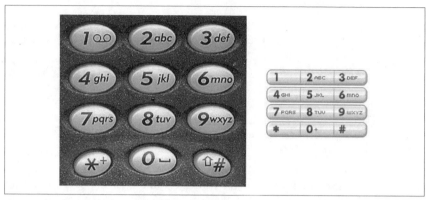

Figure 10-1. Keypad of a regular phone (left) and Skype's Dial tab (right)

Neither of these two methods of interacting with an IVR system seems to be terribly reliable. Clearly, the DTMF tones that Skype generates and transmits become distorted somewhere along the way to their destination, so they are often unrecognizable by the time they arrive at the IVR system.

However, if you are a Windows user of Skype, there is a neat little add-on called KhaosDial (*http://www.KhaosLabs.com/*) that you can use to enter DTMF codes with some degree of reliability (see Figure 10-2). It might all seem rather Rube Goldberg-ish to be playing DTMF tones from your speakers into your microphone or from the earpiece to the microphone boom of your headset; but until Skype fixes its own DTMF problems, it's worth a try.

> KhaosDial requires that you have Microsoft .NET 1.1 installed on your machine. To find out if you have .NET installed and, if so, what version, navigate to Start → Control Panel → Add or Remove Programs, and scroll down the list of currently installed programs, looking for an entry for Microsoft .NET Framework 1.1. If you don't have it, download and install it from *http://www.microsoft.com/downloads/*.

HACK #80 Find a Fax Alternative

Skype doesn't work with regular fax machines. Here are the alternatives.

Skype does not work with fax. Fax is not supported, regardless of whether it is a software or a hardware fax device. This might change, but right now, Skype doesn't support fax.

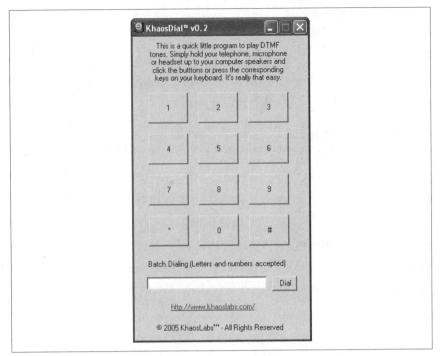

Figure 10-2. KhaosDial can generate DTMF codes independently of Skype

Suppose you've connected your regular fax machine to a USB box that acts as an audio device for Skype, and that you've signed up for SkypeOut. When your fax dials out to another fax, you can hear the wailing response from the remote fax machine and...nothing happens. Fax simply doesn't work over a Skype connection. The same is true for incoming fax transmissions to your fax machine if it's connected to a SkypeIn number.

> The reason why fax doesn't work with Skype is complex, but it comes down to the fact that fax machines are far less tolerant of any degradation in sound fidelity, even if such degradation is only transient. Skype codes and uncodes your voice (using a *codec*, so called because it codes/decodes) at either end of the transmission channel. The codec uses compression and other tricks to get your voice squeezed down into the smallest number of transmission packets. But as a result, sound fidelity suffers. This isn't such a big problem for voice transmission because the human ear and brain do a fantastic job of filling in anything that's missing. Fax, being a mindless machine technology, isn't so forgiving.

Fax might be a technology in decline—as Internet connectivity becomes pervasive—but it still has its place. Whereas the Internet promises to become pervasive sometime in the future, the simple fact is that fax technology is pervasive now. Also, fax documents with a signature (or even without) have legal force in many countries, which cannot be said for most types of electronic file transfer (Skype included).

> According to analysts, fax traffic peaked in 2000 and has been in decline since then (see *http://www.open-mag.com/features/Vol_37/FeMail/femail.htm*).

Fortunately, you have a lot of choices when it comes to workarounds for Skype's lack of support for fax.

Keep Your Fax Machine

Throughout the book, I have emphasized that switching to Skype is not an all-or-nothing proposition. You can choose to mix and match Skype services with other VoIP offerings or even with your Plain Old Telephone System (POTS). If you retain one or more regular telephone lines, connect your fax to one of them and Skype's inability to work with fax is sidestepped nicely.

> The Skype forums have reported that even though Skype's London office has no regular telephones, it nonetheless has a fax machine plugged into a regular telephone outlet. I think we can surmise from this that Skype hasn't licked the problem of fax compatibility, at least not yet.

Use Skype File Transfer Instead

If the document is in electronic form, instead of printing it and faxing it, consider sending it (or a PDF representation of it) via Skype's file-transfer function. Of course, this will work only if your recipient is also running Skype. Another plus in favor of this workaround is that it costs nothing (other than bandwidth) to send files via Skype, whereas regular fax costs money. Of course, simply attaching a document to an email is already a popular alternative to fax. But if your document contains sensitive material, sending it via Skype has the advantage that it is secure (encrypted), whereas email is typically not secure.

Online Fax Services

The move away from traditional fax machines started long before Skype even appeared. Consequently, Google on "fax service" and you'll be presented with a plethora of different types of fax services that don't require you to have a regular fax machine to send or receive faxes. Some of these services are free, but most are available at low cost—it sure is a competitive market segment, which is, of course, to your benefit.

Consider Alternative VoIP Providers

Some VoIP providers (see "Get the Best Deal for VoIP Telephony" [Hack #22]) do provide fax-compatible services, though usually at an additional cost. You might want to consider one of these providers instead of, or as a complement to, Skype.

Workarounds for 911 Emergency Service

#81 Skype doesn't provide emergency service calls. But there are some workarounds.

Works with: all versions of Skype.

Skype does not provide any access to emergency service. If you dial 911 (or the equivalent outside the U.S.) to call emergency service, you will not be connected. Period.

Skype itself is quite explicit on this issue, and therefore markets its services as an "enhancement" to regular telephone services. However, for those who switch to Skype completely, making it their sole (nonmobile) telephone service provider, some workarounds are available that can provide "911-like" service.

Perhaps it is worth repeating that the workarounds are only "911-like" and are in no way a direct substitute for real 911 service. You must weigh the pros and cons of fully switching over to Skype in light of the fact that Skype cannot provide 911 service. Switching to Skype as your sole telephone provider is a decision that you alone can make, and that you alone must live with and bear responsibility for.

911—You May Have It by Default

Most people get their broadband Internet service through one of two means: cable TV or telephone.

Cable TV uses the same physical cable through which you receive your TV channels, so it is independent of your telephone service. You can have cable Internet access without having a telephone, and vice versa.

Telephone can also provide broadband Internet access, usually at an additional cost to your regular telephone services. The most common technology for providing Internet access through your telephone line is *Digital Subscriber Line* (DSL). There are many flavors of DSL—the most common being *Asymmetric Digital Subscriber Line* (ADSL)—most of which are bundled with and ride atop a regular telephone service. Most, but not all.

If you obtain your Internet connection through a flavor of DSL that rides atop a regular telephone service you already have real 911 service as part of your regular telephone service. Thus, if you have ADSL or another flavor of DSL that piggybacks on top of your regular telephone service, you will have 911 emergency service by default (see Figure 10-3).

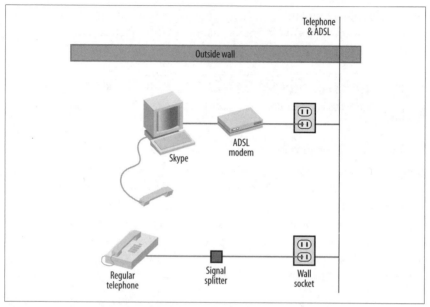

Figure 10-3. Most DSL Internet broadband services—ADSL being the most common—piggyback on top of a regular telephone line and service

Getting your broadband Internet connection through DSL with telephone services does not stop you from switching to Skype in large part to save money. Your local telephone company might not promote lower-cost service packages; indeed, it may not mention them at all! However, most telephone companies do offer "basic" or "emergency-only" service at much lower cost than their more visible offerings. In the case of "emergency-only" service, the cost may be as low as $10 to $15 per month. Depending on your local telephone company, this may be combined with DSL to reduce your regular telephone costs to the bare minimum, leaving Skype to become your principal low-cost telephone provider.

Set Up a "911-like" Service

If you obtain your Internet connection through some mechanism other than ADSL—say, cable—you can switch to Skype as your sole telephone service provider (see Figure 10-4).

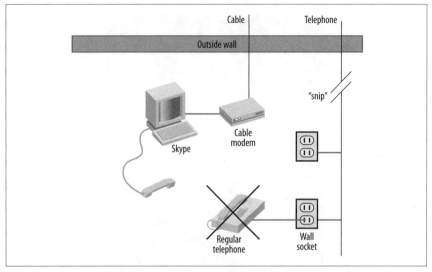

Figure 10-4. Getting broadband Internet access through cable means you can make Skype your only telephone service provider (for this configuration, you don't really have to snip your telephone wire, just cancel service instead)

SkypeOut is a paid service that enables Skype users to call regular telephones. Most local police departments and fire services have telephone numbers separate from the 911 service. Moreover, these numbers are typically manned 24 hours a day. So, in an emergency, you can call your local police or fire service and your request for help will surely be heeded.

As a matter of convenience, you should add your local police station to your Contacts list and assign it a speed-dial number. Sadly, Skype does not support three-digit speed-dial numbers—if it did, the most logical choice would be to assign 911—so, the best you can do is to assign 91 to your local police department (see Figure 10-5). In addition, you may want to add a shortcut to your desktop (see "Add Fast-Dial Shortcuts to Your Menu or Desktop" [Hack #49]) for quickly dialing your local police department in an emergency—when seconds might count!

Assigning the speed-dial number 91 to your local police department has an added advantage: if you use a USB handset or if you have connected Skype to the handsets throughout your home (see Chapter 3), you can simply dial 91# to phone your local police department. It's not quite "911," but it's close. As a courtesy to others who might visit your home, you may want to attach a label to all your handsets saying "In an emergency call: 91#" (see Figure 10-6).

Figure 10-5. Add your local police department to your Contacts list

In an emergency call:

91#

Notice: This will call the local police.
This home has no access to 911
emergency services

Figure 10-6. Add a label such as this to your handsets, telling people how to call your local police in an emergency

Test Your Emergency Phone Number

This is where the 911-like service has a distinct advantage over the traditional 911 service. You can test it whenever you like.

Your 911 service may not work when you desperately need it. You'll probably never know until you really need it. Calling 911 occasionally to make sure it's working, if not against the law, is surely in bad form and might get you into trouble.

On the other hand, nothing is stopping you from dialing 91# from time to time and asking, for example, when the next policemen's ball or fundraiser is going to take place. At least you'll know it works!

Use a Mobile Phone As a Backup

All U.S. mobile phones support 911 service. So, if your home is in an area with good mobile phone reception, it's always worth keeping your mobile phone charged and ready should you need it in an emergency.

Indeed, you can even use an old mobile phone that is no longer supported by a paid calling plan from a mobile phone company. You can use any mobile phone to call 911 without paying anything at all. Mobile phones are regulated by the Federal Communications Commission (FCC), and the FCC mandates that all mobile phones, regardless of the status of service (or even the lack of service), must be able to dial 911. Whether you have a telephone number or not or whether you have signed up for service or not, a mobile phone can connect to 911.

Location

One clear advantage of regular 911 emergency service is that when you place an emergency call from a regular phone, the dispatcher knows where you are located. This is *not* the case when you place any sort of emergency call using SkypeOut, as the nature of Skype's technology means that your location is unknown.

However, if you use a mobile phone to place a call to 911 emergency service, in many instances the dispatcher will know where you are (at least approximately), as many mobile phone networks have built-in location detection.

Workarounds for 411 Directory Assistance

HACK #82

Skype doesn't provide access to 411 directory assistance. But there are some workarounds.

Works with: all versions of Skype.

In the U.S., you can access directory assistance by dialing 411. This is usually a paid service (read moneymaker for your telephone company), and $1.25 per directory assistance call is typical.

Skype does not support 411 directory assistance. Dial 411 and you'll get nothing but an error message. That's the good news, as you'll never have to pay for 411 calls again.

The bad news is that Skype does not support 411 directory assistance. So, where are you to go now for directory assistance? If you are using Skype as an adjunct to a regular telephone line, you clearly retain the option (albeit an expensive option) of calling 411 on that line. Similarly, if you simply have money to burn, you can even dial 411 on your mobile phone to get directory assistance.

A free alternative is to use one of the many online 411 services that are now available. A search on Google with the keywords "411 directory assistance" will spit out a long list of such directory assistance web sites. But perhaps the first place to go is the list of online directory assistance services maintained by the Telecommunications Research & Action Center (TRAC, *http:// www.trac.org/tips/directory_assistance/directory-assistance-via-the-internet. html*), a nonprofit watchdog that promotes the interests of residential telecommunications consumers. Given the charter under which TRAC operates, the services listed there are among the less annoying web sites for getting directory assistance.

HACK #83   Workarounds for Home Alarm System Monitoring

Many home alarm systems are monitored remotely via telephone line, and you need not necessarily give this up when you switch to Skype.

Works with: Windows version of Skype.

Many home alarm systems are monitored over a phone line. At the risk of stating the obvious, if you intend to retain at least one regular phone line, make sure it is the one your alarm system uses.

> Cutting the phone line that feeds your alarm might set it off! After all, how is the alarm to tell the difference between you and a burglar? However, this becomes an issue only if you are configuring Skype to reuse the phone lines and wiring throughout your home (see Chapter 3 for Skype configurations that might make this necessary). So, before you cut any wires, get organized, do your homework (for example, read the manual for your alarm system), talk with your alarm monitoring service, and then (and only then) cut your wires.

Even if you decide to use Skype exclusively for phone services, this does not necessarily mean that you have to do without remote alarm monitoring. In Chapter 3, I discussed several configurations for Skype that effectively leave a dial tone on your existing phone copper wiring. If, in addition, you are a SkypeIn and SkypeOut subscriber, there's no reason why your alarm monitoring service can't dial in to your alarm system for monitoring purposes, and likewise, there's no reason why your alarm can't dial out to your alarm monitoring service in an emergency. Chances are that all you need is for your alarm monitoring service to know your SkypeIn number and for the alarm to be reprogrammed to use any special new prefix needed to dial out through SkypeOut. Note that during a power cut, your alarm will lose its connection to your alarm monitoring service.

For readers who are fully replacing their existing phone service with Skype, but who want to retain alarm monitoring services, this step-by-step check-list might prove useful:

1. Read the manual for your alarm system and learn how to reprogram it to dial out using the Skype dial format. If you don't have a manual, or if this is beyond your comfort zone, ask your alarm company to reprogram the alarm for you. Before doing anything else, you have to be convinced that monitoring your alarm system using Skype is doable. If it isn't, think again. If it is, proceed.

2. Tell your alarm monitoring service that your phone numbers are about to change. Ask them to stop monitoring until you've notified them to start again.

3. Cancel your regular phone service and then, if necessary, cut the incoming phone wires so that Skype can reuse the copper wiring in your home. Be careful to cut only the incoming phone wires (that is, cut only the wires that connect you to the outside world) and not the wires that connect your alarm system to the copper wires of your home phone wiring.

4. Connect and configure Skype so that it puts a dial tone on the copper phone wires throughout your home (see Figure 10-7).

5. Reprogram your alarm to use SkypeOut when dialing out. This will entail using the correct country code and prefix (for example, to have your alarm call your monitoring service using SkypeOut, it may have to be reprogrammed to dial something like +12035551212, rather than 5551212, which may have been the case previously).

6. Call your alarm monitoring service, provide them with your SkypeIn number, and test the new setup.

7. Tell your alarm monitoring service to start monitoring again.

Transfer Folders, Not Just Individual Files

HACK #84

You can transfer only individual files using Skype's file-transfer facility. This hack shows you how to transfer groups of files, as well as whole folders of files.

Works with: Windows, Linux, and Mac OS X versions of Skype.

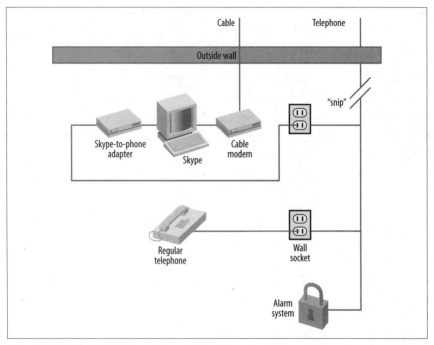

Figure 10-7. Configuring Skype to provide a phone line for your home alarm system

Skype opens one window per file transferred. This can be extremely tedious for the recipient, who must authorize every file transfer in turn. Unfortunately, you can't just specify a whole folder or directory tree to transfer. To do that, you must first bundle the folders and files into an *archive* (a special file that acts as a container for other files and folders), transfer the archive, and have the recipient unpack the archive at the other end. Though be warned, any archive you create must be easy for the recipient to unpack, so choose your archive format with care!

Here are some simple and easy-to-use options.

Transferring Folders Among Windows Machines

Windows comes with its own file archive and compression tool. Within Windows Explorer, you can select files and/or folders, and then right-click to turn them into a compressed (zipped) archive file. You can even add a password to the archive so that the recipient will have to enter the (same) password to uncompress, open, and extract the files and folders contained within it.

The Windows zip archive tool is, of course, free, as it comes with Windows. However, many people prefer other third-party archive tools, such as WinZip (*http://www.WinZip.com/*), to the one that is bundled free with Windows.

Transferring Folders Among Linux Machines

Linux, being a variant of Unix, has the ubiquitous compress and tar archive commands. Many Linux distributions also include gzip (GNU zip), which was designed as a replacement for compress, and the free zip and unzip command-line tools from Info-ZIP (*http://www.info-zip.org/*). By using these tools, it is easy to create an archive of several files and/or folders, which you can send to a Skype user using a single file transfer.

Transferring Folders Among Mac OS X Machines

Mac OS X comes with its own tool to create zipped archives. But sadly, even though the resulting archive has a *.zip* suffix, the archives it creates are incompatible with the Windows zip archive tool. However, archives generated on one Mac OS X machine can be unpacked seamlessly on another.

Mac OS X is built on top of variants of the Unix operating system (namely, the Mach 3.0 operating system and services based on the 4.4 Berkeley Software Distribution). Consequently, like Linux, it has the ubiquitous compress and tar archive commands. It also comes with the command-line tools gzip, zip, and unzip by default.

Perhaps the most popular third-party compression and archive tool for the Mac is StuffIt (*http://www.stuffit.com/*).

Transferring Folders Among Diverse Machines

Transferring folders and/or files among diverse machines—that is, machines of different architectures and running different operating systems—poses a number of problems. Differing rules for filenames and file extensions can cause problems. And finding a common archive format that all machines recognize and understand can be difficult.

One technique that seems to work well in my experience is to use the free Info-ZIP archive utility on Linux and Mac OS X, and the native Windows zip compression tool. Check your Linux and Mac OS X installations, as you will likely find Info-ZIP already installed. Just try entering the commands zip and unzip in a terminal window, and see if you get a command summary in response. Archives created by the Info-ZIP utility and the Windows zip compression tool interoperate well (see Figure 10-8).

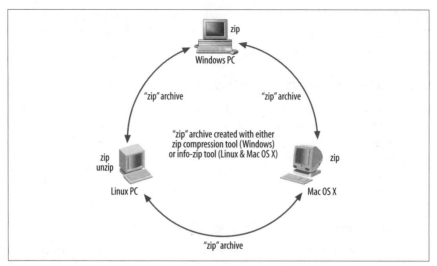

Figure 10-8. *Using a zip archive to transfer folders among diverse machines using Skype*

On Linux and Mac OS X, you can create an archive of a complete folder using the command:

```
zip -r filename.zip'your folder name'
```

You can unpack it using the command:

```
unzip filename.zip
```

Just type "zip" or "unzip" at the command prompt to see more options for manipulating archives.

You can create zip archives within Windows Explorer by right-clicking after selecting the files or folders you want to add to a zip archive (see Figure 10-9). You can unpack an archive from within Windows Explorer by double-clicking on it or right-clicking and selecting the appropriate tool using Open With.

HACK #85 Dial with More Than Just Digits

You can dial regular phone numbers with not only numbers, but also letters.

Works with: all versions of Skype.

Many companies make their telephone numbers more memorable by making their phone number digits spell something meaningful on the keypad. For example, Federal Express's principal number is +1-800-463-3339, which you also can enter as +1-GO-FEDEX using the letters on the buttons of your phone's keypad. Skype, through its SkypeOut service, offers the same

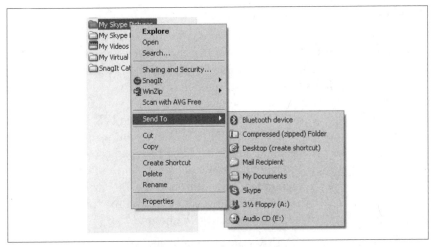

Figure 10-9. Creating a zip archive within Windows Explorer

convenience (see Figure 10-10). For those who aren't good at remembering numbers, it's nice to know that letters will work just as well.

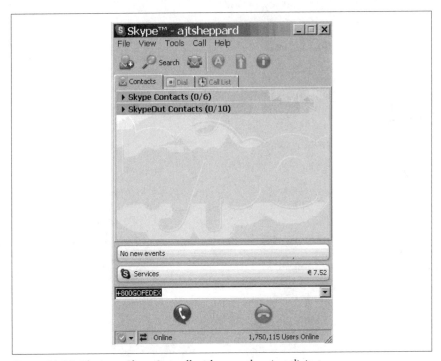

Figure 10-10. Placing a SkypeOut call with more than just digits

Hacking the Hack

Once they place your call, many of the same companies that offer a convenient moniker for their telephone number also deliver you into the clutches of their IVR system. If you're a frequent visitor, the company might have assigned a Personal Identification Number (PIN) to you so that you can authenticate yourself and access services. Oftentimes you can choose your own PIN, which effectively acts as a password for the IVR system, or you can change the company-assigned PIN to whatever you want. Again, those letters accompanying the digits on your phone's keypad can be very useful. If you can't think of a meaningful sequence of digits that are both highly personal and easily remembered, you can choose a PIN whose letters are personal and easy to remember. However, if your PIN spells a word, it should not be anything as obvious as, say, your name.

When interacting with an IVR system using Skype, you can enter responses to voice prompts using the keypad (see Figure 10-11). When it comes to entering your PIN, instead of thinking about entering digits, you can spell a secret word. For example, you might enter FIJI (3454) as your four-digit PIN, in memory of your honeymoon.

Figure 10-11. Enter numbers, or letters, using the Skype keypad

Skype Add-Ons and Tools
Hacks 86–90

There is a burgeoning market for Skype add-ons and tools that extend Skype's functionality or that leverage Skype's services. This is one of the most exciting aspects of Skype. By using Skype's Application Programming Interface (API), third-party developers are delivering neat add-ons—many of them free—that plug gaps in Skype's feature set, or just do something "completely different" (to borrow a phrase from *Monty Python's Flying Circus*). So, if there's a piece of functionality that you desperately need or want, chances are someone has had a similar idea and has built an add-on to satisfy that need or want. And if they haven't, Chapter 12 might just help you to hack your own!

Perhaps the first place to start looking for add-ons is Skype's own Extras Gallery, which is updated frequently and is located at *http://share.skype.com/directory/*.

Given the rapid pace at which all things to do with Skype are developing this chapter can only be a snapshot in time and a peek at what's available. Having said that, it is nevertheless a starting point that will help you to understand where to start looking for add-ons, how to hack and extend add-ons, and how to manage add-ons from a security perspective.

Skype Add-Ons

Broadly speaking, there are two types of Skype add-ons: hardware add-ons and software add-ons.

Hardware add-ons. A Skype hardware add-on is not just, say, a pair of USB headphones. Such things are merely generic computer devices. To qualify as a Skype add-on, a piece of hardware must interface to Skype through its API. Even though the Skype API was publicly released only a comparatively short time ago (October 2004), you already have a number of Skype-enabled hardware devices from which to choose:

Skype-to-phone USB box

Description: an adapter that allows you to use an existing phone handset with Skype—that is, to use a regular phone handset as your sound-in and sound-out device for Skype. Some have advanced features, such as call forwarding using your regular phone line, and a few have Linux drivers (still quite a rarity).

Where to buy: *http://www.echostore.com/*, *http://www.yappernut.com/*, *http://www.rapidvoip.com/*, *http://www.pcphoneline.com/*, *http://www.skypomania.com/*, *http://www.mplat.com/*, and *http://www.voip-interactive.com/*.

USB handset or desktop phone

Description: a handset or desktop phone that plugs into a USB port and interfaces directly with Skype (using software that comes with the device), and which allows you limited control over Skype from the handset or desktop phone.

Where to buy: *http://www.skype.com/store/*, *http://www.echostore.com/*, *http://www.skypomania.com/*, *http://www.mplat.com/*, and *http://www.voip-interactive.com/*.

USB Flash phone

Description: a USB memory stick with integrated audio from which you can run Skype directly. Just plug it into a USB port on a computer with an Internet connection and you can fire up Skype, and make and receive calls.

Where to buy: *http://www.echostore.com/* and *http://www.mplat.com/*.

Only some of the vendors in the preceding list offer technical support for their products. Before purchasing Skype add-on hardware, it's always worth asking some technical questions to gauge the type of after-sales support you can expect.

Software add-ons. Using the Skype API, software add-ons can control Skype or have Skype control them. Truly, it's a situation that is limited only by how quickly Skype enhances its API specification, and by the imaginative uses to which the API can be put by creative add-on software developers (or, indeed, by Skype users; see Chapter 12). If what's already been created so far is anything to go by, especially in view of the comparatively short period since the API was released, this area is going to be big! Just look at some of the add-ons that are already available.

Software Add-On Showcase

Information relating to Skype ages almost as quickly as bread on a baker's shelf. Even so, as a starting point in your own hunt for Skype add-ons, here is a sampler of many of the add-ons (including add-on services that don't use the Skype API) available at the time of this writing. The list is by no means comprehensive. It does, however, give you a sense of the breadth and scope of the Skype add-on market—even though it's clearly in its embryonic stage.

Audiomatic Skype plug-in
> Description: control Skype by using voice commands rather than the keyboard or mouse, see "Control Skype Using Spoken Commands" [Hack #86].
>
> Where to get it: *http://www.wiseriddles.com/Products/Audiomatic/index.html*

Biz.KonuSh.NET (free)
> Description: business directory (Yellow Pages) for Skype users.
>
> Where to get it: *http://biz.konush.net/*

Gizmoz Talking Headz
> Description: animated heads that give your Skype chat sessions more personality and humor (see Figure 11-1).
>
> Where to get it: *http://www.gizmoz.com/*

IPdrum
> Description: some mobile phone plans allow phones on the same network to talk free of charge within their designated home geographic region. Using a pair of mobile phones, IPdrum provides a cable and some software to connect one of them to your computer running Skype. As you move around with the other mobile phone, you can relay and route calls through your home computer using Skype. As mobile-to-mobile calls are free and Skype-to-Skype calls are free, you can effectively make mobile-to-Skype calls free of charge, or mobile-to-Skype-Out calls at rates lower than those of your mobile phone plan.
>
> Where to get it: *http://www.ipdrum.com/*

Jyve
> Description: Jyve Web Tools for Skype enable you to add Jyve-type functionality to your web site. Jyve Tag provides an HTML snippet that puts a live Skype button in a web page that shows your current online status. Jyve Card allows you to collect call-back details from people who visit your web site.
>
> Where to get it: *http://www.jyve.com/*

Pamela

Description: a productivity add-on for Skype that comprises a suite of functions, including two-way call recording, podcasts, email forwarding of voicemail, and much more!

Where to get it: *http://www.pamela-systems.com/*

Skype 3D Avatar Messenger (free)

Description: animated 3D avatars for Skype chat.

Where to get it: *http://www.vaka.com/*

Skype E911 plug-in

Description: Wireless Fidelity (WiFi) positioning for Skype users that lets people know where you are calling from. Limited geographic coverage.

Where to get it: *http://www.skyhookwireless.com/*

Skypeteer call cost calculator

Description: calculate your SkypeOut call cost in real time, without having to go to the Skype web site for current call rates.

Where to get it: *http://www.skypeteer.com/*

Figure 11-1. Liven up your Skype chat sessions with animated Talking Headz

Control Skype Using Spoken Commands

#86

You can have hands-free (and sight-free for the visually impaired) operation of Skype using only your voice.

Works with: Windows version of Skype.

Audiomatic ($29.95 from *http://www.wiseriddles.com/Products/Audiomatic/ index.html*) is a shareware tool that enables you to control Windows and applications that run on Windows using voice commands and keyboard shortcuts. If you have the Audiomatic base product, you can install a free Skype add-on (which you can download at *http://wiseriddles.swmirror.com/ AudiomaticSkypePlugin.msi*) that will more closely integrate Audiomatic with Skype.

Installing the Skype add-on for Audiomatic adds a new Audiomatic macro type called Interact with Skype, which allows you to control Skype using your voice in these two ways:

Make a phone call
> To make a phone call you must select "Place a call to" when asked by the Audiomatic Macro Wizard, "When this macro is run, I want to."

Send a chat message
> To send a chat message you must select "Send an Instant Message to" when asked by the Audiomatic Macro Wizard, "When this macro is run, I want to."

Setting up a voice command to make a phone call requires these steps using the Audiomatic Macro Wizard:

1. Open a new macro in the Macro Wizard and give it a name (select Audiomatic → File → New → Macro…); see Figure 11-2. For this example, I'll be setting up a voice command to "Call Dad"! Click Next.

2. Select Interacts with Skype from the top pull-down menu in the next window, Figure 11-3, and select "Place a call to" from the middle pull-down menu. Pulling down the bottom pull-down menu will display your Skype contacts list in numerical and then alphabetical order. Note that this pull down does not allow you to enter a new phone number or Skype name, so you can create Audiomatic macros for Skype only for existing contacts. Select a Skype contact and then click Next.

3. The next screen, Figure 11-4, allows you to set the availability of your macro. To simply have the macro available at all times, click Next.

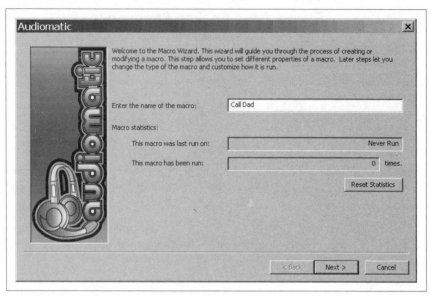

Figure 11-2. Creating a new Audiomatic macro for Skype

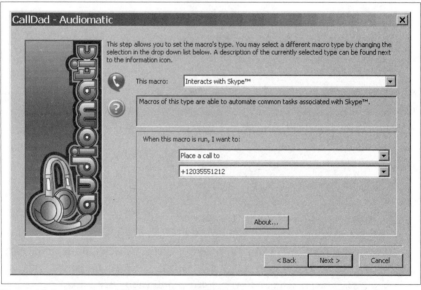

Figure 11-3. Assigning a phone number to the "Place a call to" action of the Audiomatic macro (phone numbers and Skype names can be used)

4. To assign a voice command and keyboard command to the macro, check both the "Enable Voice Commands for this macro" and "Enable Keyboard Commands for this macro" checkboxes; see Figure 11-5.

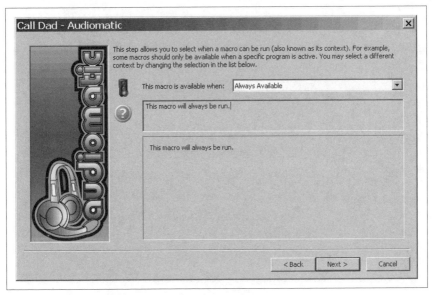

Figure 11-4. Setting availability of the Audiomatic macro

Enter a voice command and a keyboard command key sequence; in this example, "Call Dad" and (Left Shift) + (Left Ctrl) + D. Click Next.

5. Test the macro by clicking the Run Macro button in the next window (Figure 11-6). If the macro works as expected, click Finish.

6. By default, Audiomatic activates voice command mode using a keyboard hotkey (the default is (Left Shift) + (Left Ctrl) + A). However, to make macros totally voice activated, Audiomatic command mode must be activated itself with a voice command. You can do this by going to Audiomatic → Tools → Options… and in the Audiomatic Options dialog that is displayed, navigate to the Command Mode tab. In that tab, click on the "Speaking the phrase" radio button and enter the phrase "Skype" to be used to activate Audiomatic's command mode.

Now, to call Dad, all I need to do is speak the command "Skype Call Dad." Skype will open and will start a call to Dad. Look ma, no hands! Phone calls automatically are hung up when the other party exits a call, so that part is also hands free.

Alternatively, I can use the keyboard command (Left Shift) + (Left Ctrl) + D to make the call—without even looking at the keyboard!

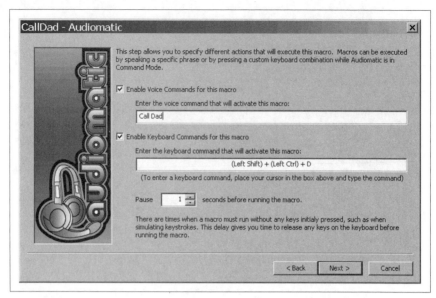

Figure 11-5. Setting the voice command and keyboard command key sequence that will run the Audiomatic macro

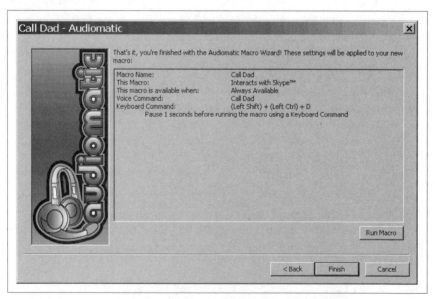

Figure 11-6. Testing your Audiomatic macro using the Run Macro button

Hacking the Hack

In Chapter 12, "Hot-Switch Among Sound Devices" [Hack #91] presents a couple of VBScripts, *logitech_API.vbs* and *c-media_API.vbs*, to hot-switch sound devices—even during a phone call. Using Audiomatic you can drive these scripts with voice commands too!

Creating an Audiomatic macro to do this requires almost the same steps as before, except at step 2 select Launches Programs instead of Interacts with Skype from the top pull-down menu in Figure 11-7. Also set "Program, file, or web site to launch" to the script file you want to run when you speak the voice command of your choice.

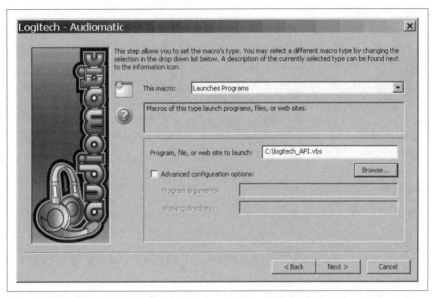

Figure 11-7. Setting up an Audiomatic macro to run a VBScript

With this slight variation at step 2, I set up two Audiomatic macros named Logitech and CMedia, which run *logitech_API.vbs* and *c-media_API.vbs*, respectively, upon my saying the commands "Skype Logitech" and "Skype CMedia." Now I can switch from my Logitech USB headset to my C-Media USB handset simply by saying "Skype CMedia," and from my C-Media USB handset back to my Logitech USB headset by saying "Skype Logitech." Moreover, I can make the switch before, or during, a call. Of course, to do this during a call requires a convenient pause in the conversation, but now I have the flexibility and convenience of switching sound devices with nothing more than a spoken command.

Using Audiomatic pretty much *any* of the scripts in this book that run on Windows—or any scripts you think up yourself—can be run with nothing more than a spoken command.

Add Video Conferencing to Skype

Skype plans to support video conferencing sometime in the future. In the meantime, use an add-on to get the functionality you want.

Works with: Windows version of Skype.

Skype video is coming! That is, video developed by Skype and built into the Skype client. But until it arrives, one of these add-on solutions may suit your needs. Indeed, even after Skype video is here, one of the solutions presented in this hack might still be what you want, as Skype's solution must necessarily span many platforms, and the solutions presented here are clearly optimized for Windows.

But before you read on, heed this word of caution. Both of the video solutions presented here are listed as "betas," so perhaps you should adjust your expectations for video with Skype accordingly. However, like the VoIP technologies that underpin Skype itself, it's a good bet that video technologies will simply get better and better with time.

Festoon

Festoon (formerly vSkype), *http://www.festooninc.com/*, boasts that you can video conference call up to 200 buddies, 8 of whom can be displayed on the screen at one time. Those who don't have a video camera can still participate, but as voice-only participants. However, the number of attendees that can video conference together is, from a practical point of view, limited by your Internet connection bandwidth. And for most Festoon users, this number will fall far short of 200; in fact, for many, one-on-one video calls will be a challenge.

To use Festoon you will have to be running Skype. Because Festoon inherits its sound devices from Skype, changing sound devices in Skype (by selecting Skype → Tools → Options... → Sound Devices) will change those used by Festoon to the same devices. Festoon also uses Skype chat to notify other video call participants that you are requesting them to join a video conference. That, and using your Skype Contacts list, seems to be the extent of Festoon's integration with Skype.

One extra feature of Festoon is the ability to share your desktop with other video call participants—indeed, not just your whole desktop, but also individual application windows. For example, open the Windows calculator on your machine and share it with your Festoon video call participants, and a regularly updated image of your calculator window will appear on their screens. How quickly the image is updated depends on how big the shared window is, but a few seconds to tens of seconds between updates is typical; see Figure 11-8.

But Festoon's shared desktop feature has its limitations. You cannot share some application windows if your machine has multiple monitors; specifically, windows that are outside your primary monitor can't be shared. Likewise, sharing your whole desktop means that others will see only the part of your desktop that is on your primary monitor.

Figure 11-8. A vSkype (now Festoon) video session with the Windows calculator as a real-time updated image from a remote desktop

Spontania Video4IM

Spontania Video4IM (beta), *http://www.video4im.com/*, works alongside Skype. Skype provides the voice component of a video call, and Video4IM provides the video component. Like Festoon, Video4IM is currently free.

Side-by-Side Comparison

To help you decide what video add-on for Skype might best suit your needs, Tables 11-1 and 11-2 compare Festoon and Spontania Video4IM side by side and feature by feature.

Table 11-1. Video for Skype hardware and software requirements

Hardware	Festoon	Spontania Video4IM
Computer	450MHz or greater	400MHz or greater CPU
Memory (minimum)	128 MB	128 MB
Operating system	Windows 2000 or XP	Windows 2000 or XP
Disk space (install)	8 MB	1 MB
Skype	1.3.0.45 or greater	Updated to be compatible with current version
Other applications	Internet Explorer 5.0 or greater	N/A
Video resolution (recommended)	320 × 240 pixels	Whatever your web cam supports
Display formats	256 color (8-bit palette)	DirectX
	16-bit color (RGB16, RGB555, or RGBH)	
	24-bit color (RGB24, RGB888, or RGBT)	
	YUV12	
	I420	
	16 shades of gray or 64 shades of gray	
Internet connection	Broadband only	Broadband only
Bandwidth requirements	"Elastic," which means Festoon will make do with what it's given, but in reality, your video session degrades rapidly below 128 Kbps per video call participant	Minimum of 128 Kbps both upstream and downstream
Sound device	Headset strongly recommended	Uses Skype for voice component of call

Table 11-2. Features comparison

Feature	Festoon	Spontania Video4IM
Video participants	Up to 200 (note 1)	One-on-one video only
Cost	Currently free (beta)	Currently free (beta)
Spyware/adware free	Yes	Yes
Secure (encrypted)	Yes	Yes
Web cams supported	Most, but not all (note 2)	Most, but not all (note 2)
Share desktop or application window	Yes	No

Notes:

1. Bandwidth permitting. Most Festoon users will be able to support only a handful of video call participants.

2. Check web site for details.

In the Author's Opinion

Sadly, you cannot literally run Festoon and Spontania Video4IM side by side, as that is not possible (they won't share the same video device). But after testing both of them, I came to some conclusions, which I share with you in Table 11-3.

Table 11-3. Side-by-side ratings

Category	Festoon	Spontania Video4IM
Integration with Skype	Good	Poor
Configurability	Poor	Good
Video quality	Poor	Better, but not good
Full-screen mode	No	Yes
East of setting up video call	Good	Poor
Test call service	Yes	No
Installation	Good	Good
Support	Poor	Poor
User forum	Yes	No
Documentation	Poor	Poor
Firewall/Network Address Translation (NAT) friendly	Yes	Yes

Both Festoon and Spontania Video4IM work, and both have something to offer Skype users who want to incorporate video into their calls. They're both quirky, and their video quality is not great, though that seems to reflect the current state of video-over-Internet technology, and is something that will clearly get better over time. Lastly, it's a shame these two add-ons won't work together, as that way you could combine the best features of both without the effort of shutting down one to use the other.

HACK #88 Show Your Online Status in a Web Page

Add your Skype online status to any web page by using this hack.

Works with: Windows version of Skype.

With this neat little add-on, you can make your Skype online status available in real time from any web page.

First, you must download and install the add-on by visiting its support page at *http://www.skyperunners.com/board/viewtopic.php?t=30*.

What you're downloading is a Windows install package that takes care of all the installation details; just follow the instructions. Once it's installed, you're ready to start building web pages that show your Skype online status.

> The add-on requires that you have Microsoft .NET 1.1 installed on your machine. To find out if you have .NET installed and, if so, what version, navigate to Start → Control Panel → Add or Remove Programs, and scroll down the list of currently installed programs, looking for an entry for Microsoft .NET Framework 1.1. If you don't have it, download and install it from *http://www.microsoft.com/downloads/*.

After starting the online status indicator, you should test it by visiting *http://www.skypestatus.com/Skypename.gif*. This URL will be created automatically for whatever your *Skypename* might be. You should see something like that shown in Figure 11-9.

The online status indicator returns a button image based on your online status (see Figure 11-10), but not all types of online status are properly indicated (see Table 11-4).

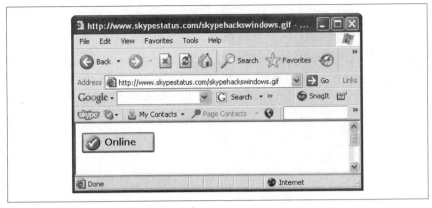

Figure 11-9. Test your online status indicator

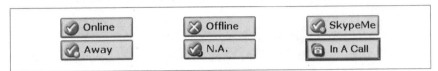

Figure 11-10. Online status indicator buttons

Table 11-4. Your online status and the button that is displayed

Your online status	Button image displayed
Online	Online
Offline	Offline
Skype Me	Skype Me
Away	Away
Not Available	N.A.
Do Not Disturb	Skype Me
Invisible	Skype Me
In A Call	In A Call

Here's how the online status indicator works. The online status add-on communicates with a remote web server to notify it of changes in your online status. Then, each time that same web server receives a request via your custom URL, it checks to see what your last online status was reported as being and delivers the appropriate button image as the response to the request. This means that wherever you use an image in a web page, you can instead use your (real-time-updated) online status button.

However, you need not stop at merely displaying your online status, as you can combine your online status with the *skype:* and *callto://* protocols (see "Make Calls from Your Web Browser" [Hack #43]) to provide any Skype user who looks at your web page the one-click convenience of calling you simply by clicking on your online status button. The following XHTML file, *online_status.htm*, shows you how to do this (you will need to replace *skypename* with your own Skype username):

```
<?xml version="1.0" encoding="UTF-8"?>
<!DOCTYPE html
    PUBLIC "-//W3C//DTD XHTML 1.0 Strict//EN"
    "http://www.w3.org/TR/xhtml1/DTD/xhtml1-strict.dtd">

<!-- File: online_status.htm -->

<html xmlns="http://www.w3.org/1999/xhtml" xml:lang="en" lang="en">

    <head>
        <title>Skype Online Status</title>
    </head>

    <body>
        <p><a href="callto://skypename">
            <img alt="Online status for skypename"
                src="http://www.skypestatus.com/skypename.gif" />
        </a></p>
    </body>

</html>
```

Hacking the Hack

There's no reason to stop at web pages! Any live document in which you can embed an image as an *http://* hyperlink that is updated is a candidate for your online status indicator. For example, this Microsoft Outlook signature file, *skype_hacks.htm*, includes an online status indicator button:

```
<!DOCTYPE HTML PUBLIC "-//W3C//DTD HTML 4.0 Transitional//EN">

<!-- File: skype_hacks.htm -->

<HTML>
    <HEAD>
        <TITLE>Skype Hacks Signature</TITLE>
    </HEAD>
    <BODY>
        <P>Skype Hacks
            <A href="callto://skypehacksbook">
            <IMG alt="Online status for skypehacksbook"
                src="http://www.skypestatus.com/skypehacksbook.gif" />
```

```
            </A>
          </P>
       </BODY>
    </HTML>
```

As long as the recipient of your email has a mail reader that can display HTML, your signature will display your online status (see Figure 11-11). However, the result might not be a real-time and up-to-date display of that status. Ever-popular web-based email will typically refresh an email message each time it is opened, which is something that regular email applications may not do. Regardless of whether your online status button accurately portrays your online status, if the recipient clicks on the button and is a Skype user (with *callto://* directed to Skype), Skype will open and start a call to you.

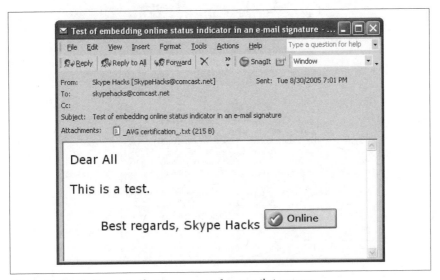

Figure 11-11. Online status button as part of an email signature

Send Skype Chat Directly from Your Browser

Send Skype chat messages from a web page, or just by entering a simple URL in a web browser.

Works with: all versions of Skype.

You're running late and you're in a rush, and all you have access to is a hotel, airport, or Internet cafe computer that isn't running Skype and runs little more than a lowly web browser. Not to worry: with this free add-on service, you can send Skype chat messages in a snap. Sadly, the service only sends messages; it doesn't receive them. But, hey, it is free!

To use this service, you will need to remember two things: a URL and the Skype name(s) of the people to whom you want to send a message.

The URL you must remember is *http://www.skyperunners.com/instant/*.

Entering this URL as the address for any web browser will bring up a simple chat page which, at the time of this writing, was available only in German, but is very, very straightforward (see Figure 11-12).

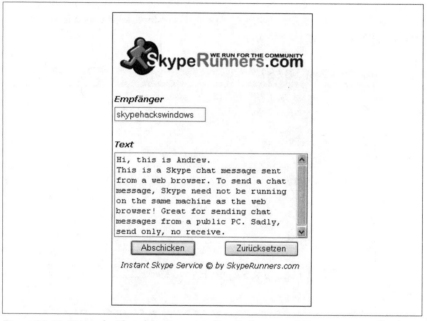

Figure 11-12. *To send a Skype chat message directly from a web browser, enter the Skype name of the intended recipient in the Empfänger box, type in your text message in the Text box, and click on Abschicken*

There is, however, a small gotcha. Your message is relayed to the Skype recipient through the SkypeRunners web server, so it will arrive at your recipient's computer as a message from an anonymous Skype user (see Figure 11-13). For that reason, you may want to start your chat message by telling the recipient who you are, so he won't be clueless as to your identity. Not knowing whom a message is from can be very confusing, especially if the message is short and cryptic.

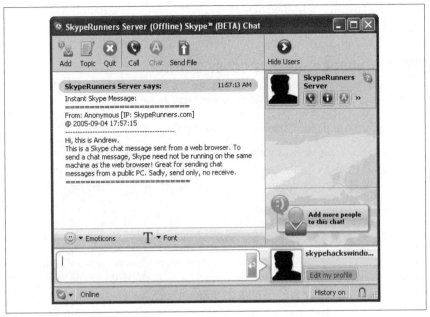

Figure 11-13. Chat message received

Hacking the Hack

If you're really in a hurry, or if your message is very short, you can send a Skype chat message from any web browser by entering just a URL alone (no web form is needed):

> *http://www.skyperunners.com/instant/*
> *?user=skypehackswindows&S1="Hi again! This is Andrew and I'll be home late for dinner - about 7 p.m."*

Pay special attention to the fact that the message (*Hi again! This is Andrew and I'll be home late for dinner - about 7 p.m.*) is between double quotes, and the recipient's Skype name (*skypehackswindows*) is unquoted.

The general format for the URL for this method of sending Skype chat messages is:

> *http://www.skyperunners.com/instant/*
> *?user=SkypeNameOfRecipient&sndr=SkypeNameOfSender&S1=*
> *"MessageText"*

Note that whereas the form method does not allow you to enter a sender's Skype name, this URL method does. This method is particularly suited to PDAs, mobile phones, and other small-form-factor devices for which the web form version might not display properly or, even if it does, might not be easy to navigate.

Manage Add-On Access Control

HACK #90

For security purposes, Skype restricts add-ons from accessing its API. This hack will help you understand and manage how your add-ons use Skype.

Works with: Windows, Linux, and Mac OS X versions of Skype.

Skype's API is a powerful tool for extending Skype's functionality and using its services. However, like any tool, it can be misused. To protect itself from malicious add-ons that might use the API, Skype provides some access control tools.

Understand Add-On Access Control

To manage intelligently how add-ons can access Skype, first you need to understand how Skype has implemented access control on the three platforms that support its API. The first thing to realize is that Skype controls add-on access at the Skype user level and not at the installation level. Put another way, the access control list is maintained in *config.xml* (user) rather than *shared.xml* (all users), so each Skype user must manage their own access control for add-ons.

Windows and Mac OS X. When an add-on tries to access the Skype API, Skype makes a digital signature of the file that was run and is requesting access. For example, when you run a VBScript, the add-on that is really making the request is *WScript.exe* (or perhaps *CScript.exe*, depending on how you are running the script). And if you give it permission to access Skype, a digital signature will be placed in *config.xml* for the Skype user currently logged on, as this fragment from *config.xml* illustrates:

```
...
<UI>
    <AccessControlList>
        <Client1>
            <Key1>073d4fafd04afde1b9cf9441a997d7cc27e43f2127
                e0f5b60a675a765dde6e27</Key1>
            <Key2>4af2cb52c5af3c568856af89f2e4cdb0</Key2>
            <Key3>65804</Key3>
            <Path>C:\Program Files\rapidSoft\rapidSoft.exe</Path>
        </Client1>
        <Client2>
            <Key1>8a85438e06e61ea46f989d478f9bb32b89279
                39f974d95796efcb5e554fb9267</Key1>
            <Key2>77ab71633cc6db19bb3366ea02ea491a</Key2>
```

```
            <Key3>263922</Key3>
            <Path>C:\Program Files\Skype Onlinestatus Indicator 2
                 \SkypeStatusClientTCP.exe</Path>
         </Client2>
      <Client3>
            <Key1>76eb3dfca1281c8cb30e2006baa678322223
                 195d9282a564f4d0aa01425bf281</Key1>
            <Key2>bf54f856b92589ad2d8c707f3e41c903</Key2>
            <Key3>460168</Key3>
            <Path>C:\WINDOWS\System32\WScript.exe</Path>
         </Client3>
    </AccessControlList>
  ...
```

By putting a digital signature in *config.xml*, even if an application with exactly the same name and file path—for example, a malicious version of *WScript.exe*—is run, Skype can tell the difference and block it.

That's all well and good for regular *.exe* files that are add-ons, but what it also means is that once you've given *WScript.exe* access to the Skype API, all scripts—yours and anyone else's—can and will run without any complaint from Skype. So, you may want to exercise a good deal of caution when giving permission to scripts and the engines that run them.

Linux. On Linux, there is no real access control; what's implemented (at least as of version 1.2.0.11_API) is an illusion. In part, this is not Skype's fault, as it's not possible to make digital signatures and the like with D-BUS (Skype's API message-passing layer on Linux) in between the add-on and Skype.

When an add-on sends the command NAME *AddonName* to Skype via the API protocol, Skype dutifully pops up a dialog like that shown in Figure 11-14. If you give the add-on permission to access Skype, an entry is placed in the *config.xml* file for the Skype user currently logged on, as illustrated by the following *config.xml* fragment. However, *any* executable add-on or script that sends the same *AddonName* as another add-on that has already been given access will likewise be granted access. By understanding this security loophole, you can better decide whether to give add-ons access to Skype.

```
    ...
    <UI>
      <API>
         <Authorizations>
            SkypeApiPythonTestClient;;;SkypeApiLogger
         </Authorizations>
      </API>
    ...
```

Manage Add-On Access Control

When an add-on first tries to access Skype via its API, Skype will ask you to give it explicit permission to do so (see Figure 11-14).

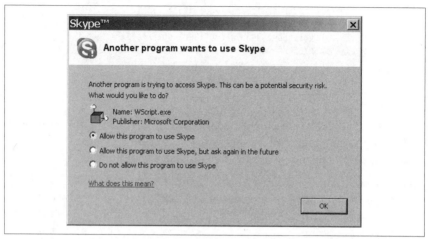

Figure 11-14. Initial permission dialog for add-on access to the Skype API

How you manage add-on access control after granting initial access then depends on the platform.

Windows. Once an add-on has been given permission to use the Skype API (the "Allow this program to use Skype" radio button should be clicked; see Figure 11-14), add-on access control is thereafter managed through a different dialog (see Figure 11-15). To access the dialog, select Skype → Tools → Options... → Privacy, and then click on the "Manage other programs' access to Skype" link).

The small double arrows in Figure 11-15 mean that that particular add-on is currently connected to Skype. Absence of these double arrows means that an add-on is under access control, but is dormant at present.

Selecting an add-on from Figure 11-15 and clicking on the Change button will open another dialog, shown in Figure 11-16, which will enable you to revoke or otherwise control the access for add-ons whose existence is already known by Skype.

Linux and Mac OS X. As of Skype version 1.2.0.11_API on Linux and 1.3.0.8 on Mac OS X, there is no dialog available through Skype's GUI to manage add-on access to the Skype API. To revoke access for an add-on, you must delete its entry in *config.xml*.

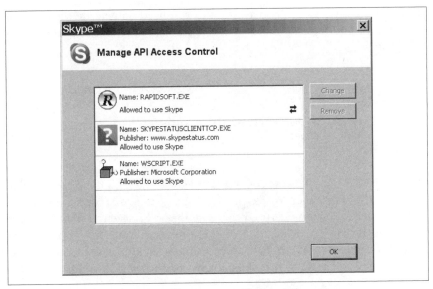

Figure 11-15. Dialog to manage add-on access to Skype's API

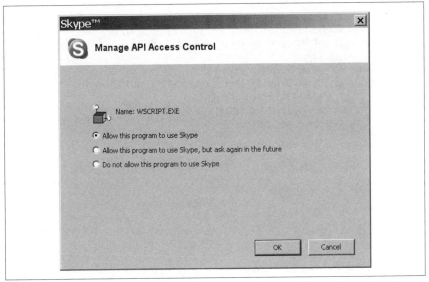

Figure 11-16. Dialog to control future access of add-ons for which you have already given permission to use Skype

To delete an entry from *config.xml* you must first stop Skype from running, delete the entry from the *config.xml* file, and then restart Skype. Otherwise, your changes won't take effect.

On Linux, to revoke access to an add-on, you need only delete the name of the add-on from the access control list, as shown in the following *config.xml* fragment:

```
...
<UI>
    <API>
        <Authorizations>
            SkypeApiPythonTestClient;;;SkypeApiLogger
        </Authorizations>
    </API>
...
```

On Mac OS X, the following *config.xml* fragment includes the access control entry for an add-on called My Skype API Tester. To revoke access to the Skype API for this add-on you will need to delete the add-on's entry (that is, delete everything between and including the `<My.20Skype.20API.20Tester>` and `</My.20Skype.20API.20Tester>` tags). If this add-on subsequently requests access to Skype, you will again be prompted to give it permission to do so.

```
...
<API>
    <List>
        <AppleScript>
            <Data1>2ACF364D256828FF6BF3680252A88880</Data1>
            <Data2>627722115D344BE8518653A885370FCF</Data2>
        </AppleScript>
        <My.20Skype.20API.20Tester>
            <Data1>39C7FB01F02DFF491174E05063DEF5F8FA20ACEE5B85F0
                   29ABB220005CFBE667</Data1>
            <Data2>627722115D344BE8518653A885370FCF</Data2>
        </My.20Skype.20API.20Tester>
    </List>
</API>
...
```

## CHAPTER TWELVE

Automate Skype

Hacks 91–100

Skype has an Application Programming Interface (API) that you can use to both extend Skype's functionality and use its services. For this chapter, you won't need to be a programmer, but you should be willing to roll up your sleeves and do some scripting. You will be using only simple tools readily available on your machine, though you might have to download a component or two from the Web to interface those tools to the Skype API.

This chapter will not discuss the *SkypeNET API* because, at the time of this writing, it had been announced but was not yet released. If you are curious, the SkypeNET API enables other third-party applications to use Skype's chat (instant messaging) and online presence infrastructure *without* having to run the Skype client (as opposed to add-ons that use the Skype API, which must have a running Skype client on the same machine to work).

We will be using scripting in three different, though complementary, ways. You can mix the three methods to accomplish what one alone cannot do. First, we will use scripting to control the Skype application, specifically through its native GUI. Second, we will use the Skype API by sending the Skype application simple text-like messages, and receiving text-like messages in return. At the heart of the Skype API is a simple, message-based "send-action-reply" protocol and we'll be using it, albeit at a simple level. Third, we will be using shell (command) scripts to automate things.

I hope the scripts in this chapter are useful as they are, but don't be afraid to hack around with them and experiment on your own. Consider these scripts as starting points for your own scripts, and as a stimulus to your imagination when inventing new scripts.

At the time of this writing, the Skype API was available only for the Windows, Linux, and Mac OS X platforms. Moreover, not all features of the API were available on all platforms and for all language bindings. For that reason, a handful of the scripts contain within them the word *experimental*, in anticipation that API support is imminent (as of the time of this writing), or that Skype has announced it will support it in the very near future. Skype's API is developing at a rapid pace, but that's no excuse for not using it now, as it already has some great features. Moreover, if you're waiting for the Skype API to reach some kind of stasis, you might have a very long wait! Experimental scripts do run and don't do anything bad, it's just that they may not work exactly as described; all other scripts work fine on the versions of Skype on which they were tested (see the Preface). If a script doesn't work for you, the first thing you should do is determine whether an updated script has been posted to the book's web site, *http://www.oreilly.com/ catalog/SkypeHacks/index.html*. You can download all scripts in this chapter from that web site.

The Skype API

Even though we're going to use the Skype API at a rather high level, there are distinct advantages to having an understanding—even if only at a conceptual level—of its inner workings. What follows is an overview of the Skype API from the scripting perspective.

The Skype API is conceptually divided into two parts: the Skype Phone API and the Skype Access API. The former is intended for hardware devices that connect to Skype, and therefore is beyond the scope of this chapter and will not be discussed further. Our focus will be on the Skype Access API, which allows an external application—that we'll refer to as an *add-on*—to extend Skype's functionality and use its services.

The choice of the term *add-on*, rather than, say, *add-in* or *plug-in* is a deliberate one. The latter two terms characteristically mean a code module that runs in the *same* memory space as the application that they extend. Skype is highly unusual in that add-ons that use the Skype API reside *outside* the memory space of Skype on Windows, Linux, and AppleScript on Mac OS X, and *inside* on Mac OS X for Cocoa and Carbon (I clarify this distinction in more detail shortly). Even so, the term *add-on* seems a better term to use for software that extends Skype's functionality, especially because such software is often associated with hardware that you add on to your computer.

At the core of the Skype API is a simple text-message-based protocol. Messages flow to and fro between an add-on and the Skype application, in a send-action-response fashion. The add-on sends a message requesting that Skype perform some *action*, and Skype responds to the add-on by sending back a message indicating success or failure (see Figure 12-1).

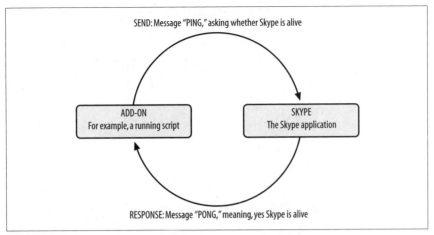

Figure 12-1. A simple Skype API message exchange on Windows

Though the message exchange protocol is the same on all platforms, the mechanism by which messages are exchanged is different depending on the platform. Here's a brief summary of how messages are exchanged on each platform that supports the Skype API:

Windows
> Messages are exchanged between the add-on and Skype by using Windows messages (which are normally messages sent to and from Windows to control their behavior), and which is the underlying method of coordinating activity within the Windows Manager (the program which controls the windows on your screen).

Linux
> Messages are exchanged between the add-on and Skype by using a message bus that is independent of the Windows Manager. This message bus is called *D-BUS* and is a component of the open source freedesktop.org project (*http://www.freedesktop.org*). D-BUS must be installed independently of Skype; that is, if you want to use the Skype API on Linux, you must install D-BUS yourself. When Skype and an add-on are connected to the same D-BUS, they can freely exchange Skype API protocol messages (see Figure 12-2).

Mac OS X
> Messages are exchanged between the add-on and Skype by using the traditional AppleScript interface to implement a "send" command for scripts, and for Cocoa and Carbon add-ons through an embeddable framework. So, Mac OS X actually supports two distinctly different message-passing methods: out-of-process in the case of AppleScript by implementing a classic AppleScript send command for Skype, and in-process

for Cocoa and Carbon using asynchronous delegate methods inside the add-on for Skype to pass messages back.

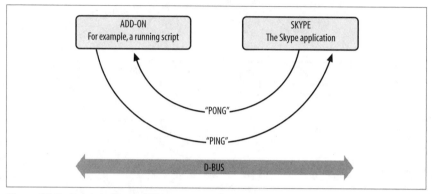

Figure 12-2. A simple Skype API message exchange on Linux

Skype protects itself from unauthorized add-ons by maintaining an Access Control List (ACL) of programs that the user has given explicit permission to use the Skype API. When an unrecognized add-on first tries to access Skype's API, the user is presented with a pop-up dialog that asks for permission to use the Skype API (see Figure 12-3). When you run a new script, you may have to give it permission to use the Skype API.

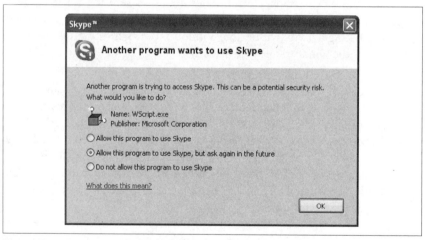

Figure 12-3. Giving permission to an add-on to use the Skype API

For readers who want to dig a little deeper into the Skype API, Skype has published a document, "Skype API: Description of Skype API and how to use it," which you can find at *http://share.skype.com/developer_zone/ documentation/documentation/*.

At a minimum, a Skype add-on should initialize its interaction with Skype's API by exchanging these messages (→ shows a message sent from the add-on to Skype, and ← shows a message sent from Skype to the add-on):

```
→ NAME NameOfAddon
← OK
→ PROTOCOL 5
← PROTOCOL 5
...
```

For Linux, during this message exchange, if this is the first time *NameOfAddon* has asked to use the Skype API, Skype will pop up a dialog asking the user to give permission for the add-on to access the API. OK will be returned and message passing will continue only if the user gives permission.

Here is a list of Skype API messages that will be used in this chapter (this is only a small subset of the commands that are available):

PING

> Message requesting that Skype respond if it's present. If Skype is running and receives the message, it will respond with PONG.

AUDIO_IN

> SET AUDIO_IN*Sound device name* sent to Skype will change the audio input device that Skype uses to the sound device specified. If no sound device is specified, this command will set audio input to the Windows default sound device. If this command is successful, Skype's reply message will be AUDIO_IN *Sound device name*.

AUDIO_OUT

> SET AUDIO_OUT *Sound device name* sent to Skype will change the audio output device that Skype uses to the sound device specified. If no sound device is specified, this command will set audio output to the Windows default sound device. If this command is successful, Skype's reply message will be AUDIO_OUT *Sound device name*.

CALL

> CALL *Skypename1, Skypename2...* with up to four Skype names and/or speed-dial codes will initiate calls to the specified Skype users. When more than one user is used with CALL, a conference call is created. If the command is successful, Skype will open, gain focus, and start the call(s). If you are a SkypeOut subscriber, you can use regular telephones in place of the Skype names; for example, you can dial numbers such as +442075551212.

CHAT CREATE

> CHAT CREATE*Skypename1, Skypename2...* with up to 50 Skype usernames will create a chat session. If a chat session is created successfully, Skype

will respond with CHAT <chat_id> STATUS <value>, where <chat_id> is a unique identifier for the chat session and <value> indicates the type of chat session created (one-on-one chat or multiperson chat).

CHATMESSAGE

Using the <chat_id> value returned by the CHAT CREATE command, you can send messages to the chat session that has been created by sending the command CHATMESSAGE <chat_id> *ChatMessage*. If this command is successful, Skype will reply with CHATMESSAGE <chat_id> STATUS SENDING.

FOCUS

Sending the command FOCUS to Skype will open it and give it focus.

MESSAGE

MESSAGE *Skypeuser Message* will send a chat message to the named Skype user. Even though Skype lists this command as "obsolete," it remains a valid command for compatibility purposes. Thank goodness, because its replacement command, CHATMESSAGE, poses a real problem for Apple-Script. CHATMESSAGE requires a chat ID, which is returned when the chat session is created, but this cannot be obtained in the case of Apple-Script because Skype has provided no means by which to receive messages from Skype!

NAME

NAME *SkypeAddonName* will notify Skype that an add-on is requesting to use its API. If the user gives permission for the add-on to access the API, NAME *SkypeAddonName* (or simply OK on Linux) is returned by Skype.

PROTOCOL

PROTOCOL*VersionNumber* sent by an add-on to Skype enables the add-on to notify Skype of the protocol version it would like to use. Skype replies with PROTOCOL *ProtocolNumber*, where *ProtocolNumber* is the lesser of the add-on or Skype's own supported protocol number. For example, if the add-on sends PROTOCOL 3, Skype will respond with PROTOCOL 3, even though it might support PROTOCOL 5. Another add-on that requests, say, PROTOCOL 7 will find that Skype replies with PROTOCOL 5. Skype will not discard messages from newer protocol versions and will try to perform the action requested by such messages, while the add-on should ignore commands it does not understand and that are sent to it by Skype.

RINGER

SET RINGER *Sound device name* sent to Skype will change the call-ringing device that Skype uses to the sound device specified. If no sound device is specified, this command will set call ringing to the Windows default sound device. If this command is successful, Skype's reply message will be RINGER *Sound device name*.

The Skype API is most distinctly a work in progress. When you can't get something to work with the Skype API, you should not immediately assume the problem is with you. Indeed, a search of the Skype forums may quickly prove it's a problem with Skype.

For example, the following tip alone might save someone a wasted day, as it cost a day of my time to find the problem and then fix it!

Skype announced support for its API with Linux in version 1.1.0.3. However, if you install the latest version of Skype (1.2.0.11 at the time of this writing) on SuSE using the RPM installation method, you may be shocked to find that the Skype API is missing! The fix is to download the *.tar.bz2* version, extract the Skype executable from that, and overwrite the SuSE version in /usr/bin with it.

The next time you have a problem with Skype, instead of stoically soldiering on against all odds, you should invest a little—or perhaps a lot—of time researching the problem on the Skype forums. The odds are that it's just as likely to be a problem with Skype as it is a problem with what you are doing.

Windows Scripting

On Windows, we will be using *Visual Basic Script*, or simply *VBScript*, which is a subset of Microsoft's popular Visual Basic language. We'll be running VBScript using the *Windows Scripting Host* (WSH), which is a runtime environment for running Windows scripts.

WSH comes with Windows XP, but must be downloaded (from *http://www.microsoft.com/*) and installed separately for Windows 2000.

VBScripts are files with a *.vbs* extension and that contain VBScript code. This is not the place to teach you how to code in VBScript. For that, O'Reilly has other books that may interest you (for example, *VBScript in a Nutshell* [2003]), but it is important for you to know how to run VBScripts. You can run VBScripts without command-line arguments by double-clicking on their filenames in Windows Explorer, from the run line (select Start → Run…), by entering their filenames (with or without the *.vbs* extension) at the command prompt, or by assigning them to a shortcut. If a script takes command-line arguments, you cannot run it by simply double-clicking on it in Windows Explorer.

Running VBScripts from the command line in a command prompt window can sometimes produce inconsistent results. It seems that sometimesthe command window grabs focus away from Skype before all the keystrokes have been sent to Skype. For this reason, I recommend that you run VBScripts that drive Skype's GUI (specifically, scripts that use the SendKeys command) either using the run line, or as the target of a shortcut. Also, be aware that the maximum length for a run-line command or shortcut target is 259 characters.

Some Windows scripts will use a neat COM component called ActiveS, which is available free of charge from KhaosLabs and which you can download from *http://www.khaoslabs.com/actives.php*. It is available in both source code and binary form under a BSD-style license.

Even though teaching you how to program in VBScript is not the purpose of this book, a few tips and tricks on hacking and making the scripts work is definitely within the book's scope. Here are a few ideas to try if you're having difficulty making a script (yours or mine) work as you want it to:

Scripting Skype's GUI

To see what your script is really doing, all you need to do is slow it down. You can do this by inserting pauses between commands, using the statement WScript.Sleep 1000, which pauses the script at that point for 1,000 milliseconds (1 second). Liberally sprinkling these throughout your script and then running it will make it look like a movie run in slow motion! And that might be enough for you to see where your script is going wrong.

Non-GUI scripting

If your script is not driving Skype's GUI, you can't actually see what's happening directly. However, by inserting commands to pop up information from time to time, you can peek at your script's inner workings. You can do this by inserting pop-up commands at important points in your code, as shown in the following script, *popup.vbs*:

```
' File: popup.vbs

Dim objShell, num
Set objShell = WScript.CreateObject("WScript.Shell")
num = 1
objShell.Popup "num = " & CStr(num)
num = num + 1
objShell.Popup "num + 1 = " & CStr(num)
```

Scripting the Skype API with ActiveS

A good starting point for any script that uses the ActiveS component (which must be installed separately) is to use the *ping_pong.vbs* script as a template. First, run *ping_pong.vbs* and make sure it works on your machine, then gradually add commands—periodically running the script to make sure it's still working—until your script is done. An interesting feature of this script is the use of the event handler, SkypeAPI_ Result, which you can modify to monitor any message returned by Skype, not just PONG. One important thing to bear in mind about a script like this one is that it won't stop until it gets the appropriate response message from Skype—in this case, PONG.

```
' File: ping_pong.vbs

Dim objShell, objSkypeAPI
Set objShell = WScript.CreateObject("WScript.Shell")
Set objSkypeAPI = WScript.CreateObject("SkypeAPI.Access")
objSkypeAPI.ConnectAndWait 15000
objShell.Popup objSkypeAPI.SendBlockingCommand("PING")
```

Unfortunately, VBScript is no longer included in ROM with Pocket PC 2003 or Windows Mobile 2003, so you won't be able to take advantage of scripting Skype on your handheld device. Scripting for Pocket PC will not be explored in this chapter.

Linux Scripting

On Linux, Skype has been developed using the Qt application framework from Trolltech, *http://www.trolltech.com/*. Qt has a scripting interface called *Qt Script for Applications* (QSA), but sadly, Skype does not support it. Nor does Skype support the standard technique for application scripting for the KDE desktop—namely, *Desktop COmmunication Protocol* (DCOP).

This sorry state of affairs leaves us with scripting the Skype API as the only option. For this, we will be using the Python scripting language, which is commonly available on the Linux platform. There is not enough space in this book to teach you Python; indeed, not enough space to give you even a quick tutorial. To learn more about programming with Python, I suggest that you read *Learning Python, Second Edition* (O'Reilly, 2003).

However, I would be remiss if I didn't offer you some help in scripting Skype with Python. So, here are a few tips and tricks you might find useful:

Slow script execution

When your script is doing a lot of things very quickly, it's difficult for you to see or understand what's going on. For that reason, it helps to slow things down by putting pauses between executable statements, as in this script, *pause.py*:

```python
#!/usr/bin/env python
# -*- coding: iso-8859-15 -*-

# File: pause.py

import time

def main():
    print "You should see this line first..."
    time.sleep(3)
    print "...and this line about 3 seconds later!"
    return 0

if __name__ == "__main__":
    main()
```

Output in a pop-up window

To see what's going on inside your script, it's sometimes useful to output stuff to the screen. This script, *popup.py*, shows you how to output data to the command terminal with print and to a pop-up window using SimpleDialog() from the Tk toolkit, which you must also have installed on your machine:

```python
#!/usr/bin/env python
# -*- coding: iso-8859-15 -*-

# File: popup.py

from Tkinter import *
from SimpleDialog import SimpleDialog

def main():
    print "Here's some output to the command terminal ..."
    root = Tk() # Initialize windowing toolkit
    SimpleDialog(root,
            "... and here's some output in a popup window!",
            buttons=["OK"], default=0, title="Popup Window").go()
    return 0

if __name__ == "__main__":
    main()
```

Scripting the Skype API using Python

Here is a very simple script, *ping_pong.py*, which you can use as a starting point for your own scripts that use the Skype API:

```python
#!/usr/bin/env python
# -*- coding: iso-8859-15 -*-

# File: ping_pong.py
```

```
import dbus, sys

class addon:
    # Name of Skype API addon (that is, name of this script addon)
    def name(self):
        return 'NAME PingPong'
    # Skype API protocol required by this addon
    def protocol(self):
        return 'PROTOCOL 1'

class skype_api:
    def __init__(self):
        remote_bus = dbus.SystemBus()
        system_service_list = remote_bus.get_service( \
        'org.freedesktop.DBus').get_object('/org/freedesktop/DBus', \
        'org.freedesktop.DBus').ListServices()

        skype_api_found = 0
        for service in system_service_list:
            if service=='com.Skype.API':
                skype_api_found = 1
                break

        if not skype_api_found:
            sys.exit('No API-capable instance of Skype was found')

        skype_service = remote_bus.get_service('com.Skype.API')
        self.skype_api_object = skype_service.get_object( \
        '/com/Skype', 'com.Skype.API')

        this_addon = addon()

        answer = self.send_message(this_addon.name())
        if answer != 'OK':
            sys.exit('Could not bind to Skype client')

        answer = self.send_message(this_addon.protocol())
        if answer != this_addon.protocol():
            sys.exit(this_addon.protocol() + ' is not supported' + \
                ' by the version of Skype you are running')

    def send_message(self, message):
        answer = self.skype_api_object.Invoke(message)
        print 'MESSAGE SENT TO SKYPE      --> ' + message
        print 'MESSAGE RETURNED BY SKYPE <-- ' + answer
        return answer

def main():
    skypeapi = skype_api()
    skypeapi.send_message('PING')
    return 0

if __name__ == "__main__":
    main()
```

You can run Python scripts from the command line, like this: `python script.py arg1`, where `arg1` and any following arguments are optional, depending on the needs of the script.

Mac OS X Scripting

The de facto scripting environment for the Mac is AppleScript. This wonderful, English-like scripting language has been around since 1993, and it is tightly integrated with the Mac operating system. We will be using Apple-Script to control Skype through its GUI and its API.

 To have AppleScript drive Skype's GUI, you must enable one of Mac OS X's universal access options. To do so, select System Preferences → Universal Access, and then check the "Enable access for assistive devices" checkbox.

To learn more about programming with AppleScript, I thoroughly recommend the book that I use, *AppleScript: The Missing Manual* (O'Reilly, 2005). In the meantime, these tips and tricks should help to send you on your way to scripting Skype using AppleScript:

Scripting Skype's GUI

AppleScript is a very powerful tool for scripting Skype through its GUI. Even though Skype can hardly claim to be AppleScript aware or even friendly (it has a miniscule dictionary of commands), by using AppleScript you can readily accomplish in a script anything you might do manually through Skype's GUI. To use AppleScript to drive the Skype GUI, you will first have to enable scripting of Apple's GUI (select System Preferences → Universal Access, and then check the "Enable access for assistive devices" checkbox). Also, if you're having problems with a script, it helps to slow it down—make it run in slow motion—by inserting pauses between commands using `delay`; for example, `delay 0.5` will pause script execution for half a second. It also helps to see what's going on inside a running script by displaying data and information at various points throughout the script, which you can do using the `display dialog` command; for example, `display dialog "Point XYZ in the script has been reached"` will pop up a window and display the message text.

Scripting the Skype API with AppleScript

Skype has support for only one AppleScript command: `send`—that's it! This unfortunately means that you can only send commands to Skype, and that you won't receive any responses back from Skype. Like many modern-day weapons, this fire-and-forget mode of operation is fine if the intended target is hit squarely; but it's no good if you miss. Not getting anything back from Skype in response to an issued command can make scripts harder to debug. Presumably, Skype will extend its AppleScript interface to its API sometime soon to remedy the situation. In the meantime, this basic script, *echo123.scpt*, may prove useful as the starting point for your own scripting efforts to automate Skype, through both its API and its GUI:

```
-- File: echo123.scpt

-- Skype API scripting
tell application "Skype"
    -- Send Skype API command to chat with echo123 and have the
    -- echo123 service call you back
    send command "MESSAGE echo123 callme" script name "echo123"
    delay 3
    -- Send Skype API command to bring Skype to the foreground and
    -- give it focus
    send command "FOCUS" script name "focus"
end tell

-- Skype GUI scripting
tell application "System Events"
    tell process "Skype"
        -- Pickup the call by clicking the "Answer" button in the
        -- "Quick Answer" window
        click button 1 of group 1 of group 1 of window "Quick Answer"
        delay 5
        -- Hangup the call by clicking "Hang Up" in the "Call" menu
        click menu item "Hang Up" of menu 1 of menu bar item ¬
            "Call" of menu bar 1
    end tell
end tell
```

Hot-Switch Among Sound Devices

HACK #91

By attaching a script to a hotkey sequence, you can hot-switch among the sound devices used by Skype—even during a call!

Works with: Windows, Linux, and Mac OS X versions of Skype.

You might want to switch from one sound device to another for many reasons. For instance, you might want to switch from a microphone and speaker to a handset for privacy from eavesdroppers during a call, or you might have a handset but you like to play your voicemail over a speaker. The scripts in this hack will show you how to hot-switch among sound devices with fast and easy hotkey sequences.

There are two ways of switching sound devices in Skype by means of scripts. First, you can drive its GUI interface to do the job, which is often ugly but avoids having to deal with the Skype API. The second method is to drive the

Skype API from a script, which, when possible, is a little cleaner and less error prone. I'll present both methods in this hack. It's your choice as to what works best for your setup.

In the case of scripts that drive the Skype GUI, in effect you will simply have the script drive those interactions with Skype that you would otherwise do by hand. You will save yourself a world of frustration if, when writing these types of script, you have a notepad and pencil close at hand. Jot down your steps, no matter how small, so that when it comes time to replay them in a script, no steps are missed. Missing a single step in a script may mean that your script simply won't work, or that it does something totally unintended. You have been warned!

Windows

Whichever method you choose—pure scripting or scripting the Skype API— it will simplify things if you first create a shortcut for *Skype.exe* on your desktop or somewhere in the Start menu and assign a hotkey sequence to it—say, Ctrl-Shift-S. This will make things easier because we'll be sending key sequences to Skype, but we can do that only if Skype is open and has focus. But Skype spends much of its time minimized in the Windows system tray. By assigning Skype a hotkey sequence of its own, we can make it open and pop up anytime we want.

 You can enable hotkeys in Skype (select Skype → Tools → Options... → Hotkeys) and assign a hotkey sequence to focus Skype. However, this method of gaining focus for Skype has the annoying side effect of minimizing Skype to the system tray when Skype is already open. This, clearly, is not the behavior required by a script that always needs to send keystrokes to an open window that has focus.

Script Skype's GUI. Here are the beginnings of our script to hot-switch sound devices through Skype's GUI. This script, *focus.vbs*, will display Skype and give it focus:

```
' File: focus.vbs

Dim objShell
Set objShell = WScript.CreateObject("WScript.Shell")
objShell.SendKeys "^+S" ' Send ctrl+shift+S
```

Now, having gotten Skype's attention, we can send it a sequence of keys to get to the sound-device setup screen for Skype. The following script, *sound_ devices.vbs*, will get you to the point show in Figure 12-4.

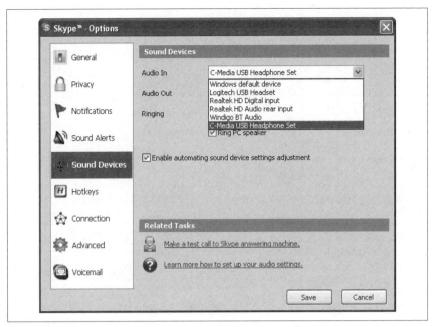

Figure 12-4. Skype sound device options screen

```
' File: sound_devices.vbs

Dim objShell
Set objShell = WScript.CreateObject("WScript.Shell")
objShell.SendKeys "^+S"      ' Send ctrl+shift+S
WScript.Sleep 1000           ' Wait for Skype to open and gain focus
objShell.SendKeys "%(TO)"    ' Tools --> Options...
objShell.SendKeys "{TAB}"    ' Move to left pane ...
objShell.SendKeys "{TAB}"    ' ... done.
objShell.SendKeys "{DOWN}"   ' Move to Sound Devices ...
objShell.SendKeys "{DOWN}"   ' ...
objShell.SendKeys "{DOWN}"   ' ...
objShell.SendKeys "{DOWN}"   ' ... done.
objShell.SendKeys "{TAB}"    ' Move to audio-in pulldown menu ...
objShell.SendKeys "{TAB}"    ' ... done.
objShell.SendKeys "%{DOWN}"  ' Pull down the menu to display devices.
```

From here on, all you have to do is replicate the key sequences you would enter by hand. In my case, the script, *logitech.vbs*, to make my Logitech USB headset the device used by Skype for all sound purposes looks like this:

```
' File: logitech.vbs

Dim objShell
Set objShell = WScript.CreateObject("WScript.Shell")
objShell.SendKeys "^+S"      ' Send ctrl-shift-S
WScript.Sleep 1000           ' Wait for Skype to open and gain focus
```

```
objShell.SendKeys "%(TO)"    ' Tools --> Options...
WScript.Sleep 100
objShell.SendKeys "{TAB}"    ' Move to left pane ...
WScript.Sleep 100
objShell.SendKeys "{TAB}"    ' ... done.
WScript.Sleep 100
objShell.SendKeys "{DOWN}"   ' Move to Sound Devices ...
WScript.Sleep 100
objShell.SendKeys "{DOWN}"   ' ...
WScript.Sleep 100
objShell.SendKeys "{DOWN}"   ' ...
WScript.Sleep 100
objShell.SendKeys "{DOWN}"   ' ... done.
WScript.Sleep 100
objShell.SendKeys "{TAB}"    ' Move to audio-in pulldown menu ...
WScript.Sleep 100
objShell.SendKeys "{TAB}"    ' ... done.
WScript.Sleep 100
objShell.SendKeys "L"        ' Set audio-in to Logitech
WScript.Sleep 100
objShell.SendKeys "{TAB}"
WScript.Sleep 100
objShell.SendKeys "L"        ' Set audio-out to Logitech
WScript.Sleep 100
objShell.SendKeys "{TAB}"
WScript.Sleep 100
objShell.SendKeys "L"        ' Set ringer to Logitech
WScript.Sleep 100
objShell.SendKeys "{TAB}"    ' Move to save button ...
WScript.Sleep 100
objShell.SendKeys "{TAB}"    ' ...
WScript.Sleep 100
objShell.SendKeys "{TAB}"    ' ... done.
WScript.Sleep 100
objShell.SendKeys "{ENTER}"  ' Press the save button.
```

During a call, Skype is busy with many things. For Skype not to miss keystrokes sent by the previous script during a call, the script pauses for 100 milliseconds before issuing each sequence of keystrokes.

Another script, *c-media.vbs*, which is identical in every respect to *logitech.vbs* except that *L* is replaced with *C*, will switch Skype's sound devices back to the C-Media USB headphone set. All that remains is to create shortcuts for *logitech.vbs* and *c-media.vbs* and assign hotkeys to them—say, Ctrl-Shift-L and Ctrl-Shift-C, respectively. Then, switching between the two devices— even during a call—is just a short hotkey sequence away.

Script Skype's API. Switching sound devices in Skype using the Skype API requires that three commands be sent to Skype: AUDIO_IN, AUDIO_OUT, and RINGER. This script, *logitech_API.vbs*, in combination with ActiveS, will have

Skype switch to the Logitech USB headset sound device. An almost identical script, *c-media_API.vbs*, which replaces the words "Logitech USB Headset" with "C-Media USB Headphone Set," will switch Skype to use that device instead. These two scripts, *logitech_API.vbs* and *c-media_API.vbs*, are the Skype API equivalents of *logitech.vbs* and *c-media.vbs* (as discussed earlier).

```
' File: logitech_API.vbs

Dim objSkypeAPI
Set objSkypeAPI = WScript.CreateObject("SkypeAPI.Access")
objSkypeAPI.SendBlockingCommand "SET AUDIO_IN Logitech USB Headset"
objSkypeAPI.SendBlockingCommand "SET AUDIO_OUT Logitech USB Headset"
objSkypeAPI.SendBlockingCommand "SET RINGER Logitech USB Headset"
```

Linux

If you want to switch sound devices on Linux using a script, you have to use the Skype API. You can invoke this script, *hot-switch.py* (experimental), from the command prompt like this: python hot-switch.py '/dev/dsp1', where /dev/dsp1 is the name of the audio device that you want Skype to use for both audio-in and audio-out functions:

```
#!/usr/bin/env python
# -*- coding: iso-8859-15 -*-

# File: hot-switch.py (experimental)

import dbus, sys

class addon:
    # Name of Skype API addon (that is, name of this script addon)
    def name(self):
        return 'NAME HotSwitch'
    # Skype API protocol required by this addon
    def protocol(self):
        return 'PROTOCOL 1'

class skype_api:
    def __init__(self):
        remote_bus = dbus.SystemBus( )
        system_service_list = remote_bus.get_service( \
        'org.freedesktop.DBus').get_object( \
        '/org/freedesktop/DBus', \
        'org.freedesktop.DBus').ListServices( )

        skype_api_found = 0
        for service in system_service_list:
            if service=='com.Skype.API':
                skype_api_found = 1
                break
```

```
        if not skype_api_found:
            sys.exit('No running API-capable Skype found')

        skype_service = remote_bus.get_service('com.Skype.API')
        self.skype_api_object = skype_service.get_object( \
        '/com/Skype', 'com.Skype.API')

        this_addon = addon()

        answer = self.send_message(this_addon.name())
        if answer != 'OK':
            sys.exit('Could not bind to Skype client')

        answer = self.send_message(this_addon.protocol())
        if answer != this_addon.protocol():
            sys.exit(this_addon.protocol() + \
                ' is not supported by the version' + \
                ' of Skype you are running')

    def send_message(self, message):
        answer = self.skype_api_object.Invoke(message)
        print 'MESSAGE SENT TO SKYPE     --> ' + message
        print 'MESSAGE RETURNED BY SKYPE <-- ' + answer
        return answer

def main():
    skypeapi = skype_api()
    skypeapi.send_message('SET AUDIO_IN '  + sys.argv[1])
    skypeapi.send_message('SET AUDIO_OUT ' + sys.argv[1])
    return 0

if __name__ == "__main__":
    main()
```

Mac OS X

On Mac OS X, using AppleScript, you can hot-switch sound devices either through Skype's GUI interface, or by using its API.

Script Skype's GUI. This script, *logitech.scpt*, will switch the sound device used by Skype to the Logitech USB headset. To make it work for other sound devices, copy the file and rename it, and then change the name of the sound device used in the script. Note that you must be very careful with device names, as the name in your script and the name of the device for Skype must match exactly. For example, to switch to my "C-Media USB Headphone Set," the name I actually had to use in my script was "C-Media USB Headphone Set " (with two trailing blank characters). Just be careful with names and you should be hot switching between sound devices in no time.

```
-- File: logitech.scpt

tell application "Skype"
    activate
end tell
tell application "System Events"
    tell process "Skype"
        click menu item "Preferences...¶" of menu 1 of ¬
            menu bar item "Skype" of menu bar 1
        try
            click button "Audio" of tool bar 1 of window "General"
        end try
        try
            click button "Audio" of tool bar 1 of window "Privacy"
        end try
        try
            click button "Audio" of tool bar 1 of window "Events"
        end try
        try
            click button "Audio" of tool bar 1 of window "Voicemail"
        end try
        try
            click button "Audio" of tool bar 1 of window "Advanced"
        end try
        try
            click button "Audio" of tool bar 1 of window "Chat"
        end try
        click pop up button 1 of group 1 of group 1 of window "Audio"
        pick menu item "Logitech USB Headset" of menu of ¬
            pop up button 1 of group 1 of group 1 of window "Audio"
        delay 0.5
        click pop up button 2 of group 1 of group 1 of window "Audio"
        pick menu item "Logitech USB Headset" of menu of ¬
            pop up button 2 of group 1 of group 1 of window "Audio"
        delay 0.5
        click button 1 of window "Audio"
    end tell
end tell
```

Script Skype's API. The API script equivalent of *logitech.scpt*, *logitech_API.scpt* (experimental), is a lot shorter and a lot cleaner. But that same warning about sound device names also applies.

```
-- File: logitech_API.scpt (experimental)

tell application "Skype"
    send command "SET AUDIO_IN Logitech USB Headset" script name "Audio in"
    send command "SET AUDIO_OUT Logitech USB Headset" script name "Audio out"
end tell
```

Automate Chat

HACK #92   If you need to send chat messages to a group of people often, why not use this script hack to create a multichat session and send messages to all participants on your behalf.

Works with: Windows version of Skype.

Sending chat to a lot of people at once can be tedious, and doubly so if you have to do this often, which can be the case for tightknit teams or groups of, say, 10 or more people that use chat a lot. So, the next time you need to send "Progress meeting, 4 p.m. today, room 101" to 50 people, consider automating sending the chat message with this script, *chat.vbs*. This is also the ideal way to start a multiperson chat session with a lot of participants, as your opening message starts the chat session, adds all participants to that chat session, and then opens the chat window (optional, see script), ready for you to continue chatting.

```
' File: chat.vbs

' Invoke like this from the command-line:
'     chat /u=skypeuser1 /u=skypeuser2 MessageText
'
' Parameters:
' /u=skypeuser1 - Recipients (up to 50) of the chat message have
'                   their Skype names prefixed with "/u="
' MessageText   - Text for the chat message

' Global variables
Dim objShell        ' Scripting shell object
Dim arrUsers        ' Array of users to send
Dim objSkypeAPI     ' SkypeAPI object
Dim objChat         ' Chat object
Dim bComplete       ' Flag to indicate when process is done
Dim strChatCmd      ' Holds the command to create the chat

' Main script begins here
Set objShell = WScript.CreateObject("WScript.Shell")
Set objSkypeAPI = WScript.CreateObject("SkypeAPI.Access")
objSkypeAPI.ConnectAndWait 15000
bComplete = False

' Count how many users are passed
Set objArgs = WScript.Arguments
iCount = 0
bUsersFound = False
Redim arrUsers(objArgs.Count)
For i = 1 to objArgs.Count
    If (Left(objArgs(i-1), 3) = "/u=") And (Not bInMessage) Then
        arrUsers(i-1) = Mid(objArgs(i-1), 4)
        iCount = iCount + 1
```

```
        If iCount > 50 Then
            Exit For
        End If
        bUsersFound = True
    ElseIf bUsersFound Then
        If Not bInMessage Then
            bInMessage = True
        Else
            strMessage = strMessage + " "
        End If
        strMessage = strMessage + objArgs(i-1)
    End If
Next

' Prompt the user if the correct parameters weren't sent
If iCount > 50 Then
    objShell.Popup "You are limited to 50 users", 0, _
        "Unable to Send Message", 48
ElseIf (iCount = 0) Or (Len(strMessage) = 0) Then
    objShell.Popup "/u=user1 /u=user2 Message to Send", _
        0, "Broadcast Chat Message Script Usage", 64
Else
    ' Resize users array
    Redim Preserve arrUsers(iCount)

    ' Connect to Skype and wait for finish
    objSkypeAPI.ConnectAndWait 15000
    If objSkypeAPI.Protocol < 4 Then
        objShell.Popup _
        "You must be running a more current version of Skype"
    Else
        ' Build and send the chat command
        strChatCmd = "CHAT CREATE " + Join(arrUsers, ", ")
        If Right(strChatCmd, 2) = ", " Then
            strChatCmd = Mid(strChatCmd, 1, Len(strChatCmd)-2)
        End If
        strResult = objSkypeAPI.SendBlockingCommand(strChatCmd)

        ' Parse the result string to get the chat ID
        sparts = Split(strResult, " ")

        objSkypeAPI.SendBlockingCommand _
            "CHATMESSAGE " + sparts(1) + " " + strMessage

        ' [Optional] Comment out if you don't want to open
        ' the chat window
        objSkypeAPI.SendBlockingCommand "OPEN CHAT " + sparts(1)
    End If
End If
```

As listing a large number of recipients on the command line can be both tedious and error prone, perhaps a better method is to wrap *chat.vbs* in a batch file—say, *team_chat.bat*—as shown here (enter the chat script command and its parameters as one, long, continuous line in the batch file). That way, you can simply invoke it at a command prompt, like this: team_ chat "Progress meeting, 4 p.m. today, room 101".

```
REM File: team_chat.bat

chat /u=TeamMember1 /u=TeamMember2 /u=TeamMember3 /u=TeamMember4
/u=TeamMember4 /u=TeamMember6 ... /u=TeamMemberN %1
```

HACK #93 Automate Your Interactions with Telephone Systems

If you interact with automated telephone systems often (the "Press 6 to access your account" sort of thing) this hack will do the work of pressing the buttons for you.

Works with: Windows version of Skype.

They're the systems we all love to hate! *Interactive Voice Response* (IVR) systems can simplify life, or make life unbearable. From renewing a drug prescription to getting your bank balance over the phone, when they work they're a boon, and when they don't they're a bust.

IVR systems respond to the keys you press (actually, the tones you hear when you press a key) on your phone's keypad (or on Skype's Dial tab) in response to voice prompts from a computer at the other end of the call. Menus for IVR systems are normally well defined and don't change often. So, grab a notepad and jot down your interactions at each step during an IVR call. Armed with this information, you're in a good position to automate the process the next time around

Of course, in tribute to Murphy's Law, the menu option you most often want is buried so deep that it's a lot of key presses away. So, if you interact often with IVR systems, automate your interaction in whole, or in part, using this script, *ivr.vbs*. Note that you will have to be a subscriber to the SkypeOut service if you want to call regular phone numbers that operate IVR systems.

```
' File: ivr.vbs

' Invoke like this from the command-line:
'               ivr +18005551212 ,,123,456,,78
'
' Parameters:
' +18005551212  - number to call
' ,,123,456,,78 - keypad keys to press with 1 second pause for
'                 each comma
```

```
' Global variable
Dim g_objShell     ' Scripting shell object

' Dial number and send DTMF tones upon connection
' SkypeHandle = handle of Skype user or telephone number to call
' DTMF = string of DTMF values (0-9,#,* and ,)
Sub DialDTMF(SkypeHandle, DTMF)
    Dim objSkypeAPI  ' SkypeAPI object
    Dim objCall      ' Call object
    Dim iStatus      ' Call status
    Dim i            ' Counter
    Dim strDigit     ' DTMF digit

    ' Create the Skype interface object
    Set objSkypeAPI = WScript.CreateObject("SkypeAPI.Access")

    ' Place the call
    Set objCall = objSkypeAPI.PlaceCall(SkypeHandle)

    ' Loop until the call is cancelled, finished or in progress
    Do
        iStatus = objCall.Status
        ' If the call is in progress, then
        ' send the DTMF characters
        If iStatus = 5 Then
            For i = 1 to Len(DTMF)
                strDigit = Mid(DTMF, i, 1)
                Select Case strDigit
                    Case "0", "1", "2", "3", _
                         "4", "5", "6", "7", _
                         "8", "9", "#", "*":
                        ' Send the DTMF digit
                        ' and wait 200 ms so
                        ' that the digit
                        ' registers properly
                        objCall.SendDTMF strDigit
                        ' If this pause isn't
                        ' here, DTMF tones may
                        ' play back too fast
                        WScript.Sleep 400
                    Case ",":
                        ' Interpret commas as
                        ' 1 sec pauses
                        WScript.Sleep 1000
                End Select
            Next
        Else
            ' Wait for the call to be picked up
            ' or cancelled
            WScript.Sleep 500
        End If
    Loop While (iStatus <> 3) and _
               (iStatus <> 5) and _
```

```
                         (iStatus <> 11)
    End Sub


    ' Main script begins here
    Set g_objShell = WScript.CreateObject("WScript.Shell")

    ' Make sure the user is sending the correct number of parameters
    If WScript.Arguments.Length <> 2 Then
        g_objShell.Popup "Parameter 1: Skype Handle to Call" & _
                 vbCrLF & "Parameter 2: DTMF to Send", _
                 0, "DialDTMF Script Usage", 64
    Else
        DialDTMF WScript.Arguments(0), WScript.Arguments(1)
    End If
```

HACK #94   Schedule Calls and Chat Using iCal on the Mac

Have you ever forgotten to make or return an important call? Well, that can be a thing of the past if you have iCal place the call for you at the right time and on the right date.

Works with: Mac OS X version of Skype.

iCal on the Mac has a neat feature whereby you can attach an AppleScript to an event and have it run precisely on a date and at a time that you choose.

To schedule a Skype call, simply create a short AppleScript—say, *call_pete. scpt*—that uses the Skype API to start the call for you. Note that after the CALL command you can have either a Skype username or a telephone number (if you are a SkypeOut subscriber). Next you must associate this script with an event in iCal. You can do this by selecting "Run script" from the "alarm" option for an event (see Figure 12-5).

At the duly appointed date and time, the script will run, and Skype will pop up and start the call. Clearly, however, scheduled calls are for times when you're sure you'll be sitting at your computer! Likewise, you can schedule conference calls in a similar way (using a command such as CALL skypeuser1 +442075551212 skypeuser2, for instance, listing up to four conference call participants after the CALL statement).

```
-- File: call_pete.scpt

tell application "Skype"
    send command "CALL +12035551212" script name "Call Pete"
end tell
```

You can also schedule chat messages in the same manner. Suppose you have a regular team meeting at noon every Wednesday. You can send a chat message reminder to all team members five minutes before the start of the meeting by attaching a script, such as *chat_team.scpt*, to a recurring event in iCal:

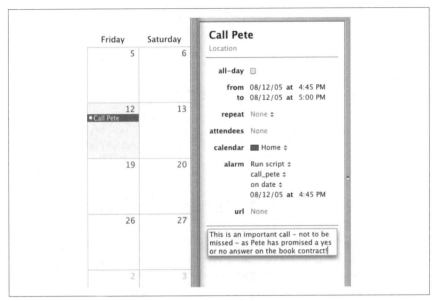

Figure 12-5. Attaching a script to an event in iCal

```
-- File: chat_team.scpt

tell application "Skype"
    set msg to "  Weekly team meeting in 5 minutes, room 101"
    send command "MESSAGE skypeteam1" & msg script name "Team member 1"
    send command "MESSAGE skypeteam2" & msg script name "Team member 2"
    send command "MESSAGE skypeteam3" & msg script name "Team member 3"
    send command "MESSAGE skypeteam4" & msg script name "Team member 4"
end tell
```

In the *chat_team.scpt* script, pay particular attention to the fact that there must be whitespace between the Skype username and the message text.

Hacking the Hack

Just as you can't call yourself in Skype, you can't send a chat message to only yourself (though the latter isn't entirely true). If you send a chat message to echo123, it will be reflected back to you. This means you can send chat messages to yourself, which at first glance seems pointless—until you realize that such messages in combination with iCal mean that you can send yourself reminders using Skype chat! This is particularly useful if you regularly log onto Skype on several machines under different Skype usernames, which might be the case if you have several machines at home or at the office and you roam from one to the next, or if you travel with a laptop. Your schedule is centralized on one machine, but your reminders are distributed. Simply attach a script such as *chat_reminder.scpt* to an event in iCal, and no matter where you are logged onto Skype, your reminder will grab your attention.

```
-- File: chat_reminder.scpt

tell application "Skype"
    set msg to "  Dental appointment at 4:30 p.m."
    send command "MESSAGE echo123" & msg script name "Self"
    send command "MESSAGE skypehome" & msg script name "Home"
    send command "MESSAGE skypeoffice" & msg script name "Office"
    send command "MESSAGE skypelaptop" & msg script name "Laptop"
    send command "MESSAGE skypepocket" & msg script name "Pocket PC"
end tell
```

HACK #95   Send Email and SMS Notification of New Voicemail

Don't let Skype voicemail languish, unheard for hours or perhaps even days. Get timely notifications of newly arrived Skype voicemail by automatically sending an email/SMS message to your handheld or mobile phone.

Works with: Windows and Mac OS X versions of Skype.

If you move around a lot with a handheld device that has email but doesn't run Skype (for example, a Palm PDA), or if you carry a *Short Message Service* (SMS)-enabled phone, you can get timely notification of the arrival of new Skype voicemail using the following scripts. Once you receive notification, go to the nearest machine running Skype, log on, and you'll be able to listen to your newly arrived voicemail.

> When you log onto Skype on a machine that is not your own, Skype downloads new voicemail and other files to that machine's hard disk. These files are not encrypted, so you might want to delete them safely before leaving the borrowed machine (see "Erase a Skype User Account" [Hack #98]).

The scripts work just as well for mobile phones. Most mobile phones with SMS have an email gateway so that any short email message sent to the gateway is converted into an SMS message and is forwarded to your phone. For example, sending an email to one of these email gateways will deliver an SMS message to the mobile phone with the number specified (*PhoneNumber*):

T-Mobile
> *PhoneNumber*@tmomail.net

Virgin Mobile
> *PhoneNumber*@vmobl.com

Cingular
> *PhoneNumber*@cingularme.com

Sprint

    PhoneNumber@messaging.sprintpcs.com

Verizon

    PhoneNumber@vtext.com

Nextel

    PhoneNumber@messaging.nextel.com

All of the scripts in this hack continuously monitor the folder into which Skype puts its voicemail files. Each time a new file appears in the folder, the scripts send off a short email to your portable device—indeed, to any device or devices that are email enabled!

The scripts in this hack work by constantly monitoring the folder that Skype uses to download voicemail files for newly arrived voicemails. Whereas the Windows and Mac OS X versions of Skype download voicemail files immediately, the Linux version does not do so until the user actually plays a voicemail message. That is why the scripting technique used in this hack won't work on Linux.

Normally, Skype stores voicemail files in these folders:

Windows

    *C:\Documents and Settings\LogonName\Application Data\Skype\SkypeName\
    voicemail*

Mac OS X

    */Users/LogonName/Library/ApplicationSupport/Skype/SkypeName/
    voicemail*

> Were Skype to make the audio format of its voicemail public (Skype, if you're reading this, that's a hint), you could easily modify the scripts in this hack to forward via email the newly arrived voicemail as a sound file attachment that could be played on the receiving handheld device. Now *that* would be cool!

Windows

This script, *new_voicemail.vbs*, will check your voicemail folder every 30 seconds or so to see whether a new voicemail has arrived. When one does, it sends off a short email message telling you so. It uses the Simple Message Transfer Protocol (SMTP) to send email, because if you try to script Microsoft Outlook, you'll soon be in a world of pain—believe me, don't go that route! To make this script work for you, you will need to make some small changes. But once you've done that, the script will run continuously in the background until you explicitly kill it or shut down your machine.

```
' File: new_voicemail.vbs

' Things you need to change in this script are
' shown like <this>.

Const cdoSendUsingPort = 2 ' Send the message using SMTP
Const cdoBasicAuth = 1      ' Clear-text authentication
Const cdoTimeout = 60       ' Timeout for SMTP in seconds
Const cdoPort = 25          ' Port number for SMTP

Dim objFSO, objFolder, objFiles, objEmail
Dim voicemail_folder, num_voicemails
Set objFSO = WScript.CreateObject("Scripting.FileSystemObject")
voicemail_folder = "C:\Documents and Settings\<YourLogonName>" & _
                   "\Application Data\Skype\<SkypeName>" & _
                   "\voicemail"
Set objFolder = objFSO.GetFolder(voicemail_folder)
Set objFiles = objFolder.Files
num_voicemails = objFiles.Count

Do
    If objFiles.count > num_voicemails Then

        Set objEmail  = CreateObject("CDO.Message")

        ' Message to be sent
        objEmail.Subject  = "You have a new Skype voicemail!"
        objEmail.Sender   = "<SenderEmailAddress>"
        objEmail.To       = "<RecipientEmailAddress>"
        objEmail.TextBody = "You have new voicemail..." & _
                            VbCr & VbCr & "...logon to " & _
                            "your Skype account to " & _
                            "listen to your new " & _
                            "voicemail message."

'-------------------------------------------------------------------
        ' SMTP server details
        objEmail.Configuration.Fields.Item _
("http://schemas.microsoft.com/cdo/configuration/sendusing") = _
cdoSendUsingPort
        objEmail.Configuration.Fields.Item _
("http://schemas.microsoft.com/cdo/configuration/smtpserver") = _
"<SMTPServerName>"
        objEmail.Configuration.Fields.Item _
("http://schemas.microsoft.com/cdo/configuration/smtpauthenticate") = _
cdoBasicAuth
        objEmail.Configuration.Fields.Item _
("http://schemas.microsoft.com/cdo/configuration/sendusername") = _
"<SMTPUsername>"
        objEmail.Configuration.Fields.Item _
("http://schemas.microsoft.com/cdo/configuration/sendpassword") = _
"<SMTPPassword>"
        objEmail.Configuration.Fields.Item _
```

```
("http://schemas.microsoft.com/cdo/configuration/smtpserverport") = _
cdoPort
        objEmail.Configuration.Fields.Item _
("http://schemas.microsoft.com/cdo/configuration/smtpusessl") = _
False
        objEmail.Configuration.Fields.Item _
("http://schemas.microsoft.com/cdo/configuration/smtpconnectiontimeout") = _
cdoTimeout
        objEmail.Configuration.Fields.Update
'-------------------------------------------------------------------

    objEmail.Send

    Set objEmail  = Nothing

  End If

  num_voicemails = objFiles.count

  WScript.Sleep 30000 ' Go to sleep for 30 seconds

Loop While True
```

Mac OS X

You can attach this AppleScript, *new_voicemail.scpt*, to a folder action—in this case, the "new item alert" action—that will run the script every time a new file is added to the Skype voicemail folder. This means that every time a new voicemail arrives, the script uses Mail to send you a notification message.

To set up a folder action, in the Finder locate the Skype voicemail folder, Ctrl-Click on it, choose Attach a Folder Action…, and then attach the *new_voicemail.scpt* script. Now, every time a new voicemail arrives, you'll know about it wherever you might be. This script will run on action until you disable or delete the folder action with which it is associated. Even after rebooting, it'll still be there, doing its job!

To have *new_voicemail.scpt* available as a folder-action script, you must put it in the folder-action scripts folder, */Library/Scripts/Folder Action Scripts/*:

```
-- File: new_voicemail.scpt

-- Things you need to change in this script are
-- shown like <this>.

on adding folder items to this_folder after receiving added_items
    try
        tell application "Mail"
            -- Send mail immediately
            set displayForManualSend to false
```

```
            -- Mail header
            set email_to to "<RecipientEmailAddress>"
            set email_from to "<SenderEmailAddress>"
            set email_subject to "You have new Skype voicemail!"
            -- Mail body
            set email_body to return & return & ¬
                "You have new voicemail..." & ¬
                return & return & ¬
                "...logon to your Skype account " & ¬
                "to listen to your new voicemail message."
            -- Create the e-mail
            set msg to make new outgoing message
            tell msg
                make new to recipient at beginning of ¬
                    to recipients ¬
                    with properties {address:email_to}
                set the sender to email_from
                set the subject to email_subject
                set the content to email_body
            end tell
            send msg
        end tell
    end try
end adding folder items to
```

H A C K #96 Convert Your Friends List to Fast-Dial Shortcuts

Convert contacts from your friends list into fast-dial shortcuts so that they're just a click away.

Works with: Windows version of Skype.

In "Add Fast-Dial Shortcuts to Your Menu or Desktop" [Hack #49], you saw how to create a shortcut that enabled you to call a contact with just a click or two of your mouse, or with a hotkey sequence. In this hack, we'll automate the process of converting everyone in your Skype friends list (also known as your buddies list) into shortcuts.

The following VBScript, *shortcuts.vbs*, constructs a list of friends and creates a shortcut icon for each one. If you have 15 or more friends, first you are prompted to confirm that you do indeed want one icon per friend. This is to prevent your desktop or menu from becoming cluttered with shortcut icons.

```
' File: shortcuts.vbs

' Global variables
Dim g_objShell          ' Scripting shell object
Dim g_objFSO            ' File system object
Dim g_strSkypePath      ' Path of Skype executable
Dim g_strShortcutPath   ' Path to store shortcuts
Dim g_objSkypeAPI       ' SkypeAPI interface object
```

```
Dim g_strPrefix          ' Prefix to add to shortcuts
Dim g_bOnDesktop         ' True=icons on desktop, False=in menu

' Return True if friends list is below 15 entries or if user approves
Function CheckFriendListSize

    Dim iFriends

    iFriends = g_objSkypeAPI.GetFriendList.Count
    If iFriends = 0 Then
        CheckFriendListSize = False
    Else
        strTitle = "Create " & iFriends
        if iFriends <> 1 Then strTitle = strTitle + "s"
        strTitle = strTitle + " Shortcuts"
        i = g_objShell.Popup( _
            "Click ""Yes"" to create shortcuts on Desktop, "+vbCr+ _
            "Click ""No"" to create shortcuts in Start Menu, "+vbCr+ _
            "Click ""Cancel"" to abort", 0, strTitle, 35)
        If i = 6 Then
            CheckFriendListSize= True
            g_bOnDesktop = True
        ElseIf i = 7 Then
            CheckFriendListSize= True
            g_bOnDesktop = False
        Else
            CheckFriendListSize= False
        End If
    End If
End Function

' Create a shortcut for the Skype User object
Sub CreateSkypeShortcut(User)

    Dim strFileName

    ' Build a file name to display
    If Len(User.DisplayName) > 0 Then
        strFileName = User.DisplayName + ".lnk"
    ElseIf Len(User.FullName) > 0 Then
        strFileName = User.FullName + ".lnk"
    Else
        strFileName = User.Handle + ".lnk"
    End If

    ' Remove any bad characters
    strFileName = Replace(strFileName, "|", "")
    strFileName = Replace(strFileName, "\", "")
    strFileName = Replace(strFileName, ":", "")

    ' Create the shortcut
    strFileName = g_strPrefix + strFileName
    set objShellLink = _
```

```
                g_objShell.CreateShortcut( g_objFSO.BuildPath( _
                                g_strShortcutPath, strFileName))
        objShellLink.TargetPath = "callto://" + User.Handle
        objShellLink.IconLocation = g_strSkypePath + ", 5"
        objShellLink.WindowStyle = 1
        objShellLink.Description = "Start Skype"
        strSpeedDial = User.SpeedDial
        If (strSpeedDial >= "0") And (strSpeedDial <= "9") Then
            objShellLink.HotKey = "Ctrl+Shift+" + strSpeedDial
        End If
        objShellLink.Save
    End Sub

    ' Main script begins here
    Set g_objShell = WScript.CreateObject("WScript.Shell")
    Set g_objFSO = WScript.CreateObject("Scripting.FileSystemObject")
    Set g_objSkypeAPI = WScript.CreateObject("SkypeAPI.Access")
    g_objSkypeAPI.ConnectAndWait 15000

    If CheckFriendListSize Then

        ' Get the location of Skype for icons
        g_strSkypePath = g_objShell.RegRead( _
                    "HKLM\Software\Skype\Phone\SkypePath")

        If g_bOnDesktop Then
            g_strShortcutPath = g_objShell.SpecialFolders("Desktop")
            g_strPrefix = "Skype - "
        Else
            g_strShortcutPath = g_objFSO.BuildPath( _
                            g_objShell.SpecialFolders("StartMenu"), _
                            "Skype Shortcuts")
            g_strPrefix = ""
        End If

        ' Delete any existing shortcuts if folder exists
        If g_objFSO.FolderExists(g_strShortcutPath) Then
            For Each objFile in _
                g_objFSO.GetFolder(g_strShortcutPath).Files
                If (StrComp(g_objFSO.GetExtensionName( _
                            objFile.Name), "lnk", 1) = 0) And _
                    (Left(objFile.Name, len(g_strPrefix)) = _
                    g_strPrefix) Then
                        objFile.Delete
                End If
            Next
        ' Or create the folder
        Else
            g_objFSO.CreateFolder g_strShortcutPath
        End If

        ' Iterate through users and create shortcuts
        For Each objUser in g_objSkypeAPI.GetFriendList
```

```
        CreateSkypeShortcut objUser
        g_iCtr = g_iCtr + 1
    Next

    ' Show an "all done" message
    g_objShell.Popup g_objSkypeAPI.GetFriendList.Count & _
        " Shortcuts Created", 0, "Process Complete", 64
End If
```

Make Chat Talk Out Loud

Sit back and just listen, as this hack uses the Microsoft Speech SDK to make incoming chat messages speak aloud!

Works with: Windows version of Skype.

Perhaps you're visually impaired and you need incoming chat messages to be read aloud so that you can participate in one-on-one or multiperson chat sessions. Or maybe you like to wander around your computer room while listening to chat sessions. Or perhaps you just think that talking chat is cool. Whatever the reason, getting chat to talk aloud is simple with this hack.

The VBScripts in this chapter use the Microsoft Speech SDK, which you can download free of charge at *http://www. microsoft.com/downloads* (search for "Speech SDK").

This hack uses two scripts, *start_talking.vbs* and *stop_talking.vbs*, to make chat start talking and stop talking, respectively. Only incoming chat is spoken aloud, the rationale being that you remember what chat messages you type in yourself; that is, you remember what you said, but you want to hear aloud what others say.

Use this script, *start_talking.vbs*, to make Skype chat start talking aloud:

```
' File: start_talking.vbs

Dim objVoice, objFSO, objSkype, objSemaphore
Dim strTempFolder, strSemaphoreName
Set objVoice = WScript.CreateObject("Sapi.SpVoice")
Set objFSO = WScript.CreateObject("Scripting.FileSystemObject")
Set objSkype = WScript.CreateObject("SkypeAPI.Access", _
                                    "SkypeAPI_")

' Skype event handler
Sub SkypeAPI_ChatMessageReceived(ChatMessage)
    objVoice.Speak ChatMessage.Body, 1
End Sub

' Main script begins here
```

```
strTempFolder = objFSO.GetSpecialFolder(2)
strSemaphoreName = objFSO.BuildPath(strTempFolder, _
                                    "talking_chat.tmp")
Set objSemaphore = objFSO.CreateTextFile(strSemaphoreName, true)
objSemaphore.Close
objSkype.ConnectAndWait 15000
Do While objFSO.FileExists(strSemaphoreName)
    WScript.Sleep 500
Loop
```

And use this script, *stop_talking.vbs*, to make Skype chat stop talking aloud:

```
' File: stop_talking.vbs

' Main script begins here
Dim objFSO, strTempFolder
Set objFSO = WScript.CreateObject("Scripting.FileSystemObject")
strTempFolder = objFSO.GetSpecialFolder(2)
objFSO.DeleteFile objFSO.BuildPath(strTempFolder, _
                                   "talking_chat.tmp")
```

The easiest way to use these scripts is to turn them into shortcuts and assign them hotkeys. Create a shortcut named Start Chat Talking that points to *start_talking.vbs* as its target, then right-click on the shortcut and choose Properties. In the shortcut properties dialog that is displayed, select the Shortcut tab, click on the text entry field opposite "Shortcut key," press the key sequence you want as your hotkey (for example, Ctrl-Shift-T for Talk), and then click OK. Do the same for *stop_talking.vbs*, giving its shortcut the name Stop Chat Talking and a different hotkey sequence (for example, Ctrl-Shift-M for Mute). Now, before—or even during—a chat session, you can switch between making chat talk aloud and making chat silent by using only a couple of hotkey sequences!

See Also

- If you need some help setting up shortcuts for the scripts in this hack, see "Add Fast-Dial Shortcuts to Your Menu or Desktop" **[Hack #49]**, as that hack shows how to set up shortcuts in detail.

H A C K   Erase a Skype User Account
#98
This hack will clear all histories, overwrite data in your personal profile, and otherwise delete all personal data associated with a Skype account.

Works with: Windows version of Skype.

Whether you've been running Skype on a borrowed machine, or you simply no longer need a Skype user account, wipe it off the face of the Earth (actually, the hard disk and the Skype network) using this collection of scripts:

erase_profile_from_network.vbs
> Erase (actually overwrite) your public profile that is stored on the Skype network.

erase_vm_history.vbs
> Erase your voicemail history.

erase_chat_history.vbs
> Erase your chat history.

erase_call_history.vbs
> Erase your call history.

erase_folders_and_files.vbs
> Erase all files and folders for a specified Skype username on the current machine.

All of the preceding scripts operate on the user currently logged onto Skype, except for *erase_folders_and_files.vbs*, which allows you to delete the Skype files and folders for a named Skype user. Most run silently, meaning that they don't notify you of what they've done, or when they're done; they just do what's asked of them and finish.

You can combine these scripts in different ways to fine-tune the erasure process. For example, if you want to erase all your voicemail and chat histories, you can run this command from the run line or a shortcut: erase_vm_history. vbs ; erase_chat_history.vbs. This command assumes you've put your VBScripts somewhere on your execution path; otherwise, you will have to include folder paths and possibly have to use quotes to encase the VBScripts.

By making the erasure process divisible through small scripts, with each script designed to perform one simple task, you gain a good deal of flexibility over what you keep, and what you throw away, in terms of Skype user data on a machine.

Lastly, you should be aware that Skype names persist forever and are never recycled or reused. So, in a sense, you can never truly erase a Skype name. However, by erasing all the data—both online and on the hard disk—associated with a Skype name, you have totally disassociated yourself from the Skype name.

erase_profile_from_network.vbs.

```
' File: erase_profile_from_network.vbs

Dim objSkypeAPI
Set objSkypeAPI = WScript.CreateObject("SkypeAPI.Access")
objSkypeAPI.ConnectAndWait 15000
objSkypeAPI.SendBlockingCommand("SET PROFILE FULLNAME ")
objSkypeAPI.SendBlockingCommand("SET PROFILE BIRTHDAY 19000101")
```

```
objSkypeAPI.SendBlockingCommand("SET PROFILE SEX UNKNOWN")
objSkypeAPI.SendBlockingCommand("SET PROFILE LANGUAGES ab")
objSkypeAPI.SendBlockingCommand("SET PROFILE COUNTRY ")
objSkypeAPI.SendBlockingCommand("SET PROFILE PROVINCE ")
objSkypeAPI.SendBlockingCommand("SET PROFILE CITY ")
objSkypeAPI.SendBlockingCommand("SET PROFILE PHONE_HOME ")
objSkypeAPI.SendBlockingCommand("SET PROFILE PHONE_OFFICE ")
objSkypeAPI.SendBlockingCommand("SET PROFILE PHONE_MOBILE ")
objSkypeAPI.SendBlockingCommand("SET PROFILE HOMEPAGE ")
objSkypeAPI.SendBlockingCommand("SET PROFILE ABOUT ")
objSkypeAPI.SendBlockingCommand("SET PROFILE MOOD_TEXT ")
objSkypeAPI.SendBlockingCommand("SET PROFILE TIMEZONE 0")

' This code is needed to erase e-mail address and
' avatar picture, as these can't be set using the API.
Dim objShell, keysequence, keystrokes, keys, pause
Set objShell = WScript.CreateObject("WScript.Shell")
keysequence = "^+S|%(FM)|{TAB}|{TAB}|{TAB}|{TAB}|{TAB}|" & _
              "{TAB}|{TAB}|{TAB}|{TAB}|{TAB}|{TAB}|{TAB}|" & _
              "{TAB}|{TAB}|{TAB}|{ENTER}|{TAB}|{DEL}|" & _
              "{TAB}|{ENTER}"
keystrokes = Split(keysequence, "|")
pause = 1500
For Each keys In keystrokes
    objShell.SendKeys keys
    WScript.Sleep pause
    If pause>100 Then pause=100 End If
Next
```

erase_vm_history.vbs.

```
' File: erase_vm_history.vbs

Dim objSkypeAPI
Set objSkypeAPI = WScript.CreateObject("SkypeAPI.Access")
objSkypeAPI.ConnectAndWait 15000
objSkypeAPI.SendBlockingCommand("CLEAR VOICEMAILHISTORY")
```

erase_chat_history.vbs.

```
' File: erase_chat_history.vbs

Dim objSkypeAPI
Set objSkypeAPI = WScript.CreateObject("SkypeAPI.Access")
objSkypeAPI.ConnectAndWait 15000
objSkypeAPI.SendBlockingCommand("CLEAR CHATHISTORY")
```

erase_call_history.vbs.

```
' File: erase_call_history.vbs

Dim objSkypeAPI
Set objSkypeAPI = WScript.CreateObject("SkypeAPI.Access")
```

```
objSkypeAPI.ConnectAndWait 15000
objSkypeAPI.SendBlockingCommand("CLEAR CALLHISTORY ALL")
```

erase_folders_and_files.vbs.

```
' File: erase_folders_and_files.vbs

' Invoke like this from the command-line:
'    erase_folders_and_files skypeuser
'

' Parameters:
' skypeuser is the Skype user name for which
' you want to erase Skype folders and files.

' Variables
Dim objShell       ' Scripting shell object
Dim objFSO         ' File system object
Dim objArgs        ' Command line arguments
Dim strSkypeUser   ' Skype user name passed on the command-line
Dim strHomePath    ' Path to home folder of current user
Dim strSkypePath   ' Path to Skype folder of strSkypeUser

' Main script begins here
Set objShell = WScript.CreateObject("WScript.Shell")
Set objFSO = WScript.CreateObject("Scripting.FileSystemObject")

' Count how many users are passed
Set objArgs = WScript.Arguments
If objArgs.Count <> 1 Then
    objShell.Popup "Parameter 1:  Handle of Skype user to delete" & _
                   vbCr & vbCr & "Skype should be closed before " & _
                   "running this script", 0, _
                   "Erase Skype folders and files", 64
Else
    strSkypeUser = objArgs(0)

    ' Get the location of the "Documents and Settings" folder
    ' First, get the system drive and profiles directory
    strHomePath = objShell.Environment("PROCESS")("HOMEDRIVE") & _
                  objShell.Environment("PROCESS")("HOMEPATH")

    strSkypePath = strHomePath & "\Application Data\Skype\" & _
                   strSkypeUser
    If Not objFSO.FolderExists(strSkypePath) Then
        objShell.Popup "Skype profile path """ & strSkypePath & _
                       """ not found", 0, "Unable to continue", 16
    Else
        ' Try to delete the folder, if there is an error, Skype
        ' is probably open
        On Error Resume Next
        objFSO.DeleteFolder strSkypePath, True
        If Err.Number = 0 Then
            objShell.Popup "Folder: " & strSkypePath & vbCr & _
```

```
                                "has been erased!", 0, "Skype folders" & _
                                " and files for " & strSkypeUser & _
                                " erased!", 64
            Else
                objShell.Popup "Skype is probably open, you need to " & _
                                "close Skype before running this script", _
                                0, "Unable to delete Skype folders " & _
                                "and files", 48
            End If
        End If
    End If
```

Spy on Skype API Messages

Use these tools to spy on the messages that pass to and fro between Skype and a client that uses its API.

Works with: Windows and Linux versions of Skype.

This hack presents a couple of tools that, if not essential to developing scripts that use the API, are pretty darn useful! Being able to interactively send API commands to Skype and see what Skype sends back in return is invaluable for both developing scripts and debugging them.

Windows

A free tool, Skype Tracer, allows you to interactively send API commands to Skype and see what Skype sends back in return (see Figure 12-6). A nice feature of this tool is that you can save your interactive session to a logfile for later analysis. You can download Skype Tracer at *http://share.skype.com/directory/skype_tracer/view/*.

Linux

Skype provides an example script, *skypeapiclient_linux.py*, as part of its API documentation for Linux. Using this script, you can interactively send API commands to Skype and see what Skype sends back in return (see Figure 12-7).

However, Skype's example script has a couple of drawbacks. First, it doesn't give you the option of creating a logfile of your session for later analysis. Although you can cut and paste text from the window and create your own logfile, this is both tedious and error prone. In addition, you can lose text for a long interactive session if the window text buffer has overflowed. Second, it doesn't provide a timestamp, so detailed analysis of exactly when things happened is not possible. To make up for these missing features, I modified the script to provide the missing logfile capability.

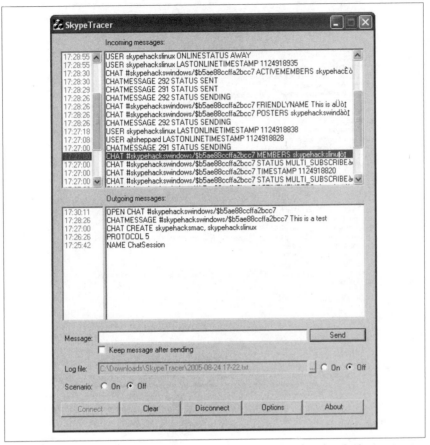

Figure 12-6. Skype Tracer allows you to conduct interactive sessions with Skype using its API

Running this new script, which I called *skypeapiclient_logging.py*, from the command line and piping its terminal output to a file—say, *log.txt*—will create a logfile of your entire session; for example, like this: *python skypeapiclient_logging.py > log.txt*.

You can construct the *skypeapiclient_logging.py* script by copying Skype's *skypeapiclient_linux.py* script (available as a zip file from *http://download. skype.com/share/devzone/example_linux.zip*) to *skypeapiclient_logging.py* and making the changes indicated in bold in the following code listing:

```
#!/usr/bin/env python
# -*- coding: iso-8859-15 -*-

# File: skypeapiclient_logging.py
```

Figure 12-7. *Skype provides an example script that allows you to conduct interactive sessions with Skype using its API*

```python
import dbus, gtk, sys, time

class MainWindow:
    .
    .
    .

class Callback_obj(dbus.Object):
    .
    .
    .

    # Skype -> Client messages
    def Notify(self, message, message_text):
        self.mainwindow.write_textbuffer(message_text)
        # Skype Hacks: Add these two lines of code
        time_stamp = time.strftime("%a, %d %b %Y %H:%M:%S")
        print time_stamp + ' MSG RECV FROM SKYPE <-- ' + \
            message_text
```

```
class Api_obj:
    .
    .
    .

    # Client -> Skype
    def send_message(self, message):
        self.mainwindow.write_textbuffer(message)
        answer = self.skype_api_object.Invoke(message)
        self.mainwindow.write_textbuffer(answer)
        # Skype Hacks: Add these three lines of code
        time_stamp = time.strftime("%a, %d %b %Y %H:%M:%S")
        print time_stamp + ' MSG SENT  TO  SKYPE --> ' + \
            message
        print time_stamp + ' MSG RECV FROM SKYPE <-- ' + \
            answer
        return answer

def main():
    MainWindow()
    gtk.main()
    return 0

if __name__ == "__main__":
    main()
```

Disable the Skype API

H A C K
#100

Perhaps corporate policy dictates it, or perhaps you just think it's a good idea. In any event, disabling Skype's API on Windows requires only a single registry setting.

Works with: Windows version of Skype.

With the release of version 1.4 for Windows, Skype included the ability to disable its API. In many businesses, disabling this function may be dictated by corporate policy, or it might be at the request of your network administrator or IT security officer. Provided you're willing to hack the Windows registry, you can selectively disable Skype's API.

Open Regedit (select Start → Run..., enter "Regedit," and press Return or click OK) and add this key: HKEY_LOCAL_MACHINE\Software\Policies\Skype\ Phone. Under this key, add a new DWORD value having the name DisableApi. Setting DisableApi to 1 will disable the Skype API, and setting it to 0 (or omitting or deleting the key altogether) will leave the API enabled. Note that you have to stop and restart Skype for this change to take effect. Also, toggling this registry entry between 0 and 1 does not delete Skype's add-on control list, as that is unaffected; instead, the Skype API simply stops receiving and sending messages.

Of course, this hack works sensibly only when regular user accounts are set up so that they can't edit the registry under HKEY_LOCAL_MACHINE themselves; that is, specifically, they should not be able to change DisableApi.

Hacking the Hack

If you don't want to hack this registry setting yourself, or if you have to roll out Skype across a large number of machines, you might find the following VBScript (*disable_api.vbs*) helpful:

```
' File: disable_api.vbs

Dim objShell
Set objShell = WScript.CreateObject("WScript.Shell")
objShell.RegWrite "HKLM\Software\Policies\Skype\Phone\DisableApi", _
                1, "REG_DWORD"
```

Here is the opposite (*enable_api.vbs*), just in case the policy prohibiting use of the Skype API changes:

```
' File: enable_api.vbs

Dim objShell
Set objShell = WScript.CreateObject("WScript.Shell")
objShell.RegWrite "HKLM\Software\Policies\Skype\Phone\DisableApi", _
                0, "REG_DWORD"
```

Note that both scripts will, if necessary, create the registry entry if it does not exist already.

Index

We'd like to hear your suggestions for improving our indexes. Send email to *index@oreilly.com*.

Colophon

Our look is the result of reader comments, our own experimentation, and feedback from distribution channels. Distinctive covers complement our distinctive approach to technical topics, breathing personality and life into potentially dry subjects.

The tool on the cover of *Skype Hacks* is an antique telephone; specifically, a tube shaft candlestick desk telephone. It has a dial, a handheld earpiece, and a solid perch with the transmitter unit attached. This style of phone was in development as early as 1894.

Colleen Gorman was the production editor and proofreader, and Audrey Doyle was the copyeditor for *Skype Hacks*. Reba Libby and Claire Cloutier provided quality control. Johnna VanHoose Dinse wrote the index.

Marcia Friedman designed the cover of this book, based on a series design by Edie Freedman. The cover image is a photograph from *Photospin Power Photos, Nostalgia Volume 9*. Karen Montgomery produced the cover layout with Adobe InDesign CS using Adobe's Helvetica Neue and ITC Garamond fonts.

David Futato designed the interior layout. This book was converted by Keith Fahlgren to FrameMaker 5.5.6 with a format conversion tool created by Erik Ray, Jason McIntosh, Neil Walls, and Mike Sierra that uses Perl and XML technologies. The text font is Linotype Birka; the heading font is Adobe Helvetica Neue Condensed; and the code font is LucasFont's TheSans Mono Condensed. The illustrations that appear in the book were produced by Robert Romano, Jessamyn Read, and Lesley Borash using Macromedia FreeHand MX and Adobe Photoshop CS. This colophon was written by Colleen Gorman.

Better than e-books

Buy *Skype Hacks* and access the digital
edition FREE on Safari for 45 days.

Go to www.oreilly.com/go/safarienabled
and type in coupon code CNGG-Z3KF-HZBY-8GFZ-R9LI

Search
thousands of
top tech books

Download
whole chapters

Cut and Paste
code examples

Find
answers fast

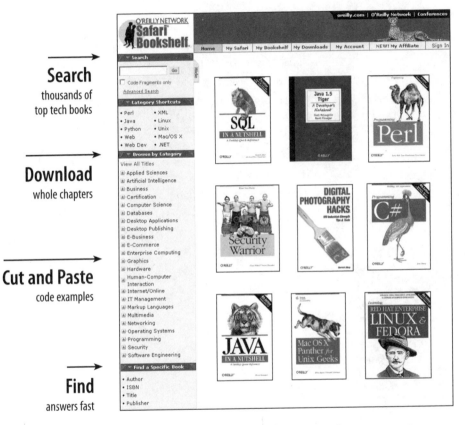

Search Safari! The premier electronic reference
library for programmers and IT professionals.

Related Titles from O'Reilly

Hardware

Blackberry Hacks

Building the Perfect PC

Car PC Hacks

Designing Embedded Hardware, *2nd Edition*

Don't Click on the Blue E!

Make: Technology on Your Time

Makers: All Kinds of People Making Amazing Things
  in Their Backyard, Basement or Garage

Nokia Smartphones Hacks

Palm & Treo Hacks

PC Hardware Annoyances

PC Hardware Buyer's Guide

Smart Home Hacks

Talk Is Cheap

Treo Fan Book

Wireless Hacks, *2nd Edition*

O'REILLY®

Our books are available at most retail and online bookstores.

To order direct: 1-800-998-9938 • *order@oreilly.com* • *www.oreilly.com*

Online editions of most O'Reilly titles are available by subscription at *safari.oreilly.com*